The Theory and Practice
of Organizational Psychology

ORGANIZATIONAL AND OCCUPATIONAL PSYCHOLOGY

Series Editor : PETER WARR
*MRC/SSRC Social and Applied Psychology Unit, Department of Psychology,
The University, Sheffield, England*

Theodore D. Weinshall

Managerial Communication: Concepts, Approaches and Techniques, 1979

Chris Argyris

Inner Contradictions of Rigorous Research, 1980

Charles J. de Wolff, Sylvia Shimmin, and Maurice de Montmollin

Conflicts and Contradictions: Work Psychology in Europe, 1981

Nigel Nicholson, Gill Ursell, and Paul Blyton

The Dynamics of White Collar Unionism, 1981

John D. Cook, Sue J. Hepworth, Toby D. Wall, and Peter B. Warr

The Experience of Work: A Compendium and Review of 249 Measures and Their Use, 1981

Nigel Nicholson and Toby D. Wall

The Theory and Practice of Organizational Psychology, 1981

In preparation

Dean G. Pruitt

Negotiation Behavior

D. R. Davies and R. Parasuraman

The Psychology of Vigilance

The Theory and Practice of Organizational Psychology

A Collection of Original Essays

Edited by
NIGEL NICHOLSON and TOBY D. WALL
MRC/SSRC Social and Applied Psychology Unit,
University of Sheffield

1982

ACADEMIC PRESS
A Subsidiary of Harcourt Brace Jovanovich, Publishers

LONDON   NEW YORK
PARIS   SAN DIEGO   SAN FRANCISCO   SÃO PAULO
SYDNEY   TOKYO   TORONTO

Academic Press Inc. (London) Ltd
24–28 Oval Road
London NW1

US edition published by
Academic Press Inc.
111 Fifth Avenue,
New York, New York 10003

British Library Cataloguing in Publication Data

The theory and practice of organizational
    psychology. — (Organizational and
    occupational psychology)
    1. Organizational behavior
    I. Nicholson, N.   II. Wall, T. D.
    III. Series
    158.7   HD58.7

ISBN 0-12-518040-3

LCCCN 81-68014

Typeset by Kelmscott Press Ltd, London
Printed and bound by T. J. Press (Padstow) Ltd, Padstow, Cornwall

Contributors

The various contributors to this volume are introduced at appropriate places in the text. Their normal addresses for correspondence are listed below.

CHRIS ARGYRIS
James Bryant Conant Professor of Education and Organizational Behavior, Harvard University Graduate School of Education, Center for the Study of Organizations and Intervention, Cambridge, Massachusetts 02138, USA

ALBERT CHERNS
Professor, Department of Social Sciences, University of Loughborough, Loughborough, Leicestershire LE11 3TV, England

DAN GOWLER
Fellow, Oxford Centre for Management Studies, Kennington, Oxford OX1 5NY, England

JERALD HAGE
Professor, Department of Sociology, Division of Behavioral Sciences, University of Maryland, College Park, Maryland 20742, USA

PAUL JACKSON
Research Fellow, MRC/SSRC Social and Applied Psychology Unit, University of Sheffield, Sheffield S10 2TN, England

FRANK LANDY
Professor, Department of Psychology, Pennsylvania State University, University Park, Pennsylvania 16802, USA

KAREN LEGGE
Senior Lecturer, Department of Social and Economic Studies, Imperial College, University of London, London SW7 2AZ, England

IAIN MANGHAM
Professor, Centre for the Study of Organizational Change and Development, University of Bath, Bath BA2 7AY, England

NIGEL NICHOLSON
Senior Research Fellow, MRC/SSRC Social and Applied Psychology Unit, University of Sheffield, Sheffield S10 2TN, England

ROY PAYNE
Senior Research Fellow, MRC/SSRC Social and Applied Psychology Unit, University of Sheffield, Sheffield S10 2TN, England

DENIS PYM
Professor, London Graduate School of Business Studies, Regent's Park, London NW1 4SA, England

SYLVIA SHIMMIN
Professor, Department of Behaviour in Organisations, University of Lancaster, Lancaster LA1 4YX, England

TOBY WALL
Senior Research Fellow, MRC/SSRC Social and Applied Psychology Unit, University of Sheffield, Sheffield S10 2TN, England

Preface

Organizational psychology, like any major area of inquiry, is well supported by literature which describes and assesses its products. There are a large number of books and articles which focus on its empirical findings, theories and methods. However, relatively little attention has been devoted to the nature of the research process, particularly to the assumptions, values, procedures and constraints which give direction and shape to the information derived. Yet such influences represent the often hidden underbelly of the body of knowledge, and their effects, for better or worse, are substantial. Periodically, therefore, it is important that researchers should stand back from their work and reflect upon the precepts on which it is based, that they should question these and, where dissatisfied, adopt a prescriptive stance. Our aim in collecting the essays which comprise this book was to provide such a perspective.

How to approach this objective proved a major problem. The number of factors which influence research processes is clearly much greater than can be adequately covered in one volume. Moreover, the typically inexplicit and often unrecognized nature of the assumptive bases of organizational psychology means that this is not a well-charted area. Thus it was not possible, nor we believe desirable, to produce a "shopping list" of topics and seek out experts willing to complete our specification. So we started out from the opposite direction. We contacted a number of individuals with highly successful research careers in organizational psychology, apprised them of the perspective we were attempting to achieve, and asked them to contribute essays dealing with those underlying issues of major concern to them. We made it clear that we did not want general reviews of the products of organizational psychology, but original reflective and prescriptive contributions concerned with the more subtle cultural, epistemological, theoretical, practical or personal influences underlying research in this area.

In an attempt to provide a range of orientations we approached researchers with differing interests and disciplinary backgrounds. The response was extremely positive. The result is this unusual collection of essays which provides interesting comment on the current state of organizational psychology and tantalizing auguries of its possible futures. We trust the reader will find these contributions as challenging and thought-provoking as we have ourselves.

Sheffield,   NIGEL NICHOLSON
September 1981   TOBY WALL

Contents

1 Introduction: Themes in the Theory and Practice of Organizational Psychology

NIGEL NICHOLSON and TOBY WALL

This book seeks to explore the nature and consequences of inquiry within a highly active field of applied social science—organizational psychology—and to examine the abiding concerns of some of its pre-eminent practitioners. Such is the force and clarity with which these emerge in the essays which follow that little in the way of additional interpretation or comment from us is needed. Our purpose here is to explain the guiding rationale for bringing them together, to delineate the major boundaries of our common cause, and to highlight some of the problems and controversies that thread thematically through this volume.

1. The research process

Within almost any field of inquiry, empirical research is undertaken with a progressively focused perspective, in which a series of implicit choices and decisions shape the nature of the enterprise at successive stages of public and private formulation; decisions that build, decisions that select, and, ultimately, decisions that bind. In whatever form, their intent is to refine and reveal an epistemological event. Typically, this process commences with a general, loosely formulated question of interest. This may be a broad theoretical issue or a more specific problem in the domain of concern, or even a question relating to the methods of research themselves. These questions and issues are reformulated into the operational terms of more particular propositions, conceptual models, and methodological strategies. These further define, guide and justify the course of subsequent research activity. Thus portrayed, the research enterprise is a multi-dimensional selection process determining subject matter, theoretical cast, level of analysis, research design and analytical strategy.

How are these decisions made? It would be comforting to think that the quality of the products of research was assured as the outcome of some "natural selection", in which those most fit for their purpose survive. Insofar as the process is evolutionary, it must be recognized that the environmental pressures to which researchers adapt are not necessarily consistent with their espoused aims. For example, the professional pressures to publish, and the criteria perceived to govern the publication policy of academic journals, may provide more explicit and compelling guidelines for research decision-making than the high uncertainty of laudable abstractions such as "making a lasting contribution to knowledge". Researchers, in the short-term at least, may find unambiguous rewards in following the fold and leaving posterity to reach its own conclusions.

There is, then, reason to be thankful that the adaptive instrumentalism of the evolutionary model is not the only determinant of the character of research, for to this must be added the teleology of researchers' purposes and values. Choices about how knowledge is pursued are not only guided by the strategic contingencies of social and professional demands but also by the values and ideals of researchers, and by their assumptions about knowledge itself. These two forces are in practice intertwined, and their interdependence constitutes culture — the yin and yang of practices and beliefs, of payoffs and values, of institutions and habits. Research both adapts to and changes the knowledge culture.

This selection process is necessary to make research a tangible and viable activity. It occurs in both explicit and implicit forms. Researchers respond not only to the traditions, desires and constraints of which they are aware, but also to those of which they are unaware. In practice, it may be observed that decisions often do not cohere into any elaborated grand design but are pragmatic working assumptions adopted as minimal requirements for the support and legitimization of efforts to produce knowledge. However conscious or complex these working assumptions are makes no difference to the fact that they determine and constraint the kind of knowledge produced.

It may be said that researchers usually recognize the existence of these processes at a general level, but, like the centipede who fears being disabled by thinking about how to run, most do not subject the details of their "guidance system" to close scrutiny when it is in active operation. This is not surprising, given the serendipitous and opportunistic ways in which research designs and practices adapt to circumstances. Indeed, it could be said to be a mark of the innovative and effective researcher that he or she feels sufficiently the master rather than the victim of assumptions and preconceptions to be able to seize the moment — to snap up the accidental or unconsidered trifle and creatively exploit its latent value. It is also worth noting, *en passant*, that it is not only the behavioural sciences that appear to drift in this semiconscious fashion towards their goals rather than with the orderly tread of precise premeditation. This kind of "sleepwalking" has been repeatedly portrayed as the *modus operandi* likewise of the physical sciences — and by no one more vividly than the writer Arthur Koestler (1959) (see also Watson, 1968).

Putting together such considerations one may form the opinion that it is important for the producers of knowledge periodically to take the opportunity to stand back from the research face and reflect upon the precepts on which their efforts are based, the efficacy of those precepts, and their wider implications for the field as a whole in which they are engaged. Arguably, this is particularly important for those disciplines whose object of study is human life and society. Researchers in the behavioural sciences or social studies are coterminous with the phenomena they investigate. If knowledge is power, and that knowledge concerns human action, then it is reflexive power. One implication of this has been called the "enlightenment effect" (Gergen, 1973), that the knowledge of behavioural "laws" can modify or even nullify their impact on those who know about them. The knowledge we seek and the problems we pursue are both inputs and outputs of our stated and unstated precepts. Appreciation of the dynamic nature of the relationship between the assumptions of researchers, the type of knowledge they produce, and its social context, has become a significant theme of modern organizational psychology — in the voiced concerns of its practitioners, in the intent underlying the training of those practitioners, and in the nature of the research involvements constructed, or rather "negotiated", with work organizations. Before we look in more detail at these concerns, which we shall preview as the central themes which run through the essays of this volume, it is important that we set the scene by briefly outlining the dimensions of the field of organizational psychology, and how this book aims to contribute to it.

2.   Organizational psychology: field or discipline?

Given its status of relative immaturity, but nevertheless fairly high sophistication, organizational psychology does not exist as a unitary academic culture in any certain sense. It is rather a meeting place for various sub-disciplinary interests. A consequence of this is that the relations between sets of ideas within the field do not constitute an orderly arrangement, nor are they always incrementally additive towards an aggregate body of knowledge. As a meeting ground, its boundaries are loose and not clearly drawn, although within them there are tighter nodes of disciplinary cohesion, and towards these there is some of the constructive accretion that is usually imagined to characterize disciplines. These nodes often represent research technologies—ideas and methods—associated with uniformities of training, theoretical schools, or operational orthodoxies. However, because of the reflexivity of the field, what intercourse there is between these often takes on the character of ideological disputes. The subjects of communication between people are beliefs and values, and ideal states for organizations, organizational members and organizational processes. Technical and operational definitions can be dispassionately constructed for such dependent variables as "effectiveness", "well-being", "viability", "dysfunction", and numerous others, but their status is always uncertain and equivocal according to usage and intent. In short, neither the theories nor the practices of organizational psychology are neutral in value. It was not our intent in acting as a stimulus for this book to provide a public display for such disputes, interesting though they may be. A more interactive and direct forum for the presentation of opposing views would be better suited to that purpose, yet this book does perhaps show what forms some of these disputes might take. Our objective was for authors to critically appraise stages or levels of inquiry within organizational psychology. Broadly, these are threefold: (1) the climate of ideas, values and beliefs within which research is undertaken; (2) the efforts of researchers to construct ordered concepts and techniques to make sense of parts of the phenomenal world; and (3) the way in which effort is behaviourally discharged in the practice of research and intervention.

It will be observed that these are closely interwoven concerns, and this recognition is the single most important unifying theme for all the essays in this book. Within this overall unanimity though, the keynote is diversity. Indeed, the diversity of the array of concerns that is displayed may be taken as a sign of some perplexity at their source, and certainly it is apparent from the essays that there is some dissatisfaction with the current state of the art. At the same time it may be seen that there is also much optimism, and justifiably so on the evidence here of a rich variety of proposals for change and the clarity with which they are conceived. Indeed, our invitation to authors to contribute was couched in terms to elicit prescriptions for change in awareness and practice among organizational psychologists.

In asking for essays of such reflective and prescriptive tenor we were also consciously not seeking a mid-career stocktaking of theoretical and empirical knowledge and an appraisal of current directions in the field. Such reviews have been numerous in recent years, notably in the comprehensive *Handbook of Industrial and Organizational Psychology* (edited by Dunnette, 1976), and in updates such as are to be found in the *Annual Review of Psychology* (e.g. Mitchell, 1979, Cummings, in press). Moreover, it is clear that the kind of portrait of the field that would emerge from a volume so conceived would depend upon what kind of cross-section of contributors it contained. Our guiding principle was to gather notable scholars with something to say on the issues. It is an interesting and indeed important corollary of this that the academic careers of all have been strongly marked by their willingness to transgress the boundaries of disciplinary orthodoxy, both within the field of organizational psychology or between it and other fields of study. We had no intent to obtain a "representative" sample of contributors, whatever that might mean in such a field. However, by eliciting the active concerns of scholars, we feel major current concerns in organizational psychology have been illuminated and some of its future ones anticipated. The nature of these concerns was only partly determined by our planned framework for the collection. The specific topics we asked authors to address were: culture and values (Albert Cherns); philosophical assumptions (Roy Payne); the problem of integration across disciplines and analytical levels (Dan Gowler and Karen Legge); theoretical assumptions (Frank Landy); theory-building (Jerald Hage); research design (Paul Jackson); the research enterprise (Iain Mangham); research as action (Chris Argyris); radical alternatives to current practice (Denis Pym); and future roles for research in organizational psychology (Sylvia Shimmin). We are thankful that authors did not suffer constraint from this route-map and that they have given their brief a sufficiently liberal reading to voice their predominant concerns at a more general level.

The question, "What is organizational psychology?" will not take up too much of our time here, for we have no intention of falling into the kinds of semantic regression that often follow such questions. Yet neither do we wish to dismiss the question by recourse to vacuous truisms of the kind — "a rose is a rose" — for names and labels do assume considerable importance as signposts for academic sub-cultures in the social sciences. First, let us make clear that our use of the term "organizational psychology" is not intended to imply any partisan disciplinary allegiance. For our purposes here "psychology" may be defined as the study of human behaviour and experience. Thus defined it constitutes more a field of study than a unitary discipline, for within that definition there are numerous "disciplines", if one takes the term "discipline" to denote coherent bodies of method and knowledge. At its various margins the sub-fields of psychology are interdisciplinary. Thus neuropsychology is a field for various biological and human sciences, and social psychology a meeting place for various social sciences. Organizational psychology then, is in no way exclusive of alternatives such as organizational sociology, organizational science and organizational behaviour. The latter are all in equally common currency for the same set of concerns. This is evidenced by the fact that our contributors' backgrounds as scholars are to be found in psychology, sociology, anthropology, industrial relations and social administration.

The term "organizational psychology" first emerged in the 1960s, reflecting a shift away from an exclusive or microscopic focus on individual behaviour in work settings, towards a more broadly contextual framework. Particularly influential in promoting this orientation was the work of Katz and Kahn (1966) and Pugh (1966), and the books by Bass (1965) and Schein (1965), which carried the title *Organizational Psychology*. The common theme of concern was succinctly captured by Kahn and colleagues (1974) who, assessing their work on organizational stress, framed the issue thus:

Knowledge can best be advanced by research which attempts to deal simultaneously with data at different levels of abstraction — individual, group and organization. This is a difficult task, and the outcome is not uniformly satisfactory. It is, nevertheless, a core requirement for understanding human organizations. Organizations are reducible to individual acts, yet they are lawfully and in part understandable only at the level of collective behavior.   (pp. 397–398)

As Payne and Pugh (1978) point out, this move to incorporate higher levels of analysis was a response to observed inadequacies of a more restricted focus:

The attempts of social and industrial psychologists in the 1950's and 1960's to explain the behaviour of small work groups and such phenomena as job satisfaction and job performance proved less than completely successful. It became clear that some of the variance was probably attributable to factors in the wider organization . . . .   (p. 350)

In 1973 this development gained recognition in psychological circles. Division 14 of the American Psychological Association, previously named the Division of Industrial Psychology, changed its title to the Division of Industrial and Organizational Psychology.

Developments in the field since the 1960s have shown increasing eclecticism and a healthy disregard for disciplinary boundaries. Organizational characteristics are less often viewed now as the mere background for the study of individual behaviour, but are brought into focus as important in their own right. The widening scope of organizational psychology can be detected in the shifts in content and interest of two of its influential texts, those of Katz and Kahn and Schein, over successive editions. In the Preface to their second (1978) edition, Katz and Kahn write:

Research is no longer contained within the boundaries of a single organization but crosses those borders to deal with environmental forces, relationships with other systems, and the effects of organizations on individual members as human beings and members of the larger society. That social psychological principles can be applied to all forms of collective organized effort is now acknowledged in many disciplines. Industrial psychology has moved towards becoming organizational psychology and not only studies behavior of people in many organizational settings but on occasion recognizes organizational or system variables in shaping that behavior.   (p. iii)

Schein (1980) in the third edition of his book sets out a similar argument:

First, traditional questions such as those of recruitment, testing, selection, training, job analysis, incentives, work conditions, and so on are now treated by the organizational psychologist as being interrelated and intimately tied to the social system of the organization as a whole. Second, organizational psychologists have begun to concern themselves with a new series of questions which derive from the system characteristics of organizations. These questions deal not so much with the behavior of individuals as with the behavior of groups, subsystems and even the total organization in response to internal and external stimuli.   (p. 7)

In his Preface Schein notes that in the fifteen years between his first and third editions there has been "an explosion" of academic endeavour in the field. In 1965 he saw the field as "new and in flux". In 1980 he says "the field has arrived". Schein notes how he has taken cognizance of these changes in his book:

I have added an explicitly developmental and sociological point of view to reflect the increasing interdisciplinarity of the field, even though the label "organizational psychology" still seems appropriate. . . .   (p. xiv)

This latter trend in organizational psychology represents an increasing convergence in all organizational sciences, for as Katz and Kahn note, in sociology there has been a trend towards using methods usually deployed by psychologists and an increased concern to integrate "psychological" levels of analysis. Terms such as "micro-sociology" have emerged to denote this movement.

In some areas, disciplinary rigidity is still in evidence, but for the most part disciplinary chauvinism is thankfully dead in organizational studies, though the same activities may often be seen under different labels: as when Gardner (1966) uses the term "organizational psychology", Pugh (1966) "organizational theory", Cummings (1978) "organizational behavior", and Mayntz (1964) "organizational science". The convergence of approach between these and other writers is motivated by an increasingly realistic problem-centred orientation, with less emphasis on purely theoretical or methodological justifications for their efforts. In short, as Sylvia Shimmin points out in the final essay of this collection, emphasis in the field is more on the "organizational" than it is on "psychology".

3.   The state of the field: science or art?

Despite the increasing overlap in the work of students of organizational processes it cannot be said that this amounts to any central consensus in the field. There is a loose common set of understandings about the nature of organizations as extensions of human intelligence and endeavour, yet beneath the span of this broad agreement there may be found a multiplicity of paradigms for the study of organizational processes. This diversity could be viewed as healthy in a young discipline if alternative views could be seen as moving towards some satisfying complementarity or if, according to a classical view of the accumulation of scientific knowledge, there was the constructive conflict of competing theories awaiting the adjudication of empirical test. Neither model fits, for in truth the field is populated on the one hand by people whose differences do not share the same universe of discourse (i.e. objectives and criteria) and consequently are unable to speak to one another, and on the other by those whose differences prescribe contrasting sets of methods and interpretive criteria and whose conflicts are philosophical rather than scientific. Is this unhealthy and unnatural? We think not. The fault lies less in what organizational psychologists have done than in the inappropriately narrow constructions of "science" that entail such negative judgements.

For some time now in the social sciences there has been a snowballing rejection of sole reliance upon the classical scientific paradigm, variously labelled "positivism", "dustbowl empiricism", "behaviourism" and "normal science". The opinion is increasingly voiced that "social sciences have been misplacing their energies by trying to ape the natural sciences" (see Weick, 1978, p. 39). This theme is one that is to be found in weak and strong forms in each and every essay of this collection. The intent in all cases is to point out alternatives, and deprecate the wilder extremes of "scientism" (for in truth "natural sciences" were never like this). However, before we bury classical science we need to quickly go through its pockets to make sure the good is not interred with the bad.[1] There is a danger in an equal and opposite reaction to positivism which leaves us with only a declamatory and unproductive anti-empiricism. The case is one which requires further examination.

One of the most startling pronouncements on the philosophy of psychology has been made by Koch. He did more than most in the adolescence of the discipline to establish its credentials as psychological science (producing through the late 1950s and the early 1960s the many-volumed *Psychology: A Study of a Science*, 1959–63). Little more than a decade later Koch issued a stinging indictment on the scientific aspirations of his colleagues. At a conference in 1971 (Koch, 1971; see also 1974) he declared:

> . . . such concepts as "law", "experiment", "variable", "control", "theory", do not behave sufficiently like their homonyms in the established sciences to justify the extension to them of the term "science". (p. 30)

He went on to say that psychology is afflicted with a "sickness of scientism" whose hallmark is a plethora of "images of man" around which "one finds a dense, scholastic cluster of supportive research, 'theorizing', and methodological rhetoric" (p. 6). Some insights have been achieved, but, he says, these are "overwhelmingly counterbalanced by the harvest of pseudo-knowledge that has by now been reaped" (p. 5). However, it is important to note that, for all their eloquence, Koch's condemnations are chiefly directed at the legacy of laboratory behaviourism, whose parallels within modern social and applied psychology tend to be oblique and infrequent. However, his analysis of the causes, consequences and remedy for the malady are potentially relevant to our concerns here.

A prime cause, says Koch, has been the striving to create a coherent discipline from so enormous a field.

Anything so awesome as the total domain comprised by the functioning of all organisms can hardly be thought the subject matter of a coherent discipline.   (p. 25)

Koch attributes psychology's striving for scientific respectability to the pressures of twentieth-century culture, which led to the constitution of psychology as a field of knowledge "by edict", something he notes that had never occurred in the history of ideas prior to the late nineteenth century.

Sciences have won their way to independence, and ultimately institutional status, by achieving enough knowledge to become sciences. . . . At the time of its inception, psychology was unique in the extent to which its institutionalization preceded its content and its methods preceded its problems. . . . Never had inquiring man been so harried by social wish, cultural optimism, extrinsic prescription, the advance scheduling of ways and means.   (p. 16)

Koch says that a corollary and a consequence of this has been the propensity for psychology to spawn "a-meaningful thinking", to be "rule-bound" and "a-ontological" in its treatment of the object of its inquiry, and to deal with man as "an ungainly and annoying irrelevance".

A great distance seems to supervene between the person and the object of knowledge. . . . They [the objects of knowledge] are dealt with, conjured with, arranged into relatively gross means–end or antecedent–consequent relations. The world, or any given part of it, is not felt fully or passionately; it is perceived as devoid of objective value.   (p. 8)

Koch believes that the institutionalization of psychology has been under the control of a twentieth-century world culture which places supreme value on "a-meaningful thinking" rather than what Polanyi (1960) has called "indwelling understanding". This intellectual alienation, argues Koch, "pervades all institutions and agencies which influence intellectual or scholarly style, habit, and sensibility" (p. 11). The consequences of this detached scientism are far-reaching, for he says that the knowledge produced

... when assimilated by a person, is no neutral addition to his furniture of confusions; it has an awesome capacity to bias the deepest attitudes of man towards Man, to polarize sensibility.   (p. 5)

Koch may have been one of the most forceful voices protesting the triviality or futility of some of our endeavours, but he has not been alone. Throughout social psychology there have been signs of a growing revolt against classically scientific conceptions of its paradigms. Specifically, Gergen (1973) has blamed the predominant ahistoricism of its concepts and methods for the insubstantiality of its theory. In a paper entitled "Social Psychology as History" he states:

Unlike the natural sciences, it deals with facts that are largely nonrepeatable and which fluctuate markedly over time . . . knowledge cannot accumulate in the usual scientific sense.   (p. 310)

Psychological knowledge not only reflects but changes its field of study. Following this train of thought Pepitone (1976) argues that psychological theories are "normative". They draw their terms and values from the social milieux in which and on which they operate. As such they are:

more characteristic of groups, classes and roles and other socio-cultural entities than of individuals observed at random.   (p. 641)

According to Sampson (1977), the fault in much of social psychology is that it has succumbed to the "American ideal of self-contained individualism", a point echoed by Frank Landy in this volume.

And what of remedies for these afflictions? The solution offered by humanistic psychology is vigorously derided by Koch (1971) as having constructed a "militant rhetoric of anti-rigour", a set of values that "challenge any conception of the person that would make life worth living", and "a passion for unending collection and elaboration of group engineering *methods*" (pp. 45 and 46, emphasis in the original), and in their review of organizational psychology Blackler and Brown (1978) similarly see positivism and humanism as the devil and the deep blue sea. Koch, however, admits to being sanguine about the feasibility of a

fruitful middle path. Psychology, he says, should be dissolved into relatively autonomous "fields of study", which may be collectively denoted
as "psychological studies" rather than psychological science. These, he
says, should maintain a fundamental empiricism in striving towards
"the rational classification of observed events" and "essay shrewd,
tough-minded, particulate, and differentiated analyses of interdepen-
dencies [of those events]" (p. 29).

Let the teaching of psychological studies and humanities be a matter of men exploring
the meanings of human experience, actions, and artifacts at their most value-charged
reaches, among men.   (p. 47)

A desire to reduce the gap between the representation of human
action and its meaning to the actors is a theme that is also prominent
among the objectives espoused by Gergen and other social psychologists, for whom this entails a more active recognition of changes over
time in the psychological dispositions of individuals and collectives, and
a heightened awareness of context. Gergen is explicit that social psychology can best grapple with these problems by taking the subject
matter out of the laboratory into the world of field research.

According to these views, organizational psychology could be seen to
be among the most promising of psychology's "fields of study" in following this route. In so doing, it admits a plurality of approaches to its focal
issues. According to a liberal definition of science most of these may be
considered "scientific" insofar as they make use of controlled observation and use feedback from empirical enquiry to modify ideas and future
empirical activities. We would argue that this view of science merely
commits one to the use of empiricism as a form of sense-making, and
does not entail the logic of positivist verification. Furthermore, the
better forms of "armchair theorizing" may be considered scientific insofar as they use explorations of symbols and meaning to understand
human behaviour, or test understanding by trying to change it through
the creation of new symbols and meanings. Indeed, the philosophical
pluralism of organizational psychology may indeed be considered one
of its chief sources of strength. This is evident from the range of its philosophical underpinnings. In his essay on this question Roy Payne reviews five "world views" which he finds are all represented in organizational psychology, and each could be seen as pragmatically appropriate
to different and legitimate objectives within the field. It may also be
argued that the "science" parts of "behavioural or social science" pose
less of a threat of stifling orthodoxy in applied fields where a major por-

tion of the impetus for problem generation is beyond the purview of theory and method, for it is in laboratory-based human research that the danger of game-like recursions of problem invention and resolution has been most evident. This is not to say that organizational psychology is immune from what Koch calls "truth by trivialization" or from research that is method-driven rather than method-using, and in a number of topics (such as leadership) there has been an immense volume of research effort for very little substantive return. However, what has emerged from such endeavours has been a widening appreciation of the requirements for further advances in the field. This could be said to anticipate a new paradigm for organizational psychology, composed of three interrelated themes or elements: individualized theorizing, contingent analysis, and interactionism. These themes recur throughout the essays of this volume, so we shall only briefly attempt to characterize here what they entail.

4. A new paradigm for organizational psychology?

It is a moot point whether the developments to which we refer already constitute a new paradigm, for even where there is agreement about what kinds of explanations for phenomena are needed, there is no clear agreement about the methodological innovations that these entail. The latter issue is raised with particular clarity in the essays by Paul Jackson and Jerald Hage, so let us here merely seek to establish on what set of common understandings such methodological efforts are based.

First, what we have called "individual theorizing" is the recognition of the limits to generalization about organizational phenomena and the temporal insubstantiality of our theories. As has been pointed out by the social psychologists to whom we have already referred, the cause lies in (a) the historical specificity of observed processes, and the tendency for apparently stable relationships to change with developments over time; and (b) the culturally normative character of behaviours, constructs and usages. The effect of these forces is the attenuation of so-called "laws" over time, shrinkage in explainable variance, and failures to replicate significant findings. Rather than chasing the chimera of bigger and better replication studies, researchers are increasingly pursuing three alternatives, each potentially more demanding of time and resources than conventional methods: (i) longitudinal designs to record changes over time and aid causal interpretation; (ii) comparative studies to define understanding of the contextual limitations of findings; and (iii) cross-validation in field-settings of ideas and findings generated by theory or laboratory research. The common thrust of these approaches is towards what Lawler (1974) has called the "individual organization".

Lawler notes that one of the founding emphases of academic psychology, the study of individual differences, has been overshadowed in the organization-behaviour literature by its counterpart, the study of similarities. He notes the density with which the management literature is populated by prescriptions of ideal organizational types and appropriate managerial practices. Lawler proceeds to reveal how individual differences can be observed to moderate the impact of job design (e.g. not all workers respond favourably to enriched jobs), pay systems, leadership styles, training methods, and selection instruments. The need for organizational theory and organizational design to achieve a more differentiated recognition of this is urgent.

It is increasingly recognized that conventional analytical methods and research designs have in the past been too locked into predisposition to reveal normative generalizations. They typically suffer from three afflictions: first, the triviality of inconsequential common sense; second, the simple-mindedness of bivariate associations or the "billiard-ball causality" of much model-building; and third, the insubstantiality of conclusions whose reliability decays with any move in space or time from their point of origin. In his essay, Jerald Hage grasps this nettle by exploring ways of departing from linear and additive approaches to theory-building. He draws attention to the need for attention to move towards deviant cases, and the development of grounded typologies of such phenomena. Denis Pym's interest in the study of "misfits" and disenchantment with the revelations of conventional methodologies parallels this concern.

The second element, contingent analysis, is the realization that the principal kind of complexity with which research must grapple more effectively is that of context. This is no new concern, for it has a pedigree which may be traced back through Brunswik and Lewin to William James. Its reawakening as a major concern may be observed in the controversies over how multivariate analytical techniques should cope with intervening variables such as mediators and moderators (e.g. Saunders, 1956; Zedeck, 1971). In his essay, Paul Jackson explores the analytical innovations that are necessary for further progress in the construction of valid findings, as does Jerald Hage from the design perspective. At the level of theory, it is clear that a change in conceptual framework must accompany such analytical developments. Specifically, Roy Payne sees this as entailing a shift away from the dominant paradigm of "mechanism" towards those which are better suited to a dynamic treatment of organizational reality.

Third, and finally, is the issue of interactionism, which to hark back to our quotations of Koch (who was citing Polanyi), refers to the need for a more "indwelling" understanding of the human world. A strongly emergent issue within most essays in this volume is how ultimately deceiving, but seductively convenient, many of the divisions that are drawn and accepted within the social sciences are. Dan Gowler and Karen Legge show how the internal boundaries of the knowledge process — between disciplines and levels of analysis — are a serious impediment to the evolution of inquiry, though unfortunately well entrenched through professional and institutional mechanisms. The distinction between subject and object, and knowledge of the world from the world itself, is viewed as a major problem by many writers. For Denis Pym, increased use of case methods is recommended. Roy Payne's advocacy of a philosophical pragmatism in organizational research, and the appropriateness of "selectivism" as a tool of interactionist thought, finds elaboration in the reflections of Frank Landy about the need for organizational modellers to be awakened to the reciprocation between the images of man they pursue and their choice of inferential strategies for scientific inquiry. Albert Cherns sees this interaction as operating at the level of culture, where social scientific thought has taken the place of theology and demonology, but without, perhaps, equivalent self-awareness and power.

At the level of research practice, it could be said that the interactionist concern is for more of what Chris Argyris in his essay calls "usable knowledge", and that which escapes the "single-loop" learning trap of many research interventions (i.e. those that fail to produce fundamental changes in the ways organizations adapt to their experience, or grow in their capacities). With parallel intent, symbolic interactionist and ethogenic approaches find strong advocacy in the essays of Iain Mangham and Dan Gowler and Karen Legge, who view them as paths to the goal of greater integration between knowledge and action. As we have already noted, the latter authors see some powerful vested interests standing in the way of the kinds of integrations they propose. A similar recognition is implicit in Sylvia Shimmin's call, in the closing essay of the volume, for the dissolution of the scientist/practitioner dichotomy. Some years ago, Miller (1969) urged that psychology be "given away" to ensure its continued vitality and social usefulness. Although Miller's clarion call is often quoted, there is little evidence that the kinds of direct knowledge and activity-sharing with a non-specialist public that this entails have taken place in mainstream psychology. To the extent that it shows an ability to do this, organizational psychology may enjoy greater vitality in the future than other fields of study. The essays that follow supply an abundance of ideas about how we can try to ensure that what we have to give away is both valuable and usable.

Notes

1. We are indebted to Frank Heller and William Shakespeare for this apt metaphor.

References

BASS, B. M. (1965). *Organizational Psychology*. Boston: Allyn and Bacon.

BLACKLER, F. H. M. AND BROWN, C. A. (1978). Behind conventional wisdom in organizational psychology. *Human Relations*, **31**, 333–351.

CUMMINGS, L. L. (1978). Towards organizational behavior. *Academy of Management Review*, **3**, 90–98.

CUMMINGS, L. L. (1981). Organizational behavior. *Annual Review of Psychology*, **32** (in press).

DUNNETTE, M. D. (1976). *Handbook of Industrial and Organizational Psychology*. Chicago: Rand McNally.

GARDNER, G. (1976). Organisational Psychology. *Occupational Psychology*, **40**, 101–106.

GERGEN, K. J. (1973). Social psychology as history. *Journal of Personality and Social Psychology*, **26**, 309–320.

KAHN, R. L., WOLFE, D. M., QUINN, R. P., SNOEK, J. D. AND ROSENTHAL, R. A. (1964). *Organizational Stress: Studies in Role Conflict and Ambiguity*. New York: Wiley.

KATZ, D. AND KAHN, R. L. (1966). *The Social Psychology of Organizations*. New York: Wiley.

KATZ, D. AND KAHN, R. L. (1978). *The Social Psychology of Organizations* (2nd edition). New York: Wiley.

Koch, S. (1971). Psychology as science. (Paper delivered at the Philosophy of Psychology Conference sponsored by the Royal Institute of Philosophy, held at University of Kent, England.)

Koch, S. (1974). Psychology as science. In S. C. Brown (ed.), *Philosophy of Psychology*. London: Macmillan.

Koestler, A. (1959). *The Sleepwalkers*. London: Hutchinson.

Lawler, E. E. (1974). The individualized organization: Problems and promise. *California Management Review*, **16**, 31–39.

Mayntz, R. (1964). The study of organizations—a trend report and bibliography. *Current Sociology*, **13**, 95–176.

Miller, G. A. (1969). Psychology as a means of promoting human welfare. *American Psychologist*, **24**, 1063–1075.

Mitchell, T. R. (1979). Organizational behavior. *Annual Review of Psychology*, **30**, 243–281.

Payne, R. L. and Pugh, D. S. (1978). Organizations as psychological environments. In P. B. Warr (ed.), *Psychology at Work* (2nd edition). Harmondsworth: Penguin.

Pepitone, A. (1976). Toward a normative and comparative biocultural social psychology. *Journal of Personality and Social Psychology*, **34**, 641–653.

Polanyi, M. (1960). *Personal Knowledge: Towards a Post Critical Philosophy*. Chicago: University of Chicago Press.

Pugh, D. S. (1966). Modern organization theory: a psychological and sociological study. *Psychological Bulletin*, **66**, 235–251.

Sampson, E. E. (1977). Psychology and the American ideal. *Journal of Personality and Social Psychology*, **35**, 767–782.

Saunders, D. R. (1956). Moderator variables in prediction. *Educational and Psychological Measurement*, **16**, 209–222.

Schein, E. H. (1965). *Organizational Psychology*. New York: Prentice-Hall.

Schein, E. H. (1980). *Organizational Psychology* (3rd edition). New York: Prentice-Hall.

Watson, J. D. (1968). *The Double Helix*. New York: Mentor.

Weick, K. E. (1978). *The Social Psychology of Organizing*. Reading: Addison-Wesley.

Zedeck, S. (1971). Problems with the use of "moderator" variables. *Psychological Bulletin*, **76**, 295–310.

2 Culture and Values: The Reciprocal Influence between Applied Social Science and its Cultural and Historical Context

ALBERT CHERNS

As soon as we begin to examine the relationship between a science and its cultural and historical context we plunge into deep water inhabited by strange and menacing creatures — philosophers of science, historians of science, scientists of numerous stripes, cultural historians, epistemologists and sociologists of knowledge. If we succeed in scrambling back to land we may be forgiven for resolving never to approach the water again. But we shall emerge without some of the certainties we took with us. No longer shall we take the "problems" of science as given nor accept methodologies as the cognitive derivatives of a universal scientific method.

We shall have been persuaded that what we take as science was the product of a particular, if protracted, period in the development of a particular form of society. We shall note especially that the notion of experimental science prospered in the intellectual climate of Europe in the seventeenth century in which discoveries had changed the shape of the world, in which the experience of the growing possibilities of man's control over his world suggested a new way of understanding by controlling.

The effectiveness of capitalism as a mode of acquiring control over the world by the creation of industries ensured that the growth of physical science was entwined with the growth of industrial capitalism. In its most vulgar form this fact is expressed in statements to the effect that science exists to serve the interests of the rich and powerful and therefore is an instrument of oppression of the weak. Less tendentiously it is pointed out that science requires resources and organization, that to obtain resources it has to assert and substantiate its claim to be fit and worthy to be entrusted with them by those who control the resources. Fitness and worth have two aspects: the first is concerned with the returns that may be expected, the other with the credentials of the particular subject matter and the particular people for whom the resources are sought. Science has to project itself as the way to acquire valuable knowledge, the scientists must substantiate their claim to practise true science. That this is more than a requirement that "scientific method" be used is clear from the history of psychical research or parapsychology. To defend themselves against the charge of charlatanry its practitioners have embraced the most rigorous and dreary forms of experimentation and control. Their negative outcomes are accepted as confirmation of the sterility of their enterprise; their occasional positive findings are greeted with a combination of scepticism and boredom. The status of parapsychology as a science has made little advance; the subject forms no part of the syllabus of psychology taught in our universities.

The disciplines of the social sciences claim areas of "knowledge". As we have seen, these claims are not necessarily validated simply because they are made. Indeed, even those which today appear secure and prestigious were forced to struggle hard to obtain that position. As recently as 1957, the *Cambridge Review* conducted a debate on whether sociology should be accepted in Cambridge as a fit subject to be taught to students. Intervening in that debate, George Homans declared that the question was no longer whether sociology was a university subject but whether Cambridge was a university. Resistance was finally overcome in 1960.

But the universities have not obtained a monopoly of validating knowledge. Instruments of the State have a stake, greater of course in centrally controlled societies, but considerable in all. As research in all sciences becomes more expensive and as universities and professors can no longer finance any but library research from their own resources, so the sources of research-funding determine what is and what is not science, what is and what is not potentially useful. Because the links between academies of science and research councils on the one hand and universities on the other are close, the latter providing the core of the membership of the committees of the former, the differences may not be great. In Britain, professors have been able to be more welcoming to the claims of new sub-disciplines or interdisciplines in research councils and committees than in the senates of their own universities. Of course the risks are less; an unsuccessful research team is easier to disband than a university department. There is now a well-worn path to respectability: first a research project, then a research group or unit, the award of higher degrees, the establishment of a course at Master's level and finally acceptance as a subject to be taught to undergraduates. The history of organizational behaviour in Britain is an excellent example of this process, culminating in the establishment of a Department of Behaviour in Organizations in the new University of Lancaster in 1969.

The acceptance of a discipline as "science" is an easier matter in a culture whose language makes no distinction between science and knowledge. *"Les sciences"* in France and *"Wissenschaft"* in Germany embrace the human and social as easily as the natural sciences. Indeed, in French cultures the term *"sciences humaines"* includes the "humanities" along with the social sciences. These differences are not merely linguistic; in France the more literary, historical and philosophical approaches are more firmly established within the social science disciplines than they are in English-speaking societies. And France is more hospitable than Britain to Freudianism and to structuralism in theory and to, for example, psychoanalysis and graphology in practice.

Again, law is firmly located among the social sciences in all societies except those which follow the English common-law tradition. This reflects the difference in the way in which the function of law is perceived. In England, in particular, where the rule of *Stare Decisis* is most strictly observed, the separation of legal thinking from social analysis is most obvious. Tangentially it may be observed that the modification of that rule by the House of Lords in 1966 has been paralleled by a growth in the association of law with other social science disciplines in university courses.

Psychology underwent far less pressure in the societies of continental Europe to become "scientific" than in the English-speaking world, where experimental psychology became the leading edge with the social and applied branches of the discipline, both assigned and accepting an inferior status, trying to mimic the method of the experimentalist. Denied the opportunities for direct experiment open to the psychologist,

sociologists sought scientific status through empiricism: the gulf between European and American and British sociology yawned wider and
wider until the 1960s when the retreat from "scientism" accompanied
the attack on positive science generated by the war in Vietnam.

Positivism and scientific empiricism ("critical" sociologists and
"humanistic" psychologists will have to forgive my use of the term
"scientific" in this context in preference to the more partisan, tenden-
tious and ugly "scientistic") were two sides of the same coin, both stress-
ing the uniqueness of information obtained through experience as the
basis of knowledge and the invalidity of judgement of value as untest-
able by experience. Durkheim (1895) defined the sociological method as
the study of social facts. And as to social facts, "[It] is, however, the
collective aspects of the beliefs, tendencies, and practices of a group that
characterize truly social phenomena" (p. 7). Thus no "social fact" can
exist outside of its historical and cultural context. "Applied" social
science is, then, both positivist and culturally bound — positivist because
it seeks the efficient causes of social phenomena and the laws or relationships which link the cause with the outcome, culturally bound because
it deals with social facts. It is positivist also in its Comtean belief that
scientific method provides the basis for more rational social life. In that
tradition have been such widely varied enterprises as the attempts to
apply Marxist theory to social and economic development, the search
for the personal and cultural roots of criminal behaviour and the application of tests of capacity to selection for industrial jobs. All, whether
macro- or micro-, represent forms of social engineering, improving the
operation of society by the application of knowledge derived from the
use in the social sciences of scientific method. Of course the concealed
term in the equation is whose is the definition of what the outcomes of
the operation of society are to be. If greater efficiency in matching tasks
to be learned to learning ability is the value sought, then educational
selection appears to be rational; if greater social equality is sought, it
does not. (Of course those simple arguments may be wrong because
intervening variables have been omitted, for example the stimulus to
learning of social competition or social facilitation or whatever.) But
that leads to another difficulty: an aim or objective may be stated, a
value enunciated, but outcomes are not simple. If all anticipated outcomes are specified, they may prove incompatible and, worse, new un-
anticipated and unwanted outcomes may be their accompaniment.

The retreat from positivism has not been solely the consequence of disappointing outcomes, though that has surely played a part. Its other causes have been a questioning of the right of authority to define the outcomes to be sought and a questioning of the validity of the empirical, scientific method. The attack on scientific method has many roots. Revolt against the apparent determinism of science is common to religion and romanticism, to mysticism and the artistic sensibility. The attack on the social system of science comes from various left-wing political sources, whose principal objection lies in the organization of science which, they claim, ensures that the choice of topic for investigation and the method of enquiry serve the ruling class. It is the attack on method which is the most radical. The easier target is method in social science, but scientific method itself has not escaped challenge. Phenomenologists and ethnomethodologists criticize the positivist base of empirical study of structures which, they argue, claim a privileged position for the mental maps of the rulers and managers. By emphasizing the meaning that the situation has for the actors in it, and the equal validity of each actor's interpretation, they assert the impossibility of an objective reading of any situation. By denying all striving for objectivity they deny all striving for a cumulative science. (For discussion of these issues, see Phillips (1973) and Gouldner (1971).)

The boldest challenge is to the objectivity of science and scientific method in the physical sciences as well, pointing to the commitment of great scientists to beliefs beyond the reach of test about the nature of nature, and to the interrelationships of method with objective, of means with ends. Wrapped in rhetoric and packaged in politics, the exact nature of this challenge is difficult to grasp; exactly how the beings in white coats would do their science differently in a different political system is unclear. Maybe they would not wear white coats.

Still nobody can deny that science despite all criticism has advanced and has associated with it enormously powerful technologies. Social science has few and shaky social technologies. And while much technology is under intense and critical scrutiny, partly because of its unintended consequences, the social technologies are in total disarray. Macro-economic methods are a mess and mental testing is presented as naked oppression.

The easiest retreat is into criticism. But if that criticism takes the form, as it inevitably does, of a denial of "objective laws", it is branded as bourgeois sociology fearing the destruction of its world,[1] a sharp attack from the rear.

In Britain, the high faith in the possibilities of social engineering which characterized postwar politics has declined, and with it the belief in the capabilities of applied social science. The prestige of the social sciences, high in the hopeful 1960s, is today lower than it has been since the days of the Clapham Committee (1946) which feared that their recognition would precipitate "the premature crystallization of spurious orthodoxies". With the loss of prestige and the ebbing of hope in the capacity of social science to reshape the world closer to the heart's desire has come a reorientation among social scientists themselves. It has not been enough to abandon the social engineering: it has become fashionable to decry what had been thought to have been achieved in the past. Thus, for example, we now know that the famous Hawthorne experiments were naively conceived, badly conducted, poorly controlled and do not sustain the conclusions drawn from them. In any case, the experimenters accepted the managerial perspective in the topics they chose for examination.

Here we need to pause to reflect on the problem of discussing the "cultural context" of applied social science. None of us is likely to find difficulty in giving meaning to the statement that what is taken to be a social problem is culturally determined. In a culture where sexual relations before marriage are discountenanced, teenage sex is a social problem; where they are acceptable, it is no problem. But can we assume culture to be unitary? Are all agreed on what is right and what is wrong, what is acceptable and what is a problem? Absenteeism is a problem for the management; is it a problem for the workforce? It is a problem for the foreman, is it a problem for the worker? As social scientists are we to accept that absenteeism is a problem we may be able to throw light on and perhaps help to reduce? It is the managerial culture that defines the problems on which applied social scientists work. And since management controls the resources of its organization it can divert some of them to paying for social science. The ethical question for the social scientist is obvious, if not always explicitly recognized in the past. Many have no difficulty in answering it. Their work, however sponsored, and under whatever auspices, will benefit all—workers as well as managers, prisoners as well as prison officers, public as well as officials, and so on. Furthermore, the humanist assumptions underlying their approach will ensure that its outcome will likewise serve humanist goals. Others are not so sure and strive to hedge their work with assurances; some disdain the entire enterprise. A few vociferously attack it as supporting and maintaining a system of which they disapprove. There is also a culture in which the social scientist works and one which defines for him what is and what is not an appropriate topic on which, and an appropriate method with which, to work. That culture, too, has been changing, and in Britain in recent years has become more estranged from a managerial culture.

At any time, then, there is a set of topics and problems which are understood to constitute the subject matter of an applied discipline. The set changes over time less because the topics are exhausted and the problems solved, than because they are differently perceived; the cultural context has changed.

Culture defines science but science revises culture. The disciplines, the sciences, are the chosen instruments through which society explores its own nature. In past centuries societies perceived themselves through the lens of history; the nature of man himself was to be found through theology. The twentieth century chose the social sciences as the mirror in which to view itself. To comprehend man the social sciences enter and help to shape our consciousness; our vocabulary of motives today derives from Freud not from Aquinas; from psychology and sociology, not from theology and demonology. When we are faced with a problem we search until we find an acceptable answer. What makes the answer acceptable? The acceptable answer fits our presumptions about causal relationships. We accept that the butler did it when we understand the motive; if he was about to be unmasked as a traitor or if his legacy under the will was about to be revoked, the motive is plain. If he was about to be unmasked as a philatelist or his legacy was about to be doubled, the causal chain appears defective. If he was possessed by demons we have been cheated. Our understanding of what causes what has been profoundly affected by social science. Many years ago I was working with problems of youth-training in the Royal Air Force. Officer after officer working with the apprentices and boy entrants reported that those with disciplinary difficulties came largely from broken homes. In fact, while boys from broken homes were indeed more likely to appear "on a charge", they accounted for a minority of charges. The explanation of the officers' misperception lay in their theories of causation. When a boy appeared on a charge the officer would try to understand the reason for the offence. He would ask questions until he received an answer which "explained" the offence for him. The discovery that a boy came from a broken home was such an explanation and was indeed the single most frequently occurring "reason". To make the point: if they had all had red hair, that would have been noticed, but if all their names began with a letter after R in the alphabet, that would not. We have learned a "vocabulary of motives" which we use to "explain" our behaviour. That a man of high status could kill another to protect his "honour", or a woman kill herself to protect hers, were acceptable motives in the eighteenth century, they would be considered evidence of mental disturbance today. Moral degeneracy through bad heredity "explained" crime in the nineteenth century, bad environmental conditions "explained" it yesterday, the oppressive structure of society "explains" it today.

Thus the "problems" on which social science works are in two ways the products of the social sciences themselves. On the one hand, they are framed in terms which express our understanding of the phenomena and their contexts—in other words, in the vocabulary of causation derived from the understanding of society provided by, or contributed by, the social sciences. On the other hand, they are rephrased in terms which make them accessible to the methods and predilections of the social scientists, both those who work on the problems and those who advise how the money available for research on problems should be spent.

The history of occupational and organizational psychology is a good example of the interaction of problem with method and of problem with a perspective progressively offered by the discipline itself. In tracing these interactions we need to be aware also of their relationship to the developments in the external society. Since I cannot here undertake a serious review of the history of organizational psychology, the picture I present will be both partial and schematic. It is fashionable, and may nevertheless be right, to begin the history of organizational psychology with F. W. Taylor (1911, 1923), who was not a psychologist but an engineer, and to include contributions from physiologists, anatomists (or functional anthropologists) and sociologists. I shall do the same. I shall also try to relate at each stage the present problem, the model of man in organization and the broader context.

We start, then, with Taylor and scientific management. Katz and Kahn (1978) assert that:

Industrial psychology began with a narrow focus; it accepted organizational variables as givens and tried to learn how people could best be selected and adapted for the required organizational roles. The orientation was pragmatic, and the organization was viewed as a machine. The dominating interest, explicit or implicit, was how the organization could be made more efficient. The scientific management school of Frederick Taylor (1923) conducted time and motion studies, investigations of temperature and illumination, rest intervals, and other conditions of work — always in relation to the criterion of productivity. This concern with ways of increasing productivity went hand in hand with personnel procedures for developing an appropriate fit between a particular role and its incumbent, preferably without modifying the role.   (pp. 9–10)

But their statement is over-emphatic and, to some extent, misleading. Taylor certainly sought to give to the human the attention which had formerly been reserved to the mechanical. But his system in practice consisted of:

1. The development of a science for each element of a man's work to replace the old rule of thumb methods.
2. The selection of the best worker for each particular task followed by a program for training the workman to replace the practice of allowing the worker to select his own task and train himself as best he can.
3. The development of a spirit of hearty co-operation between the management and the men in carrying on their activities in accordance with the principles of the developed science.
4. The division of the work in almost equal shares between the management and the workers, each department taking over the work for which it is better fitted as a substitute for the condition in which almost all the work and the greater part of the responsibility were thrown on the men.   (Babcock, 1917 p. 17)

In elaborating practice 4, Taylor paid attention to the role of foremanship, the establishing of a planning department, the "exception principle" in management, routing systems, cost systems, and so on. He can hardly be said to have taken the organization as given. In reflecting on the evil consequences of Taylorism and his managerial viewpoint on productivity we too easily forget his insistence that its benefits must include higher wages and that "no system or scheme of management should be considered which does not in the long run give satisfaction to both employer and employee" (1911, p. 21).

The context was a rapidly industrializing country, the United States at the turn of the century, with a largely immigrant workforce with no industrial experience. The model of man was that of a somewhat wayward, uncalibrated machine, economically motivated, and of organization as the most effective instrument for the division of labour.

The perception of worker as a machine was shaken by the failure of the women who replaced the men in the Royal Ordnance factories in the First World War to do twice as much work in sixteen hours as they did in eight. The medical physiologists who were asked by the Health of Munitions Workers Committee to study the problem investigated the onset of fatigue, the effects of hours of work, rest pauses and other conditions of employment. The impact of their findings was less to change the model of man than to initiate a tradition of work on the environmental factors affecting performance at work. The same context of war gave an impetus to the use of psychology in the selection and classification of the civilians called to, or volunteering for, military service. Special tests for special tasks were developed and in the United States the army instituted group methods of testing for all who were called to the colours. The army "Beta" test was devised for illiterates, instituting the methods of non-verbal testing. The model of man as a peg and job as a hole was triumphantly confirmed.

The model of man-in-organization as having an emotional and irrational side to his nature which had to be allowed for and worked around was one of the many outcomes of the Hawthorne studies. The concept of the "informal" organization with its norms, its modes of social control, the emphasis on the importance of the relations between worker and supervisor can be seen against the background of the growth of collectivist ideas during the 1920s and 1930s, the emphasis in explanations of behaviour on the unconscious, the irrational and the need to be loved. Giving the executive the lever to fix responsibility for morale on to his subordinate managers helped to delay the consequences for organization design of rising standards of education. The Second World War interrupted and its aftermath accelerated this.

Like the First, the Second World War as a context brought a new set of problems. Among them were the difficulties encountered in operating and maintaining new technologies. That experience forced our reconceptualization of weaponry as man–machine systems in which each component required "fitting" to the other. And it was the abrupt transition from the planned economy of war to the economy of the peacetime market that drew attention to the influence of the environment on organization functioning (Burns and Stalker, 1961), with the accompanying concept of the organization as an "open system". The postwar impact of mechanization on traditional industrial systems of work resulted in the new model of organization as a sociotechnical system focusing on the problems of job and organization design.

And as the consequences of widespread education became felt, so did the model of "complex" man with his hierarchy of needs obtrude itself,

directing the organizational psychologist to the problem of job enrich-
ment. Finally, in a context of growing challenges to established power,
we observe the emergence of the model of the organization as a power
system and the problem of "industrial democracy". The relationships
of context, problem, model and response are roughly schematized in
Table 1.

This schematic treatment gives less than full value to the contribution
of the psychology of organizations to our conceptualization of industrial
man. The work of the scientific management school emphasized the
notion of man as machine, but also as a poorly utilized one. The work
on selection, huge in quantity, emphasized — indeed overemphasized —
individual differences in capacity and ability to learn, reinforcing the
hierarchical concept (see Jaques, 1976) both of organization and of
society. The concept of the informal organization and the associated

TABLE 1

The interaction of context, problem, model and response

Context	Problem	Model	Response
1. Rapid industrialization	Inexperienced workforce	Economic man	Scientific management
2. Wartime pressure for production	Fatigue	Machine man	Work and environmental design
3. Wartime rapid change in occupation structure	Allocation	Man as peg, task as hole	Testing — fitting man to job
4. Interwar social conflict	"Informal" organization	Emotional man	Human relations
5. Wartime rapid advance in technology	Misfit between man and technology	Man–machine system	Ergonomic design
6. Transition from planned to market economy	Adaptation to changing environment	Organization as open system	Contingency approach
7. Impact of advanced technology on mature systems	Misfit between organization and technology	Organization as sociotechnical system	Job and organization design
8. Educated society	Dissatisfaction with work	Complex man — hierarchy of needs	Job enrichment
9. Challenge to established authority	Industrial conflict	Organization as power system	Industrial democracy

concept of "resistance to change" both emphasized the irrational and emotional in man and influenced understanding of the processes of innovation, contributing to the two-step theory of diffusion. The concept of a hierarchy of needs, originated outside but receiving its support and apparent validation from inside organizational psychology, has exercised great influence in the interpretation of society and, in particular, of social change. And half a century on from scientific management the "quality of working-life" school has demonstrated that man is indeed poorly utilized in organizations, but this time round it is his skill as a social and judgemental animal that is stressed, a contribution to anti-hierarchical views about society. And as organizations themselves have undergone change along with change in the values and attitudes of managers and workers towards themselves and each other, so have the preoccupations of organizational psychologists changed.

Over the 70 years that span the history of industrial, occupational and organizational psychology, the nature of industry has changed substantially. The heyday of the mass-production assembly line has come and gone, the shift towards process-flow production, computer control and the robot continues. The growth of white-collar jobs in industry and of the service and government sectors in employment have changed the scene in which organizational psychology is studied and practised. Hospitals, schools, banks, insurance companies, government offices are very large employers. In Britain, according to official statistics (*Social Trends*, 1979, HMSO), 45% of all employees are non-manual. As non-manual work has become more commonplace, so have the distinctions between manual and non-manual weakened. White-collar employment has in many areas become deskilled as was blue-collar employment in the transition to mass production. And as the computer takes over in the bank, so the problems emerge of a fit between the computer and the user. When the distinctions between white and blue collar were wide, the white-collared employee was close to management and largely shared management's perspective, attitudes and values. As white-collar employment grew and became less prestigious, more controlled by systems and even by machines, the wedge between it and management grew wider. Unionization was the response: white-collar membership of unions now approaches 40% of all union membership in Britain. The attention paid by organizational psychology has shifted too, although possibly less rapidly than these developments might warrant. At the same time much more attention is now paid to managers and management, and to the organization in its environmental context, paralleling the growing awareness of society's legitimate concern with what organizations are and do. Organizational psychology has not followed public concern in respect of industrial relations. Partly because industrial relations constitutes a separate discipline, and partly because unions have seen organizational psychology as management-oriented, this has become an area which organizational psychologists have found hard to penetrate. Also their approach is not historical enough, tending to focus on the forces in the present rather than on residues from the past which are less easy to fit into models of negotiation. Since industrial relations and particularly industrial conflict focus national attention, the work of the organizational psychologist has seldom captured national attention, nor had the opportunity of influencing public consciousness in the way open to economists and sociologists concerned with industrial relations.

Nevertheless, organizational psychology has contributed to the way in which our society understands the nature of the industrial revolution through which it has passed and the industrial society which it has become. The questions that are now posed betray this influence and the vocabulary of motives which derive from it. Among the most persistent is the question of "job satisfaction", a good example of the albatross. Having fashioned it, psychologists cannot get rid of it; the more elusive and unsatisfactory the concept turns out to be, the more firmly it enters the non-technical literature. It is, of course, seldom that scientific concepts are understood in precisely scientific form outside of science; the more influential they become, the less they cleave to their scientific origins. That is partly due to the change in context as they pass from the world of science to the world outside. But it is also partly due to the inherent subversiveness of scientific ideas. So much do we expect them to be subversive that we suspect any tendency that appears to support existing modes of understanding. Durndell (1977) considers the question of whether psychology inevitably supports the *status quo*, as claimed by its most assertive critics:

What is to be considered here is whether psychology, as some of its left-wing critics would argue, has and will necessarily play a part in the subjection of, for instance, women, blacks, and homosexuals. The argument that psychology is *necessarily* an oppressor of women is very hard to accept. Whereas it is true that many psychologists have incorporated much of society's and their own views about the inferior position of women into vocational tests . . . and ideas of normality, it is equally true that the reverse occurs. . . . To try and assess the stereotypes and perceptions that are held by various sections of the population about maleness and femaleness does not imply at all that the investigator feels women to be inferior or accepts these stereotypes — the reverse could be the case. Attempting to increase our knowledge about the way that socialization, genetics and hormones affect human sexuality can just as easily be seen in the context of helping to change sex roles as in the context of preserving them.

It has also been argued that psychology oppresses blacks, in particular through the use of IQ tests to prove that they are less intelligent than whites and therefore deserve an inferior place in the world *vis-à-vis* whites. Whilst it is undoubtedly true that Jensen and his allies have done a great deal to provide racialist groups with ammunition, it is also true that a very great deal of opposition to these ideas has come from within psychology.   (pp. 320–321)

Turning to industrial psychology, he argues:

Industrial psychology is another area that radicals often assume is necessarily conservative, conning more out of the workers. On the basis of much industrial psychology it could be argued, however, that frustration and alienation at work can be lessened by involving the workforce in decision-making and giving them control over their working environment. How does realizing the importance of good communication, good working, good job-design and accident prevention necessarily exploit the workers? The problem is of course whether this takes place within a context of increasing production to increase profits or making work more beneficial and pleasant for the workers. (p. 321)

And he concludes:

The conclusion from all this is that psychology as a whole is not necessarily oriented towards the *status quo*, but it has a strong tendency to be so, particularly because of the pressures that employers of psychologists are liable to put on them in guiding research areas and techniques which are to be used towards the ends the employers desire. The extent to which individual psychologists are able to question the *status quo* would depend on the culture in which they live. . . .   (pp. 321–322)

Ford (1977), on the other hand, argues that occupational psychology has reinforced the dominant economic view of man at work:

This traditional conception of work may have generated a certain convergence in the practising occupational psychologist's vision of his role, i.e. the employers' role-expectations would be oriented towards increasing productivity by improved work-adaptation and making working conditions more tolerable, not necessarily to examine the overall effect of the nature of work on an individual's personality. . . .

. . . occupational psychology has tended to depart from its general psychological disciplinary roots by perpetuating an economic framework of occupational adjustment — in other words concentrating on ergonomics, wages, promotion, hours and conditions of work, training, advertising effects and so on — at the expense of de-emphasizing the wider psychological framework of occupational choice and adjustment. . . .   (p. 374)

And:

Perhaps the imbalance in favour of an economic framework rather than a psychological framework of occupational adjustment is a sequel to the experimental psychologist's value of controlled observation, replicability, theoretical developments and scientific objectivity.   (p. 374)

Kelly and Llewelyn (1978), in their prescriptions for the British Psychological Society, clearly believe that applied psychology is political in its impact:

In many of our activities as psychologists, especially in the applied field, we are acting *politically*. We should therefore recognize this fact and become conscious of what we are doing. The issue confronting us then becomes one of differentiating *between* political beliefs, rather than avoiding them *in toto* with naive formulations about politics and well-being. Therefore we do not believe that the Society should place all political beliefs on a par and accord them equal treatment.

. . . we believe it *would* be legitimate to stipulate minimal criteria for the avoidance of certain actions and results. Specifically, we would suggest that the Society ought to condemn psychological work (however defined) which in any way impairs the actual or perceived interests of groups in society which are disadvantaged in terms of access to . . . education, income, authority, etc. Political beliefs underlying work of this kind, such as racialism, should be unequivocally condemned. . . .

Whilst the criterion above *may* involve the subordination of some people's well-being to that of others we should recognize . . . that both the unequal distribution of rewards and opportunities, and the presence of conflicts in society, render this inevitable.   (p. 260)

Occupational and organizational, along with other applied psychologists have always thought they were doing good, were on the side of the angels, and alleviating the lot of man. The views I have quoted above reflect changes in the ideas in good currency in society generally, rather than changes in organizational psychology itself. Insofar as those ideas owe their origins to social science thinking, it is to sociology rather than to applied psychology. The subversive ideas in organizational psychology have been largely confined to the field of organizations, although they may have influence outside it. The concepts of non-hierarchical organizations, of power to the periphery, are largely subversive. They link with other ideas drawn from ecology in the "small is beautiful" fantasia. But they have not given rise to an organizational anti-psychology. You can think of madness outside of asylums; psychologists do not think of work outside of organizations. The psychology of sport and leisure takes over, although with the increasing organization of both it should perhaps be the other way about. Maybe psychologists have, like everyone else, fallen into the trap of confusing work with employment. And while we have psychologized and philosophized about the place of work in the life of man we have with our ergonomic hats on colluded in taking the work out of employment. Much of what is written about work is actually about employment. The subversive thoughts lead to an anti-organizational psychology of work, not to an organizational anti-psychology. Sociology brewed with them does not give the lethal draught that it provides when brewed with psycho-pathology: you can prove that madness does not exist but you cannot banish the idea of work. The really significant difference is that by the nature of his work the clinician's client is his patient, the organizational psychologist's client is not the worker.

That brings us back to the context in which organizational psychology is performed. Although part of psychology and influenced—as is psychology—by the adjacent disciplines of economics and sociology, organizational psychology as an applied discipline is unfree of its context. Much of its knowledge is gleaned from work in large organizations, usually stable and moderately progressive. I do not know of any account of work in a failing or disappearing organization, yet many fail each year.

The dominant paradigm of social science during the early period of organizational psychology was a structural functional one, eminently appropriate for the examination of stable societies and organizations. That paradigm is now unpopular, discredited in favour of those giving more prominence to conflict. While in the past the gap between the "pure" and applied disciplines was small, it is widening today. In the past that gap was more one of prestige than of paradigm; the applied psychologist like the applied scientist has less status than his "pure" colleague. But in the past the parent discipline was experimental psychology; today the parent discipline of organizational psychology is social psychology and a sociological social psychology at that. After the gap between psychology and social psychology we cross another to organizational psychology, an "applied" discipline, and another to the world of the practitioner. And as the academic climate turns critical, a wedge is driven between the academic organizational psychologist and the practitioner which has not been removed by the emergence of action research. Action research, indeed, creates new problems. Claiming a special dispensation for scientific publication from the requirement of replicability, action research is hazardous for those who seek academic advancement and renders its followers second- or third-class academic citizens. Action researchers *do* acquire clients among those with whom they work. Not surprisingly, then, they are more likely to acquire the critical perspective that has troubled some of their clinical colleagues. Prone, too, to a humanist perspective which rejects the implicit goals and measurements of the organizations with which they engage, they are embarked on a course whose destination is as yet unclear. This unclarity and uncertainty is surely characteristic of our times; when the ability to select goals and chart the route is lacking, all we can hold to is our values; the goals, as in action research, are emergent.

Note

1. See *The Foundations of Marxist Leninism*, Foreign Languages Publishing House, Moscow, p. 141.

References

BABCOCK, G. D. (1917). *The Taylor System in Franklin Management*. New York: The Taylor Society.

BURNS, T. AND STALKER, G. M. (1961). *The Management of Innovation*. London: Tavistock.

CLAPHAM COMMITTEE (1946). Report of the Committee on the Provision for Social and Economic Research. Cmd. 6868, July. London: HMSO.

DURKHEIM, E. (1885). *The Rules of Sociological Method*. New York: Free Press.

DURNDELL, A. (1977). Does psychology support the *status quo? Bulletin of the British Psychological Society*, **30**, 320–322.

FORD, R. G. (1977). A further look at the role of the occupational psychologist. *Bulletin of the British Psychological Society*, **30**, 373–375.

GOULDNER, A. W. (1971). *The Growing Crisis of Western Sociology*. London: Heinemann.

JAQUES, E. (1976). *General Theory of Bureaucracy*. London: Heinemann.

KATZ, D. AND KAHN, R. L. (1978). *The Social Psychology of Organizations* (2nd edition). New York: Wiley.

KELLY, J. E. AND LLEWELYN, S. P. (1978). Abuses of psychology for political purposes: Some critical remarks on the Working Party Report. *Bulletin of the British Psychological Society*, **31**, 259–260.

PHILLIPS, D. L. (1973). *Abandoning Method*. San Francisco: Jossey Bass.

TAYLOR, F. W. (1911). *Shop Management*. New York: Harper.

TAYLOR, F. W. (1923). *The Principles of Scientific Management*. New York: Harper.

3 The Nature of Knowledge and Organizational Psychology

ROY L. PAYNE

Success in the pragmatic sphere is a matter of the avoidance of affective mishaps and the attainment of affective satisfaction through the effective guidance of the actions of a being emplaced within a difficult and generally unco-operative world. (Rescher, 1977)

Rescher's comment seems particularly apt at this moment. It is proposing the validity of pragmatism as a way of understanding the human situation, a view which I also support. His comment conveys my present intention, which is to provide guidance in the epistemological domain and to provide it in a way which is, I hope, affectively satisfying. I introduce some of the basic concerns and concepts of epistemology, but a modest innovation is that they are derived from a psychological model of learning. The essay, in this sense, is largely pedagogical. But there is also a polemical element in that I argue for the primacy of pragmatism as the appropriate epistemology for organizational psychology. In this sense, I believe I provide an epistemological justification for the views of some of the other authors in this volume, whether they realize they are being pragmatic or not.

The detailed implications of pragmatic thought are not dealt with here, but the reference section provides enough information for the interested reader to explore it. There is much to be done to develop the links between pragmatic philosophy and research practice, so even these readings provide the tools rather than the prescriptions. The books by Rescher (1977) and Pepper (1966) are particularly important, and we can finish this introduction, as we began, with a quotation from Rescher that makes the point: ". . . the epistemology of what might be called the lesser degrees of cognitive warrant remains a relatively "undeveloped area" (p. 114).

1. How do we acquire knowledge?

Kolb *et al.* (1974) have proposed a model of human learning which is portrayed in Fig. 1. It describes the process by which we acquire cognitive knowledge. I distinguish this from the acquisition of habits: the acquisition of habits is better described by Skinner's (1974) theories. Usually, but not necessarily, the knowledge process starts with our *concrete experience*. Something happens which surprises us in the sense that it doesn't fit neatly with our present knowledge or understanding. We have noticed this deviant signal/phenomenon and we may *observe* it more, or *reflect* on what the event might mean and how it came about. If we are able, and sufficiently motivated, we may then generate a hypothesis or hypotheses about what caused the event and, by implication, what might explain this event and others similar to it. We have

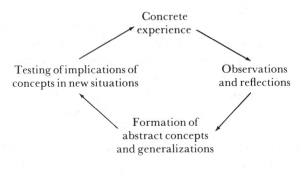

Fig. 1.

started to make the explanation *abstract*. We might speculate in passing, that this is partly because past experience has conditioned us to appreciate that the capacity to generalize has survival value. This is true only if the generalization works, of course, so we now move to *test* our hypothesis, possibly by an experiment. If successful, the hypothesis (verified or at least not refuted) can be tested further against our concrete experience and so on until our knowledge becomes more and more refined. If a sufficient number and variety of iterations around this process occur, it is likely that the hypothesis will change its status to a theory, something more general. It is perhaps worth a small digression to make clear how *I* am using some of these terms.

Figure 2 contains a simple (oversimple?) table which attempts to distinguish four basic terms: fact, hypothesis, theory and law.

	Particular	General
Constructions of the mind	Hypothesis ←——→	Theories
Observed/Discovered	Facts ←———→	Laws of nature

FIG. 2. A way of seeing some epistemological concepts.

The table suggests a classification into particular versus general and observed/discovered versus constructions of the mind. It shows also that each of these four concepts has effects on its immediate neighbours and that the effects are in both directions. Facts lead to hypotheses, but hypotheses expose new facts. Hypotheses lead to theories, but good theories lead to new hypotheses.

Facts then are particular things or events which do exist or have existed.

Hypotheses are particular statements (not yet known to be true) which can be used to explain particular occurrences. They are required to be consistent with natural laws and relevant theories. Theories are overthrown by theories, not hypotheses.

A *theory* is a unified system of hypotheses with explanatory power. It contains more than the facts that have been observed and leads to the observation of new facts.

Natural laws, like facts, are observed or discovered. They are invariant relations in nature, e.g. the boiling point of water at sea level. Ayer (1976) emphasizes the distinction between generalizations of law and generalizations of fact by arguing that the former entail unfulfilled conditionals. He uses the example that because all living men are warmblooded we can predict that unborn or undiscovered men will be warm-blooded. But whilst we can make the generalization of fact that if a meeting passes a motion unanimously every person voted for it, we cannot infer that anyone else who had gone to the meeting would have voted for the motion. Thus, whilst we can make generalizations of fact, they are ultimately judged by the particular.

Apart from getting a particular perspective on some basic terms, this excursion has also served to emphasize that the learning process described by Kolb is time-bound. It is only by repeating this process many times that knowledge advances to theories and laws. The iterations usually involve different people, of course. My reason for emphasizing this is that I wish to use Kolb's model as the core of knowledge acquisition and then move from it to consider the kinds of knowledge produced by this process and the relation of methodology and epistemology to it.

2.   Knowledge-acquisition, methodology and epistemology

Figure 3 illustrates the relationships between the knowledge-acquisition process (method), methodology (which informs the method), and epistemology (which informs methodology). The diagram also shows three kinds of knowledge which are produced by this process of inquiry. They are the three kinds of knowledge commonly distinguished by epistemologists. The diagram contains feedback loops from the criteria for evaluating this knowledge to emphasize the connection with epistemological principles. Before describing the three forms of knowledge and the criteria for evaluating them, I shall define methodology and epistemology.

Methodology, according to Abraham Kaplan (1964) is:

. . . to describe and analyse methods, throwing light on their limitations and resources, clarifying their presuppositions and consequences, relating their potentialities to the twilight zone at the frontiers of knowledge. It is to venture generalizations from the success of particular techniques, suggesting new applications, and to unfold the specific bearings of logical and metaphysical principles on concrete problems, suggesting new formulations. It is to invite speculation from science and practicality from philosophy. In sum, the aim of methodology is to help us to *understand*, in the broadest possible terms, not the products of scientific inquiry but the process itself.

Epistemology might be defined in contrast as helping us to understand, in the broadest possible terms, not the process of scientific inquiry, but the nature and possibility of its products (knowledge). What is knowledge, truth or reason? What possible forms can knowledge take? In Fig. 3 I have indicated the three conventional answers to this last ques-

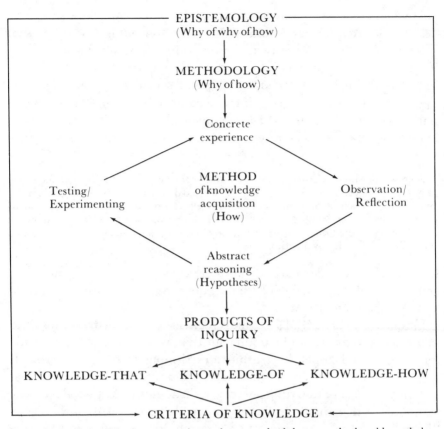

FIG. 3. The relationships between epistemology, methodology, method and knowledge.

tion and will now turn to the more substantive issue of what these three types of knowledge mean.

3. Kinds of knowledge

Knowledge is often held to be of three types: knowledge-that, knowledge-of and knowledge-how (e.g. Pears, 1971; Hamlyn, 1971). Hospers (1967) refers to the same three types as propositional, acquaintance and know-how knowledge. "Knowledge-that" is sometimes called "factual knowledge", and Phillips (1973) sub-divides factual knowledge into facts as things and facts as propositions. Russell (1912) divides "knowledge-of" into knowledge by acquaintance and knowledge by description. Acquaintance knowledge refers to what is directly present to a person when he/she is aware of something. Russell held such knowledge to be direct, immediate, certain and incorrigible, and all other knowledge, which would be knowledge by description, would be founded upon it. Knowledge by acquaintance can, therefore, only entail sense data, memory data, the self and universals. It specifically excludes knowledge of objects. Hamlyn (1971) gives short shrift to this suggestion:

> This knowledge must be essentially contentless, since any attempt to say what one knows must be to go beyond the immediate experience and desert knowledge by acquaintance. In this sense, therefore, the concept of knowledge by acquaintance [Russell's sense of it] is both useless and misguided. There is no such thing as knowledge by acquaintance in this sense, since what one knows must always be identifiable under a description and this implies knowledge by description.   (p. 106)

In fact, Hamlyn had earlier almost rejected the value of the more general use of "knowledge-of" by arguing that it is really a variant of "knowledge-that".

Similarly, Pears (1971) virtually converts "knowledge-how" into "knowledge-that" when he points out that as soon as one can provide meaningful and hopefully truthful descriptions of how something is done (knowledge-how), one has actually moved to a state of factual knowledge-that. Both writers, however, distinguish what I believe to be states of intra-individual knowledge which are distinguishable as "knowledge-of" (acquaintance of a person, for example) and "knowledge-how" (to balance on a bike without being able to explain how one does it). For this reason, the distinctions are retained by them and other epistemologists, but when it comes to knowledge that is available to more than one person, "knowledge-that" seems to be the proper designation. A sophisticated discussion of these forms of knowledge can be found in Rozeboom (1972) who argues that knowledge-how and knowledge-of can both be subsumed under knowledge-that.

The purpose of this brief description is to illustrate the complexity surrounding these issues and the fact that there is no precise, universal agreement about different kinds of knowledge. I wish, therefore, to return to Kolb et al.'s model of the learning process and use it to show how there are different kinds of knowledge emerging from this process. Happily, they parallel the types already described.

As we saw in Fig. 1, Kolb et al. suggest that human learning derives from a process of concrete experience, reflection, hypothesis-building and testing out of hypotheses. Obviously, the amount of effort put into each phase will vary with the problem and with the individual. Any one part could be minimal or perhaps even non-existent. In day-to-day learning, abstract theorizing is likely to be of low priority, which is perhaps why it has become the province of specialist institutions like universities. Kolb *et al.*'s model and the developments from it that I now wish to describe appear in Fig. 4. I have altered Kolb *et al.*'s terms slightly so that they are all given as verbs. This seems more suitable to a process and consistent with pragmatism as a guiding epistemology (Pepper, 1942).

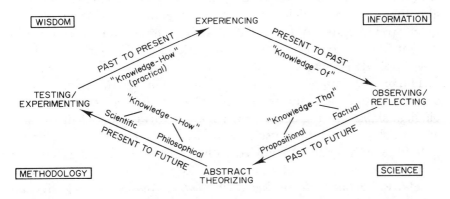

FIG. 4. Forms of knowledge and the learning cycle.

The concrete experience phase of this process is dependent on our individual sensations and perceptions. The knowledge we have is that of the "facts of the situation" — that of which we are aware. This stage of the learning cycle involves "knowledge-of" or acquaintance knowledge. Knowledge-of, as Hamlyn (1971) expresses it, arises from "a confrontation between subject and object". It might be described as personal knowledge. It is worth noting that a common-sense understanding of knowledge might involve dismissing this as true knowledge. A common-sense view of "true knowledge" might be regarded as concerning publicly available facts. Some of the difficulties surrounding the definition of kinds of knowledge may be illuminated if it is recognized that "knowledge-of", acquaintance knowledge, is intra-individual knowledge.

Continuing our path around the learning cycle, the next stage involves observation of and reflection on our awareness. This involves comparing present awareness with past experience. We are drawing on factual knowledge. It may be personal to us, but this part of the process could entail a search for facts about situations similar to this one. From this comparison of "knowledge-of" and "knowledge-that" (factual) we begin to build ideas about how situations like this may be more generally explained. We begin to build propositional knowledge about similar situations and phenomena. This division of "knowledge-that" into facts and propositions is not dissimilar to Ayer's distinction between primary and secondary systems (Ayer, 1976). The primary system deals largely with facts and the secondary system "goes beyond the facts in that it legislates for possible as well as actual cases, and can also contain terms which are not directly related to anything observable" (p. 33). Later, Ayer (p. 210) describes the secondary system as a "scientific one", being a further justification for the descriptive label I have applied in Fig. 4.

The propositions now need to be evaluated or tested, which involves our ability to actually do the testing. Good tests involve our methodological skills. For the actual experimenter this is "knowledge-how". Methodology as a subject itself, of course, exists outside the particular individual and is really "knowledge-that" (factual). The separation of methodology as a type of knowledge may be unusual, but it may be timely. In his book *Methodological Pragmatism* Rescher (1977) offers an epistemology in which pragmatic criteria are applied to methods of inquiry in such a way that method is an absolutely central part of the knowledge process. Rescher expresses it (p. 70) in this way: "Our knowledge, after all, is not just a matter of theses (of propositional *knowledge-that*), but also—and perhaps even more fundamentally—a matter of ways of doing things (of *how-to knowledge*)." And he adds that, "pragmatic considerations provide the requisite *controls*, the proper standards of operative efficacy for our cognitive methodologies" (p. 286).

If the tests are reasonably satisfactory and the propositions are consequently regarded as sound, the knowledge may then be further tested against concrete experience. At this stage we return to knowledge within an individual, and such knowledge is "knowledge-how". All these kinds of knowledge are refined by iterating around this process. For "knowledge-that" it is mandatory that this occurs and preferable that different people take part in the process: in Pepper's (1942) phrase, the evidence involves "multiplicative corroboration".

Time is an important and neglected variable in our understanding of knowledge. In Fig. 4 I have indicated the different time-orientations of the stages of learning and the types of knowledge associated with them. The time-direction of acquaintance knowledge ("knowledge-of") is from the present to the past. Our awareness is of the facts of the current situation, but that awareness is conditioned by and relative to the past. The present calls on the past, and present meaning is derived largely from a comparison with past experiences.

This is also true for one aspect of "knowledge-that". Factual knowledge is rooted in the past. The comparison between present awareness and the past may involve a comparison with a similar experience/situation, but it will also be informed by our factual knowledge of the world. And factual knowledge is derived from the past even though it is operative in the present.

The time-orientation of propositional knowledge is from the past to the future. Propositional knowledge concerns stating the relationship amongst variables, and the propositions may contain, and usually imply, a reason or explanation about the relationship. They are also predictions: x is related to y and will continue to be so (usually, anyway). That's why propositional knowledge is so useful and psychologically comforting—it reduces anxiety. Science is often defined as the ability to predict and control and, in this sense, scientific knowledge is propositional knowledge. Much factual knowledge is also regarded as scientific.

The epistemological journey round the learning cycle has so far revealed the value of dividing "knowledge-that" into factual and propositional knowledge. It has also revealed a distinction in "knowledge-how": methodology versus practical action. It is a difference in degree rather than kind, but the knowledge process depends greatly on sound and rigorous attempts to refute propositions, as the reference to Rescher emphasizes. This is the province of the technology of knowledge—of methodology as it was earlier defined. It's time-orientation is from present to future. Experiments are conducted to establish the validity of a current proposition so that our future knowledge will be increased.

The learning cycle returns us to present experiencing, and to further application of the knowledge obtained. At this stage the knowledge, if it is used at all, is used to solve practical problems. It becomes practical know-how knowledge and actual application and utilization may involve creative, tactile, auditory and kinaesthetic skills and experience which were less obvious at the testing/experimenting stage. At that stage, cognitive processes and factual knowledge usually dominate. In practical situations, success may depend more on wisdom than on science. The time-orientation of practical knowledge is from past to present. The wisdom gained from the past is used to solve problems in the present. And more often than not, the attempt raises new problems and the cycle starts again.

In summary, knowledge is of several types; "knowledge-how: practical" and "knowledge-of" lie within the individual; "knowledge-that" and "knowledge-how: scientific/philosophical" are extra-individual. Since knowledge depends on individual learners, however, it is obvious that all types of knowledge are necessary to the successful working of the knowledge process. Furthermore, each type of knowledge has a different time-orientation reflecting its different role in the knowledge process.

So far, we have discussed how knowledge is created and the different kinds of knowledge involved in the process. We have done so without really asking what knowledge is.

4.   What is knowledge?

The answer will vary according to the type of knowledge. For "knowledge-of" the answer must contain references to the beliefs and declarations of the person whose awareness is in question. For "knowledge-how" reference must be made to the success/failure of the attempt to solve the problem or perform the act: can the claimant actually ride a monocycle to the satisfaction of a group of "reasonable men", and can he do it on more than one occasion?

It is obvious that these criteria alone would not be satisfactory for those interested in propositional and factual knowledge, and this is reflected in the greater consideration these forms of knowledge have been given by philosophers. Adequate answers, and they are no more than that since there are differences amongst thinkers about them, would require even further elaboration of the types of knowledge. The interested reader can discover some of these subtleties by comparing some of the writers already mentioned (e.g. Hamlyn, Ayer, Pears and Hospers). I wish to present one approach to the corroboration of knowledge and I have argued elsewhere (Payne, 1975) that this view satisfactorily covers and reconciles many of the issues raised by several contemporary philosophers of science—e.g. Popper (1963), Kuhn (1962) and Toulmin (1972).

A. STEPHEN PEPPER'S "WORLD HYPOTHESES"

Burtt (1943) commenced a review of Pepper's book with these words: "A volume has just appeared which, should the time prove ready for it, may well inaugurate a new era in the writing of systematic philosophy" (p. 590). Amongst the many fine things Pepper achieves in *World Hypotheses* (1942) are the distinctions amongst the various kinds of evidence about the world which can be used to corroborate claims to knowledge. These can be classified into two broad types which Pepper calls "multiplicative corroboration" and "structural corroboration". Before describing these, however, it must be noted that Pepper believes that knowledge is ultimately rooted in our "common-sense" appreciation of the world. The search for knowledge starts with common sense, but when we have questioned, doubted and refined that common-sense knowledge, we may be forced to return to it to defend ourselves from the determined sceptic who may claim we can never know anything. Thus Pepper refers to common-sense knowledge as *dubitanda*—claims to be doubted. The development of knowledge is therefore defined as the process of "cognitive refinement": the criticism and improvement of common-sense claims. One of the advantages of this definition is that it avoids the question as to whether something is or is not scientific: i.e. the demarcation dispute (Magee, 1973). In principle, poetry, drama, intuition, and divine revelation are acceptable cognitive refinements. The confidence we would have in such evidence would be judged by the procedures inherent in multiplicative and structural corroboration.

1. *Multiplicative corroboration: empirical and logical data*

This simply means that a claim to cognitive refinement is validated if many men/women argue that such and such is the case. Pepper agrees that such multiple agreements can be obtained about two sorts of things —empirical facts and logical facts. Pepper calls these "data". An example of empirical data would be that men and women all over the world have observed that water boils at 100°C. Similarly, Euclid's geometrical laws provide a universal example of logical data. Data are not usually so well established as these two examples. Many of our data are what Pepper would call "rough" — empirical claims for the existence of Unidentified Flying Objects have been made by many people, but not by enough people for most of us to be convinced of their existence.

Positivists would claim that multiplicative corroboration is the only sure way to refine cognitions about the world. Pepper disputes this because the areas of knowledge for which it works are very limited — physics and chemistry — and furthermore because even in these subjects the data are often "rough", relying ultimately upon common sense. A second argument is more complex but ends in demonstrating that a person wishing to propose that data are the only reliable form of knowledge must have a hypothesis as to why his position is held. The grounds for any such argument could not be based on data, but only on some hypothesis about the structure of the world. Thus we arrive at structural corroboration and world hypotheses.

2. *Structural corroboration : world hypotheses*

Pepper uses a concrete example to distinguish between multiplicative and structural corroboration. The claim is that a chair is strong enough to be sat upon and not broken. Multiple corroboration would be obtained by having many persons sit upon it. Structural corroboration would be achieved by having a theory about what is required of a chair to achieve this. What wood, of what dimensions, of what arrangement, would be required? If a chair exists or is constructed to satisfy this theory/hypothesis, then structural corroboration has been achieved.

Each of the components of structural corroboration rely ultimately on multiplicative corroboration, and in this sense data might appear to take priority over danda. There is, however, fluctuating tension between the two sorts of evidence. The problem with highly refined data is that they have been refined to such an extent that they commit themselves to very little. In Karl Popper's terms they have a very low probability of being falsified, but as a result have a very low information content (Magee, 1973, p. 36). Furthermore, a refined datum would most likely be interpreted also as part of a more encompassing structural hypothesis. Returning to the strength of our chair: if the evidence suggests the chair is weak, but someone actually sat on the chair without breaking it, would one be inclined to assume the hypothesis was wrong, or would one interpret this datum in the light of the structural hypothesis? That is, assume the person was too light to break the chair, or he didn't put all his weight on it. Unless such an event occurred many times, the evidence would be interpreted in terms of the structural hypothesis, or the dandum. As Pepper puts it,

The question is one of proportion and it appears that structural evidence does not give way to multiplicative evidence, unless the latter is based on very considerable agreement among many observers and unless it cannot be interpreted to fit the hypothesis which organised the structural evidence.   (p. 51)

The conjecture would have been refuted, and as Popper (1963) has taken pains to point out, even this does not lead to a victory for data, but to another opportunity for a better conjecture. The tension between data and danda reappears.

One of Pepper's main concerns is with the nature of structural hypotheses and how they may influence attempts to corroborate claims to knowledge. There are potentially hundreds of such hypothetical structures and two of those that have ultimately been found wanting are animism and mysticism. Four have been found to be relatively adequate, and they are only regarded as relatively adequate because each has some weakness. These four are discussed in *World Hypotheses* and the title itself implies their universal validity.

B.   FOUR WORLD HYPOTHESES

Figure 5 presents Pepper's outline of the various paths to knowledge, which include the four world hypotheses as four types of danda. None of these four are superior to the others, and there is much discussion in the book about the criteria by which such a judgement is made. Simply, the criteria are precision and scope. A precise hypothesis fits all the facts exactly, and one adequate in scope covers all known facts. A hypothesis which does not cover all the facts is not a world hypothesis, but can probably be subsumed under one of the four relatively adequate world hypotheses which are: formism, mechanism, contextualism and organicism.

Pepper is able to reduce the multitude of possible world hypotheses by constructing a theory of the origin of world hypotheses which he calls the "root metaphor theory". Burtt (1943) describes it this way,

the philosophic imagination has drawn from experiences of common sense only a very few fundamental clues to world interpretation. Each of the main schools of philosophy has cognitively refined one of these basic clues, that is, has codified the implications of

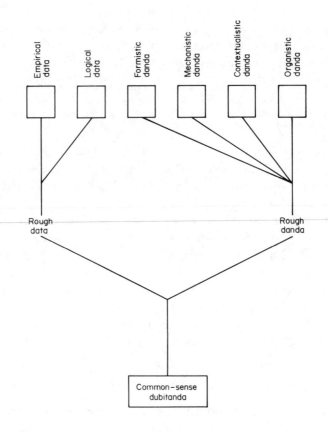

Roots of knowledge

Fɪɢ. 5. A tree of knowledge.

that chosen idea into a set of categories that hang together and claim power or corroboration by all evidence of every kind. That clue is its "root metaphor".   (p. 592)

Pepper uses "analogy" as a synonym for "metaphor", and the analogies turn out to be surprisingly unprepossessing. The root metaphor of formism is similarity. Objects and phenomena are often very similar and thus can be classified into categories or types. The truth theory of formism is the correspondence theory: things are truer as a result of the degree of similarity which a description has to its object of reference. Maps and pictures are examples of close correspondences though ultimately the correspondence can be expressed in symbolic form as in a mathematical equation. Formism is better known philosophically by the terms "realism", and "Platonic idealism", and its best-known exponents (dogmatic exponents at that, as is true of all exponents of the world theories) are Plato and Aristotle.

The alternative names for mechanism are "naturalism" and "materialism" and its major champions are Hobbes, Locke and Hume. The root metaphor of mechanism is the machine, and cognitive refinement is obtained by interpreting the world as if it were a machine. Put oversimply, this involves three steps: first, the machine consists of a configuration of parts and it is necessary to define the precise *locations* of these parts. Treating a lever as a simple machine would thus involve stating precisely the length of the lever and the distance of one end of the lever from the fulcrum. The second step involves identifying the *primary qualities* of the machine. In the case of the lever this would be the weight exerted to work the lever. The actual weight could be a load of bricks or a tree stump, but when working with the machine analogy one merely wants the weight or force applied, so as to describe the quantities necessary for the efficient functioning of the machine. Thirdly, mechanism requires the statement of a *law* of the interrelationships amongst the parts of the machine. In the case of the lever this would entail an equation stating the required weights for balancing a lever with a given fulcrum length. The truth theory of mechanism is whether the machine works. Pepper uses the term "workability" or the phrase "causal adjustment", but it comes down to whether or not one's knowledge allows one to predict the outcomes of any causal adjustments made in the system.

On the face of it workability sounds a very pragmatic criterion, but pragmatism as philosophy has contextualism as its world hypothesis, and its root metaphor is the historic event. This is the event alive in its present; or the act in its context. Pepper says (p. 232) that only verbs should be used in the language of contextualism — doing, enduring, enjoying, etc. Weick (1974) refers to Bateson (1972) who has sounded the more evocative clarion call, "stamp out nouns" (p. 334), but his reasons imply a contextualist's view of understanding the world. One of the major derivatives of such a philosophical stance is that change is endemic. The context will change and thus knowledge will need to change also. Consequently the truth theory of contextualism is "qualitative confirmation" or verification, though such verification demands a thorough exploration of the context and texture of any event. Strictly speaking it is not the event but a hypothesis about the event that is verified, so hypotheses, not events, are regarded as being true or false. Nevertheless, "A true hypothesis, does in its texture and quality give some insight into the texture and quality of the event it refers to for verification (p. 277)." William James, C. S. Peirce and G. H. Mead are the founding fathers of pragmatism.

Pepper cites Hegel and Royce as the main originators of the organicist cognitive attitude. Its alternative philosophical name is "absolute idealism", which is sometimes called "objective idealism". Burtt (1943, p. 593) describes its root metaphor as "harmonic unity". It too is concerned with understanding the historical event, but it differs from contextualism in that time is regarded as unimportant. It is the integration in the process rather than the duration of the process that concerns the organicist. His ultimate aim is to describe the enduring structure that processes realize. Its truth theory is called the "coherence theory of truth". The criteria of the coherence theory are, "the categorical features of the organic whole — inclusiveness, determinateness and organicity — and the ideal of truth is the absolute itself " (p. 310). Organicism thus proposes the existence of degrees of truth dependent on the amount of facts known, and when all facts are known — as in principle they can be — then absolute truth has been obtained. This is a very different conclusion from the contextualists who will always believe that change is just around the corner, so that "truth" may turn out to be false, and thus there is no absolute truth.

C. A FIFTH WORLD HYPOTHESIS: SELECTIVISM

In 1963 Pepper proposed a new world hypothesis which is elaborated at length in a book entitled *Concept and Quality* (Pepper, 1966). It is in fact a radical revision of contextualism. Pepper calls it "selectivism". Its root metaphor is the goal-seeking or purposive act and Pepper drew from the writings of psychologists such as Tolman (1932) in developing his theory. Choosing or selecting the path which will achieve quiescence for an activated drive state is the central concept in selectivism. It sounds as if it might apply only to humans and animals but as a world hypothesis it must allow one to study anything and Pepper asserts that full understanding of an act will involve human physiology and hence the chemistry and physics of the universe.

The truth theory of selectivism is the operational-correspondence theory which is a unification of the truth theories of contextualism and formism, respectively. Our claims to truth are held to be more viable if we have a set of conceptual categories which are directly linked to the processes actually at work in purposeful conceptual and qualitative categories (Pepper, 1966, pp. 28–30). Argyris and Schon's (1974) distinction between "espoused theories" (correspondences) and "theories in use" (operations) appears to be a distinction which parallels Pepper's.

In Table 1 I have summarized the five world hypotheses and listed examples of research from organizational psychology which I believe illustrate the kind of research that would arise from the pursuit of any particular world hypothesis.

I am not claiming that the researchers were aware of the epistemological underpinning to their ventures. Indeed, some of the research examples quoted are very poor attempts at working within the prescriptions of the world hypothesis, and research could be much improved if some of the conceptual and analytical categories described in Pepper's work were more closely followed. This is most evident for contextualism and selectivism though little research has actually been carried out in these traditions.

The greatest activity has occurred in the formistic and mechanistic traditions. Personnel selection and the leadership-style literature contain two of the largest bodies of empirical data in organizational psychology, but neither has succeeded in maintaining significant empirical or theoretical progress. They are formistic in the sense that they have tried to compare people and situations and to match one to the other to see which "forms" are congruent. The Aston studies (Pugh and Hickson, 1976; Pugh and Hinings, 1977; Pugh and Payne, 1977; Hickson and McMillan, 1980) similarly created ways of typing organizations and then relating them to their contexts. Starbuck (1980) acknowledges the attractiveness of the idea, admires the quality of their efforts, but wonders now whether it was worth the effort since it has revealed little new about organizations and their functioning. As he vividly expressed it, "The Aston researchers set out to find the holy grail, and they came back with a broken tea cup" (p. 25).

Mechanism has been the dominant metaphor in organizational psychology and in some senses some of the research I have identified as formistic could even be seen as mechanistic. The notion that more consideration will lead to higher group productivity, or that greater size

TABLE 1

World hypothesis and its chief philosophers	Root metaphor	Truth theory	Examples from organizational psychology
FORMISM Plato Aristotle	SIMILARITY and DIFFERENCES	CORRESPONDENCE e.g. maps, pictures, plans, equations, models	TRAIT THEORY (Personality types, leadership styles) PERSON–ENVIRONMENT FIT TAXONOMIES OF ORGANIZATIONS (Aston studies)
MECHANISM Locke Hume	THE MACHINE a lever/weight a computer	CAUSAL ADJUSTMENT workability, prediction	BEHAVIOUR MODIFICATION SCIENTIFIC MANAGEMENT ERGONOMICS
CONTEXTUALISM (Pragmatism) James, Peirce	THE ACT IN CONTEXT	OPERATIONAL qualitative confirmation pragmatic working	ORGANIZATION DEVELOPMENT INTERACTIVE PLANNING (Ackoff)
SELECTIVISM Pepper Tolman	THE GOAL-SEEKING ACT	OPERATIONAL–CORRESPONDENCE	MODEL II LEARNING (Argyris and Schön) "GARBAGE-CAN" DECISION MODELS APPRECIATIVE BEHAVIOUR (Vickers)
ORGANICISM Hegel Royce	HARMONIOUS UNITY timelessness enduring structures	COHERENCE determinateness absoluteness	NEED THEORY PRINCIPLES OF MANAGEMENT (Fayol)

will lead to increased specialization, can be interpreted in mechanistic terms, though their underlying philosophy seems to me to be formistic. Behaviour modification and scientific management are more compelling examples of the machine metaphor. Experimental psychology of most kinds would fall into this category as would most of ergonomics. Not surprisingly, it has been most successful where man is used as if he were a machine, but once one moves to situations where persons interact to achieve something or where the environment allows the human freedom to select what he will do to satisfy his needs, the machine metaphor breaks down.

Herbst (1970) has proposed that mechanism assumes (a) that measures are invariant and (b) that relationships between measures are invariant. He argues convincingly that these conditions do not apply to behavioural systems, and proposes that we concentrate on the study of single cases. I have shown elsewhere (Payne, 1976) that studies in the positivistic tradition have enabled us to account for so little of the variance in individual, group and organizational behaviour that their methodology can no longer be regarded as an adequate way of investigating human behaviour in organizations. Larger samples and more adequate statistical methods have only emphasized the poverty of this approach and increased our confidence that the effects we have been studying really are small ones (Cohen, 1978). This *should* be seen as a valuable refinement of our cognition, and encourage us to try something else.

As I indicated in my introduction, I believe we should try a contextualist/pragmatic approach. In Table 1 I have used organization development (Beckhard, 1969) and what Ackoff (1979) calls "interactive planning' as examples of contextualistic epistemology. They portray the spirit of contextualism in that they focus on understanding how individuals perceive their situations and try to make the organization work better, if not perfectly. They are very "loose" ways of understanding the world since they contain no systematic way of analysing events. This makes it difficult to generalize from the particular cases studied. But in his analysis of contextualism Pepper (1942, 1966) provides sets of categories which could enormously facilitate this.

D. THE CATEGORIES OF CONTEXTUALISM

The root metaphor of contextualism is the act in and with its setting:

"These acts or events are intrinsically complex, composed of inter-connected activities with continuously changing patterns. They are like incidents in the plot of a novel or drama. They are literally the incidents of life" (Pepper, 1942, p. 233). The stress on "continuously changing patterns" is what distinguishes contextualism from the other world theories, for if there are unchangeable structures in the world such as the forms of formism, or the space-time structure of mechanism, then contextualism would be a restricted hypothesis, and hence a false world hypothesis.

The basic, fundamental categories of contextualism are quality and texture, and although it is conceivable that some future states may not contain these two categories in the world as we know it, it is quality and texture that provide the structure the world does have.

Pepper says that it is impossible to understand quality and texture separately, but they can be contrasted. The quality of a given event is its intuited wholeness or total character; the texture is the details and relations which make up that character or quality. The quality of con-textualism itself is its root metaphor — the historic event. The texture is the categories of quality and texture. The quality of a performance of a ballet is the total effect it produces — the actual dancers, props, and orchestra are the texture of the event. As the gestalt psychologists would argue, we see the whole (quality) and it is only in later analysis that we see the parts (texture). Quality has three sub-categories: spread, change, and fusion.

(1) *Spread.* The contextualist believes that an event can only be under-stood qualitatively by assuming that the event is located both in the past and the future, as well as the present. They do not accept the primacy of linear time as the mechanists do. They accept linear or schematic time as useful, but for them qualitative time is more useful. Indeed, schematic time is regarded as a derivative of it. In an actual event the present is the whole texture which directly contributes to the quality of the event (p. 242).

(2) *Change.* This refers to changes in the quality of events. Even as events occur, each part of the event extends forwards and backwards in the specious present. As the event unfolds, the quality of the event may change. Permanent structures may appear to exist, but these are interpreted as historical continuities which are not changeless. Whilst fundamental to the contextualistic position, change itself appears like a backdrop — it is there, but the event is still interpretable.

(3) *Fusion.* The quality of an event is determined by the degree of fusion in the details of its texture. This idea is well illustrated by some of the visual illusions used in the psychology of perception. The vase figure which is also the outline of a face shows a higher degree of fusion than the three rows of dots formed into a square. The former is always seen as a vase or a face, whereas many people may just see three vertical or three horizontal lines of dots rather than a square. A team of players who co-ordinate their play are more fused than a team of equally skilful individuals who are not "getting together". It is this degree of fusion which determines the unity of an event. In other world theories, fusion is interpreted as vagueness, failure to discriminate, but it is a central feature of contextualism, since the contextualists believe that even the simplest things are fusions of details.

In practice, its centrality is somewhat ignored since "the analysis and practical control of events goes on in terms of the categories of texture. . . . But, without qualities, textures would be as empty as sentences the words of which had no meaning" (p. 246). This interdependence is not confined to quality and texture. Pepper also takes the stance that the first two categories of texture, strands and context, are so interlocked with the notion of texture itself that all three must be considered together.

The categories are indeed complexly interlocked as the following quotation illustrates:

A texture is made up of strands and it lies in a context. There is, moreover, no very sharp line between strands and context, because it is the connections of the strands which determine the context, and in large proportion the context determines the qualities of the strands. But by way of definition we may say that whatever directly contributes to the quality of a texture may be regarded as a strand, whereas whatever indirectly contributes to it will be regarded as context. (p. 246)

Taking the decision-making activity of a group of senior executives as an event, it might be said that the executives themselves are the strands of the event. But they are based in a context represented by their departments and in a wider context represented by their professional reference groups. These contexts of the strands obviously bring something of their quality into the texture of the event. Therefore, each of these strands can be reconceived as an event or a quality which will have its own texture and strands, etc. This interdependence is so clear to the contextualist that he ridicules the idea of analysing things into their elements since elemental analysis so easily distorts the real quality of the

event. It is thus "pragmatic" or practical to limit analysis to the degree
to which it reveals the quality of the particular unity being studied. This
pragmatic choice as to where the event ends is akin to having to decide
where the boundary of a system lies when following a systems-theory
model. Both are, in an absolute sense, arbitrary decisions. It is perfectly
legitimate for the contextualist to "intuit" where the wholeness lies.

The third category of texture concerns references of the strands: these
are a detailed specification of strands and there are four of them — linear,
convergent, blocked and instrumental.

(a) A *linear reference* has a point of *initiation*, a transitive *direction*, and
achieves an ending or a *satisfaction*. The direction is forwards and backwards and is consistent with the "spread" of the event. Returning to our
group of executives, the chairman's activities to keep to the agenda
exemplify a linear reference. They start from the agenda, and as the
group proceeds the agenda moves them forwards and backwards both
directly and indirectly through its relations to past events. Finally, the
meeting ends and the satisfaction of that particular linear reference is
achieved.

(b) A *convergent reference* describes a situation where several linear
references converge on one satisfaction. It is a contextualist's version of
a form since the convergence implies some similarity. A consensus
decision would be an example. The executives only have this similarity
on this one issue, and become dissimilar, non-convergent, on others.

(c) *Blocking* refers to the blocking of a linear or convergent reference.
Strands do not always run smoothly from their initiation to their satisfaction. When they do we have order, and it is blocking that creates
novelty or disorder. Usually the blocking is due to another strand conflicting with the original strand. It is therefore likely that investigation
of the blocking strand will show how the two strands arrived in conflict.
It is thus not absolutely new or novel and is called "intrusive novelty".
Most novelty is of this kind, but the contextualist allows the possibility
of an absolutely inexplicable blocking which would be called an
"emergent novelty".

(d) *Instrumental references* are secondary acts which remove the blocking reference, or at least circumvent it. Once again this can become very
complicated if instrumental references build one upon another, but
what retains the integration is the original linear reference which was
seeking satisfaction when the blocking occurred. In a sense, any instrumental reference is a texture in its own right with its own satisfaction,

but it is guided by the terminal action it is serving and also by the blocking action it is trying to neutralize. This pattern can become so interlocked that what was originally a blocking strand can become like an articulated linear reference itself, giving the appearance of a total quality. Because of this, what appeared to be discrete textures can become fused so that they far outreach the contextualistic present. This is how contextualism extends beyond the present event even though its categories are all derived from such an event.

E.   A CONTEXTUALIST ANALYSIS OF THE MOTIVATION TO PRODUCE

As already indicated, the categories of quality play little part in contextual analysis although they are always there as a background. Thus in studying a person who had decided to be a high producer the contextualist would be interested in how the past and the future had been relevant to the decision. He would also be concerned to consider that the decision might be changed or might have changed in the past, and the pressures which might have created the change (the strands) would be investigated. He would finally examine the degree of *fusion* in the act which might lead to questions about how well integrated the total person was with the work he did. But these wider questions, all of great importance with reference to the "quality of working life", take a back seat in relation to the more detailed analysis of the texture.

The first step would be to identify the strands in the event and then to describe them in their contexts. The first strand might be:

$$\text{To produce} \longrightarrow \text{More}$$

and if this actually happened the event would lead to satisfaction and whatever had been done to produce more could be said to have verified the hypothesis behind it. What might the hypothesis have been? A simple one might be "to work harder". What then is the context of this strand?

Figure 6 lists some of the indirect factors which may affect this strand. Some of these may themselves become blocking strands. Eventually the individual's capacities to work may reach a limit, or the machinery may reach a limit. What might happen if the former occurred? Figure 7 depicts some possibilities.

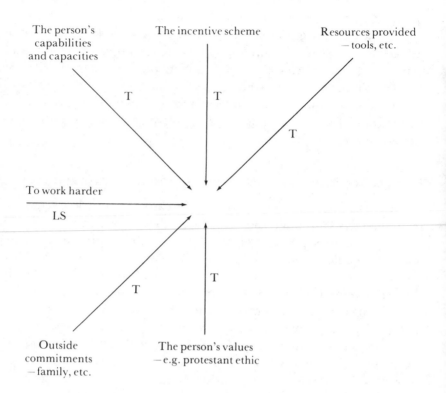

FIG. 6. The texture of a linear strand. T = texture; LS = linear strand.

Figure 7 contains a relatively superficial analysis. Let us pursue the instrumental reference (IS) "change design of task". This analysis appears in Fig. 8. This traces what the textures of each of the strands (T, etc.) and also the functions of the strands (BS = blocking strand; IS = instrumental strand) are. It shows that in order to remove the original blocking strand it is necessary to change the supervisor's attitudes and remove the technological constraint which is also a block. This requires the boss, motivated by organizational goals, to put pressure on the supervisor to ask for more resources to change the technological constraint. In addition, this requires the supervisor to change his attitude and this is achieved by using pressure from the unions and pressure from the subordinates as instrumental references. These are of course a convergent strand, even though they are totally different, but they converge on the supervisor for the same reason. This illustrates how strands

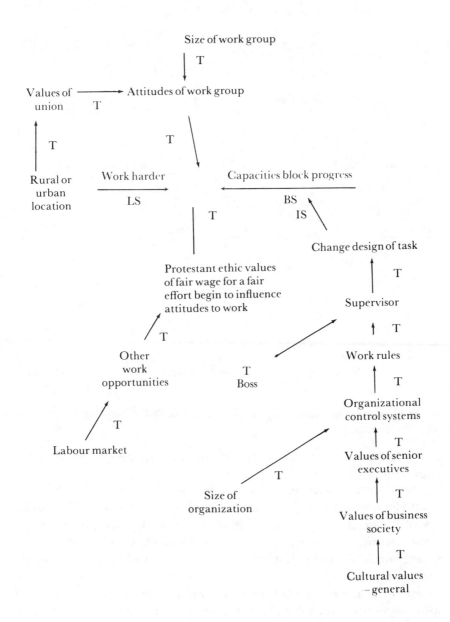

FIG. 7. A contextualist analysis of the effect of a blocking strand on motivation to produce. LS = linear strand; BS = blocking strand; IS = instrumental reference strand; T = texture.

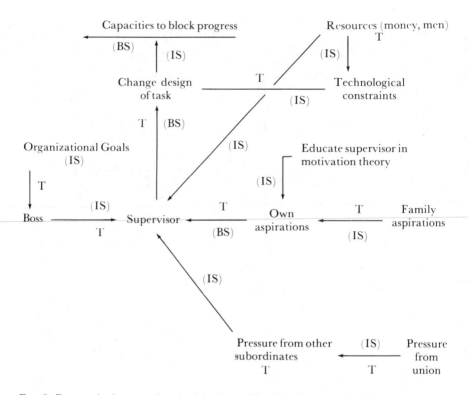

Fig. 8. Removal of a second-order blockage. BS = blocking strand; IS = instrumental reference strand.

which are textures at one point in the analysis become qualities at another point.

The strands described in Figure 7 are only examples. The blocking strand for another individual might not be his capacities but the capacities of the machinery or tools. The analysis would then proceed to see what instrumental strand could remove the block, what was its context, what strands blocked it, how they could be removed, what made up the context of the blocking strands and so on. In a case such as the breakdown of machinery the provision of a maintenance fitter might be an instrumental strand which would eventually become so routine as to look like a linear strand contributing to the main linear strand of increased output. The main value of using the various forms of strands is that it forces one to pursue the way the system is working, not only in terms of what is happening, but also in terms of what it is that makes it happen. The focus on linear, blocking and instrumental references is particularly potent here since it compels an understanding of the texture of the main strand. The fact that each also requires the setting up of a hypothesis (a) about what the blocking strand may be, and (b) about what instrumental reference may remove it, encourages strongly the conjectural and refutational stance so valued by Popper. This perpetual concern for hypothesis-testing and the "qualitative confirmation" that goes with it makes contextualism much less dependent on multiplicative corroboration (data) than the other world theories. If the hypotheses are verified for that particular event, in that particular context, then that's good enough. This does not mean that statements of a general kind are not possible. If many instances of the same linear references are found to produce the same blocking references and the resulting instrumental references solve the problem, then a general solution can be offered. But the possibility of something changing is never to be disregarded. Nor must the quality of the event be forgotten since it may always be possible to produce a better fusion or more intuited wholeness by a different arrangement of references.

Figure 7 also illustrates the need to make a pragmatic decision as to when to stop. In a practical sense one would probably stop in Fig. 7 with the values and attitudes of the supervisor's boss in relation to whether to change the work rules. Similarly, it would probably not be worthwhile tracing the values of the union on the values of the work group.

In summary, a contextualistic approach to organizational psychology requires a focus on acts and events rather than contrived experiments, though one might profitably study experiments as events themselves. Sarbin (1977) has argued that it is the appropriate world view for psychology in general. It has a systematic way of analysing events which can lead to generalizations about what controls the events and the values/qualitative judgements that determine the boundaries to understanding them. Spencer and Dale (1979) provide an example of a contextualistic, empirical study, and detailed analysis of quantitative versus qualitative research (see Appendix).

Since *selectivism* is a revision of contextualism, it implies a similar research approach. Indeed, its refinements seem to me to be more philosophical than practical, but as I have indicated in Table 1, some recent ideas and conceptual frameworks seem to fit quite neatly into it. March and Olsen's (1976) work on ambiguity and choice, "garbagecan" models of decision-making, etc., provide good examples of the

kinds of selection inherent in purposive acts. Vicker's (1968) concept of
appreciative systems and the criteria they imply for selection match
nicely too. He also links appreciation to instrumental action and thus
unites both correspondence and operational theories of truth. Instru-
mentality-expectancy theory should in principle be classified here, but
it has been pursued rather fruitlessly (Campbell and Pritchard, 1976). I
would suggest this is because it has been researched within a mechanistic epistemology where the concern has been for generalization
across populations rather than for the understanding of particular
purposive acts.

Because it is a synthetic theory, the categories of *organicism* are very
like those of contextualism and for practical purposes one would act as
an investigator in a very similar way. The crucial difference would be a
commitment to discover the underlying unity that determines any particular event. This may direct the researchers to explore similar events
in other epochs and other milieux in order to discover the absolute truth
that any particular event should be capable of revealing. Thus I have
selected Maslow's need theory and the principles of management as
examples of organicist positions since they would claim to have universal validity. All men will be motivated to self-actualize if other needs are
satisfied, and all organizations will be effective if the principles are
properly applied. This is so because these are held to be absolute truths
about the way men and organizations are.

5.   Conclusion

I have tried to describe and interpret some fundamental epistemological
concepts and show how they may help us to understand the organizational psychology of the past, and the design of the organizational psychology of the future. I personally believe empirical work has to be
much more of the case-study kind, though carefully contrasted cases
may be more powerful than the single-case study common in the past.
Contextualism and selectivism are the two structural theories which
provide the necessary concepts and epistemological justifications for
making a systematic attempt at this style of cognitive refinement. The
reader may disagree with me and prefer formism or mechanism, but I
hope he or she does so with a clearer awareness of the strengths and
weaknesses of these different approaches to knowledge acquisition.

Appendix

NOTES ON "QUALITATIVE" AND "QUANTITATIVE" RESEARCH

1. The distinction itself seems pre-scientific, since categorization into qualities is the first step in measurement.
2. When one looks at what the proponents of the "two" approaches are actually concerned about, it seems to include the following:

"QUALITATIVE"	"QUANTITATIVE"
2.1 MEANING IS SITUATIONAL	**MEANING IS UNIVERSAL**
A concentration on emergent concepts/categories. The properties which they describe are thus known to be salient for the organism(s) studied. Measurement proceeds by first listing, then counting, identifying directions (valencies) where appropriate, and only then to scaling, which can only be done for properties which have intensity (are divisible).	A concentration on pre-existent concepts/categories. The salience of such categories may or may not be checked. Similarly, measurement may proceed through listing to scaling, or may proceed directly to scaling.
2.2 MEANING IS DECIDED BY THE ACTORS, NEGOTIATED, OR THERE ARE MULTIPLE PERSPECTIVES	**MEANING IS DECIDED BY THE RESEARCHER**

The researcher may try to ascertain the concepts and meanings of the actors, either taking them as paramount or engaging in a "hermeneutic spiral" with them: i.e. trading concepts and meanings. That is, the approach is
    emic,
    idiographic,
    phenomenological,
    "social construction of reality".
	The researcher concentrates on his own concepts, and attributes meanings to the actors. That is, the approach is
	    etic,
	    nomothetic,
	    positivistic.

2.3 HOLISTIC CONCEPTION OF ORGANISM	**ATOMISTIC/AGGREGATIVE CONCEPTION OF ORGANISM**
The unit of analysis is the whole-in-context, leading to a concentration on relational/structural, global and contextual properties.	The unit of analysis is the part, leading to a concentration on analytical properties of organisms.
2.4 GENERALIZATION BY COMPARISON OF PROPERTIES AND CONTEXTS OF INDIVIDUAL ORGANISMS Study is focused on many properties of an organism in context. Interactions between such properties in other organisms are only assumed when there is careful comparison of properties and contexts in each case.	**GENERALIZATION BY POPULATION MEMBERSHIP** Study is focused on a few properties of many organisms with or without regard to context. Interactions between such properties are assumed to apply to all population members.

3. It seems clear that so-called "soft" and "hard" data/research are found in both columns, assuming that by "hard" we mean rigorous, or something like that. Similarly, we can have a "hard" treatment which is invalidated by "soft" (sloppy) assumptions or the omission of necessary preceding steps, such as checking for salience. Furthermore, we may find quantitative research in both columns.
4. Approaches in either column may be appropriate to particular research aims and situations. However, whilst the approach of the left-hand column can nearly always produce *something* meaningful (provided the researcher is competent, of course), in the right-hand column it is not only possible but common to find research which is largely meaningless. (For example, measuring people's attitudes to objects of which they are both ignorant and uncaring; or using an aggregate of individual scale scores to make statements about social collectivities.)

References

ACKOFF, R. L. (1979). Resurrecting the future of operational research. *Journal of the Operational Research Society*, **30**, 189- 199.

ARGYRIS, C. AND SCHÖN, D. A. (1974). *Theory in Practice: Increasing Professional Effectiveness*. San Francisco: Jossey-Bass.

AYER, A. J. (1976). *The Central Questions of Philosophy*. Harmondsworth: Penguin.

BATESON, G. (1972). *Steps to an Ecology of Mind*. New York: Ballantine.

BECKHARD, R. (1969). *Organization Development: Strategies and Models*. New York: Addison-Wesley.

BURTT, E. A. (1943). The Status of "World Hypotheses". *Philosophical Review*, **LII**, 590- 601.

CAMPBELL, J. P. AND PRITCHARD, R. D. (1976). Motivation Theory in Industrial and Organizational Psychology. In Dunnette, M. D. (ed.), *Handbook of Industrial and Organizational Psychology*. Chicago: Rand McNally.

COHEN, J. (1978). *Power Statistics for Behavioral Sciences* (2nd edition). New York: J. Wiley.

HAMLYN, D. W. (1971). *The Theory of Knowledge*. London: Macmillan.

HERBST, P. G. (1970). *Behavioural Worlds: The Study of Single Cases*. London: Tavistock.

HICKSON, D. J. AND McMILLAN, C. J. (1980). *Organization and Nation: the International Aston Programme*. Farnborough: Saxon House.

HOSPERS, J. (1967). *An Introduction to Philosophical Analysis*. Englewood Cliffs: Prentice-Hall.

KAPLAN, A. (1964). *The Conduct of Inquiry: Methodology for Behavioral Science*. San Francisco: Chandler.

KOLB, D. A., RUBIN, I. M. AND McINTYRE, J. M. (1974). *Organizational Psychology: An Experiential Approach*. Englewood Cliffs: Prentice-Hall.

KUHN, T. S. (1962). *The Structure of Scientific Revolutions*. University of Chicago Press, Chicago.

MAGEE, B. (1973). *Popper*. London: Fontana.

MARCH, J. G. AND OLSEN, J. P. (1976). *Ambiguity and Choice in Organizations.* Bergen: Universitetsforlaget.
PAYNE, R. L. (1975). *Epistemology and the Study of Behaviour in Organizations.* Unpublished Memo No. 68, MRC Social and Applied Psychology Unit, University of Sheffield.
PAYNE, R. L. (1976). Truisms in Organizational Behaviour. *Interpersonal Development,* **6,** 203–220.
PEARS, D. (1971). *What is Knowledge?* New York: Harper and Row.
PEPPER, S. C. (1942). *World Hypotheses.* Berkeley: University of California Press.
PEPPER, S. C. (1966). *Concept and Quality.* La Salle: Open Court.
PHILLIPS, D. (1973). *Abandoning Method.* San Francisco: Jossey-Bass.
POPPER, K. (1963). *Conjectures and Refutations.* London: Routledge and Kegan Paul.
PUGH, D. S. AND HICKSON, D. J. (eds) (1976). *Organizational Structure in its Context: The Aston Programme I.* Farnham: Saxon House.
PUGH, D. S. AND HININGS, C. R. (eds) (1976). *Organizational Structure: Extensions and Replications: The Aston Programme II.* Farnham: Saxon House.
PUGH, D. S. AND PAYNE, R. L. (eds) (1977). *Organizational Behaviour in its Context: The Aston Programme III.* Farnham: Saxon House.
RESCHER, N. (1977). *Methodological Pragmatism: A Systems-Theoretic Approach to the Theory of Knowledge.* Oxford: Basil Blackwell.
ROZEBOOM, W. W. (1972). Problems in the psycho-philosophy of knowledge. In J. R. Royce and W. W. Rozeboom (eds), *The Psychology of Knowing.* New York: Gordon and Breach.
RUSSELL, B. (1912). *The Problems of Philosophy.* London: Butterworth.
SARBIN, T. (1977). Contextualism: A World View for Modern Psychology. *Nebraska Symposium on Motivation.* Lincoln: University of Nebraska Press.
SKINNER, B. F. (1974). *About Behaviourism.* New York: A. A. Knopf.
SPENCER, L. AND DALE, A. (1979). Integration and regulation in organisations: A contextual approach. *Sociological Review,* **27,** 679–702.
STARBUCK, W. H. (1980). A trip to view the elephants and the rattlesnakes in the garden of Aston. To appear in A. H. Van De Ven and W. H. Joyce (eds), *Assessing Organization Design and Performance.*
TOLMAN, E. C. (1932). *Purposive Behavior in Animals and Men.* New York: Appleton Century.
TOULMIN, S. (1972). *Human Understanding* (Vol. I). Oxford: Oxford University Press.
VICKERS, G. (1968). *Value Systems and Social Process.* London: Tavistock.
WEICK, K. E. (1974). Middle-range theories of social systems. *Behavioural Science,* **19,** 357–367.

4 The Integration of Disciplinary Perspectives and Levels of Analysis in Problem-oriented Organizational Research

DAN GOWLER and KAREN LEGGE

Social scientists, including organizational psychologists, who are engaged in applied "problem-oriented" research in organizations, seldom enjoy the luxury of a neatly bounded area of interest. Organizational "problems" (for example, labour turnover) often cannot be satisfactorily analysed (in the sense of providing both identification and explanaof the variables and relationships relevant to the "understanding" and "solution" of the "problem") from one theoretical orientation within a discipline, or even from one disciplinary perspective alone (Price, 1977). For example, if labour turnover was analysed purely from a psychological perspective, it is likely that more than one theoretical orientation within that discipline would be relevant. If it was to be examined "in the round", economic and sociological perspectives, in addition to psychological ones, would be required. The question then arises of whether it is desirable and, if so, how may different theoretical orientations within one discipline could be integrated and, even more crucially, how may different disciplinary perspectives could be harmonized? Nor does the matter stop here. "Problems", although surfacing at one level in the organization, are likely to have antecedents and effects at different organizational levels. The individual's decision to leave the organization may reflect his relationship with his work group, which in turn may reflect organizational structure and control systems. Conversely, organizational structure and control systems may be influenced by individual employees' decisions to leave. How then, if desired, may analyses at these different levels — individual, group and organization — be integrated? What are the problems involved and how are they expressed and constructed? (Spector and Kitsuse, 1977).

It is on these sorts of issues that this chapter is focused. Basically, three questions are examined. First, what are the advantages of (and drawbacks in) attempting to integrate or synthesize different disciplinary perspectives and levels of analysis? Secondly, what approaches may be employed? Thirdly, what are some of the problems associated with integration attempts? However, before embarking on these questions and discussion, it is necessary to examine in more detail what is meant by the key concepts involved, i.e. disciplinary perspectives and levels of analysis.

1. Disciplinary perspectives and levels of analysis

A researcher's "disciplinary perspective" has three facets. First, there is the *general branch of learning* in which he has been trained, within which he works and with which he is "professionally" identified, as a psychologist, sociologist, or economist, for example. Secondly, within the relevant branch of learning there is generally a division of labour or *specialism* reflecting the focus of interest, for example, "organizational psychologists", who are interested in work behaviour and "climate" in organizations; "educational psychologists", who are interested in the learning development of children, and generally work in educational institutions; "clinical psychologists", who are interested in the pathology of personality and behaviour, and who work in a professional/client relationship, generally in hospital and clinic settings and so on. Thirdly, there is the *theoretical orientation* that the researcher as psychologist, sociologist or economist brings to his area of interest. Thus, a "neo-classical" and an "institutional" economist, while both analysing problems of employment, will view them from radically different theoretical perspectives, although working within the same branch of learning (economics) and with the same focus of interest (labour markets). Murray (1979) provides a good illustration of this in his discussion of football hooliganism, pointing out that this phenomenon, even within one discipline (sociology) has been analysed from three different perspectives. He argues that sociologists who embrace an ethnomethodological approach "spiced with interactionist and anthropological positions" tend to see football hooliganism as a "game"; those analysing it in terms of "class consciousness" as a "protest", while those interested in deviancy focus on the extension of "class consciousness" into "cultural crises" and the police as amplifiers of deviance, and examine football hooliganism as an expression of a "youth cult".

Yet such overt issues in defining disciplinary perspectives cannot be divorced from more covert "political" issues. Spector and Kitsuse, when discussing the "competition" between disciplines, provide some critical insights here. Thus they comment that

Ideas about causation are basic to how the work of the scientific community is organized. The division of work into special ties or disciplines, including the departmental structure in universities, reflects these ideas about where different parts of the world fit in the overall body of scientific knowledge. Some phenomena are the exclusive property of one discipline. Others are considered multi-dimensional, with complex causal structure, and may be claimed by more than one discipline or by an interdisciplinary program. Those who presume to research a problem outside of their discipline may be accused of reductionism, suggesting a disrespect for the nature of the phenomenon, or of dilettantism. (1977, p. 64)

Moreover, they go on to point out that the commonplace belief that

. . . scientific inquiry may determine the causes of a phenomenon and provide the basis for adjudicating the validity of competing causal statements ignores the fact that such statements are the *social constructions of social scientists*. As such, they must be treated as objects to be explained, and the form and content of those constructions must be taken as problematic. (1977, pp. 64–65)

Thus, Spector and Kitsuse argue that competing causal analyses may be seen as the ideologies of professions that have adopted the language of science to further their professional interests (1977, p. 65). They also conclude that this somewhat cynical view of academic disciplines

. . . provides a new perspective on social science theories. By viewing sociology, psychology, social psychiatry, economics and social work as ambitious social movements, disciplines, or professions, we may apply to them and their knowledge the same tools we bring to bear on the activities of any social group. *Statements about causation, levels of analysis, or the nature of a phenomenon are efforts to stake claims to certain subject matter.*
(1977, p. 65, emphasis added)

This critical orientation towards different disciplinary perspectives is introduced here to make the point that disciplinary integration is not solely a conceptual or methodological question but also involves professional and monopoly interests. Indeed, we suggest that any realistic form of integration will have to respect both theoretical and professional interests, and our subsequent argument for "multiple triangulation" owes much to this pragmatic consideration. In the meantime, however, we turn to the "levels of analysis" question, since this apparently technical term is often used, *inter alia*, to avoid conflict over vested academic interests.

Conventionally, "levels of analysis" refer to the units of analysis delineated by the researcher's professional, theoretical and methodological preferences. Among organizational researchers, *this process of selection usually delineates the three levels of individual, group and organization. Moreover, there has been a tendency for these three levels of analysis to become associated with different disciplines.* For instance, Roberts *et al.* (1978) suggest that the industrial/organizational psychology paradigm assumes that "individual differences [are] more relevant to individual responses than characteristics of occupational settings" and hence concentrates on the individual as a unit of analysis. On the other hand, they claim that the social psychological paradigm "implies that a person's responses cannot be studied adequately without reference to the social groups to which that person responds" and consequently takes the group as a unit of analysis. The sociological paradigm, they argue, "is based on the premise that organizations are forms of social collectives with enduring patterns of social interaction", and where "social interaction is assumed to continue unaltered when individual members of the collective leave and others are added". Thus sociologists' units of analysis tend to be the group, organization, institution, society or culture.

It must be emphasized, however, that the frequently assumed match between certain disciplines and levels of analysis is more apparent than real. For instance, *as theories*, levels of analysis not only involve explicit or implicit ideas about causation, but they also define a range of empirical referents. Consequently, while an organizational psychologist and a micro-sociologist might agree upon an empirical referent, e.g. employee performance, they are more than likely to disagree about causal attribution. Consequently, even if one simply considers the distinction between cause and content (which varies with epistemological assumptions) the likelihood of a neat fit between disciplines and levels of analysis not only becomes uncertain but also a source of interdisciplinary misunderstanding and competition. In other words, the "integration" or "synthesis" of different disciplinary approaches has to operate simultaneously at the level of cause *and* content. Furthermore, in applied work, the subjects of investigation and intervention will probably hold relatively strong, if not well-formed, opinions on these issues. It is therefore not surprising that problem-solving in organizations involves a protracted process of negotiation about the nature of reality. We return to this vexed question in our conclusions to this paper.

A related assumption lying behind the constellation of ideas comprising the "levels of analysis" concept is that one level, operating in a hierarchical or vested manner, provides the context or environment for another. Thus, the group is often seen by organizational psychologists as providing the context for individual behaviour, while sociologists might treat the organization as the context for the emergence, structure and functioning of groups. As Roberts *et al.* (1978, p. 39) put it, "The sociologist's unit of analysis is the industrial organizational psychologist's environment". Emphasis on one level of analysis providing a "context" for another is particularly notable in the work of organizational researchers, whether sociologists or psychologists, who adopt some form of "systems" perspective (e.g. Gowler, 1969; Rousseau, 1977; Wall, 1980). Rousseau, for example, treats an organizational-level variable, technology (classified in terms of Thompson's (1967) typology), as the context for two individual-level variables, perceived job characteristics (measured by a modified version of Hackman and Oldham's (1974) Job Diagnostic Survey) and affective responses of employees to their jobs (measured by the Brayfield–Rothe satisfaction index, Miller's alienation questionnaire, and Patchen's measure of involvement in the job) (Brayfield and Rothe, 1951; Miller, 1967; Patchen, 1965). Her hypotheses predict that perceptions of job characteristics and levels of employee satisfaction (individual-level variables) will vary according to technological context, and multivariate analyses of variance are employed to test the hypotheses.

Although Rousseau explicitly rejects any suggestions that this study demonstrates causal relationships, "since static correlational analyses were employed" (1977, p. 40), implicit in the "levels as context" approach is an assumption that the "context" may act as an independent variable *vis-à-vis* the focus of the analysis (in this case job characteristics, which in turn provide the "context" for individual affective responses). Where a fully fledged systems perspective is employed, inferences of causality are made doubly complex by the assumption of feedback in the system (Gowler, 1969; Legge, 1970). In other words, the "contextual" independent variable at one point in time (e.g. production targets for a work group — Wall, 1980) may become the focused level of analysis, the dependent variable, at a subsequent point in time.

This raises a familiar problem of integration. Levels of analysis may be differentiated conceptually (individual, group, organization) but, when these distinctions are applied empirically, *a time dimension becomes involved.* However, the time dimension appropriate to measuring behaviour at one level (e.g. the individual level) may be very different from that used at other levels (e.g. group and organization). For example, individual attitudes to work may be measured at one point in time by a questionnaire, whilst the cohesiveness of the work groups, which provide the "context" for these individual attitudes, may be measured by observation of patterns of interaction over a much longer time period. Given the different time dimensions involved, are the results achieved from such measurements strictly comparable (in the sense of being capable of being compared)? Moreover, if one level is to be treated as the context (independent variable) of another (the dependent variable) the time period over which variation in the independent variable is likely to result in variation in the dependent variable needs to be identified. This raises serious integration problems if more than one independent variable is hypothesized (which is likely if several disciplinary perspectives are being brought to bear on one "problem") and serious identification problems (of appropriate time dimensions) if feedback is hypothesized.

Additionally, levels of analysis may refer not just to the "concrete" levels of individual, group and organizational and their "related" disciplines, but to the fact that one unit of analysis, typically a set of processes, such as "planning events" or "choice situations" (McClintock *et al.*, 1979) or an event such as a strike, may be analysed from different perspectives, both within and between disciplines, to achieve different layers of meaning or levels of measurement. An analogy would be peeling an onion, where each layer represents a different (and deeper) interpretation of one set of data, rather than the organizational layers or levels from which the data were drawn.

Thus the problems of integration in organizational research can be seen to be extremely complex. First, there is the problem of integrating different disciplines (sociology, psychology, etc.). This is complicated by the fact that different orientations within one discipline may also require integration. Secondly, even if this can be achieved, the question still remains of how these different disciplines, and orientations within disciplines, may be integrated across different levels of analysis, particularly when, for example, the time spans required for the meaningful measurement of the different concepts involved may differ. Stated like this, it is obvious that any integration that can practicably be undertaken must be limited in scope and in the degree to which synthesis is achieved.

In one sense though, researchers who attempt any form of integration often find that their approach inevitably becomes more ambitious than they might have wished or initially intended. For, in theory, it might appear possible to limit the exercise by adopting one of several partial designs: (i) to use concepts from two or more disciplines but focused on one level of analysis; (ii) to integrate two orientations from one discipline, again focused at one level of analysis; or (iii) to use concepts from one discipline and one theoretical orientation across several levels of analysis. But, in the first two cases, the different disciplinary concepts selected may be relevant to different levels of analysis (for example, as in an attempt to integrate psychological and economic concepts in the analysis of labour turnover), while in the third case the concepts and methods from one discipline (for example, psychology) may be inadequate for analysing responses at certain levels (for example, organizational) leading to potential aggregation problems, on the one hand, and the need to move outside one discipline on the other.

Finally, as commented upon above, the integration of different disciplinary perspectives and levels of analysis presents more than a complex theoretical problem. For not only are "professional" monopoly interests at stake, but questions of "identity" and "commitment" also emerge with the active encouragement of bureaucratic arrangements. As Platt comments,

... there are strong institutional forces pulling people towards distinct disciplinary approaches; the pressure to disciplinary conformity is probably particularly strongly felt by younger people who do not yet have a securely established base or identity in any particular field. To the extent that this is so, the effects of different patterns of intellectual training and socialisation are reinforced by personal needs, and conflicts and disagreements are likely to follow. ...   (1976, p. 42)

2. The case for integration

In the light of these complexities, is it really worth attempting integration between disciplinary perspectives and levels of analysis? What are the *theoretical* arguments for such an exercise? In the opening paragraph of this paper we gave some indication of why such an attempt was desirable in problem-oriented organizational research and a discussion of this rationale is necessary before proceeding further.

Riley (1964) distinguishes between four types of analysis: *individual analysis*, where measurement is carried out on the unit alone (e.g. measurement and correlation of an individual's attitudes and behaviours); *group analysis*, where measurement is carried out on properties of groups, sometimes relative to other groups of the same kind (e.g. as in ranking); *structural analysis*, where data and conclusions focus on the group, but where individual variables are used either for specifying the result or for checking its validity; and *contextual analysis*, which differs from structural analysis in that the main focus is on individuals, but individual relationships are checked or specified by accounting for differences between the groups to which the individuals belong (cf. Lazarsfeld and Menzel, 1961). Using these distinctions, Allardt (1969) makes the observation that structural and contextual analysis (i.e. analysis involving more than one level or to put it in Allardt's terms (1969, p. 51) "containing variables from different levels of a social system . . . variables dealing with entirely different subject matters or chosen from different theoretical systems") is likely to prove more fruitful than group and individual analysis. The reason for this, he suggests, is that structural and contextual analysis enhance the informative value of a finding.

Following Popper (1959), the informative value of a finding relates to the degree to which it can be falsified: the larger the number of ways in which a statement can be proved false, the greater its empirical content and the higher its informative value. Allardt argues that when analysis is contained at one level there is a greater likelihood for the statements generated to be trivial, almost tautological, and to involve arbitrariness or instability in the use of operational definitions. For example, take the finding that "workers interested in industrial relations issues are more likely to become shop-stewards". It is clear that the "generalization is trivial because the generalizing term (interest in industrial relations) must be operationalized in such a way that it expresses a predisposition towards the predicate (becoming a shop-steward) in terms of all our common-sense notions" (Allardt, 1969, p. 48). Furthermore, not only are the number of ways in which such a generalization can be falsified small, but if one operationalization of the generalizing term, such as balloting in union elections, fails or does not confirm the generalization, another can easily be selected, such as attendance at union branch meetings. "When a generalization is very narrow in scope and accordingly not too tied to other and different phenomena, there are actually no guides and few restrictions on how operational definitions should be chosen" (Allardt, 1969, p. 49).

Another argument for "the value of generalizations containing variables from different levels" (Allardt, 1969, p. 49) is that it enhances procedures of specification. Put simply, *if generalizations are to be of any use, they must be specified, i.e. their conditions of validity must be assessed.* This is best done, in the sense of increasing the number of potential falsifiers, if the specifying variables are selected from different levels. If selected from the same level, concerning the same type of phenomena as the generalization, the dangers of a low degree of falsifiability and a high arbitrariness in selecting operational definitions will not be checked. "Structural and contextual analyses (i.e. analyses involving more than one level) involve in practice a systematic specification" (Allardt, 1969, p. 50).

Given these arguments, it is suggested that single-level analysis (and single-perspective analysis, as the two are related) does not produce fruitful hypotheses. Against this, however, it must always be borne in mind that the conditions which increase the possibility of the *generation* of such hypotheses does decrease the likelihood of being able to draw stringent *causal inferences*. To draw causal inferences about the relationship between two variables, A and B, we need to know three things: "that A and B tend to appear together; that A precedes B in time; and that the relation between A and B is not a result of their common relation to a third variable" (Allardt, 1969, p. 42). With the exception of the first, these requirements can only be established with certainty through the use of an experimental method. Use of such a method — even quasi-experimental — is difficult enough in organizational research at one level, but control problems become magnified if more than one level of analysis is involved. Furthermore, if the researcher wishes to involve more than one disciplinary perspective, it is by no means certain that they will all be compatible with the experimental, or quasi-experimental method. In these circumstances stringent testing of hypotheses ("stringent" in the sense of conforming to the positivistic paradigm) may be difficult, if not impossible, to achieve.

Thus, using Allardt's (1969) distinction, in pursuing integration between levels and disciplines, our attentions are probably better directed towards *generating* causal *interpretations* rather than in seeking (and failing) to *establish* "strong" (Platt, 1966) causal *inferences*. Moreover, given the reservations expressed earlier about the feasibility of simplifying the integrative task by *either* integrating by level *or* by disciplinary perspective, the control problem is especially difficult to resolve.

In the light of this position, we now intend to discuss three approaches to integration, namely: aggregate analysis; ethogenic analysis (Harré, 1978, 1979) combined with structural analysis (Gowler and Legge, 1980); and strategies of multiple triangulation (Denzin, 1970). Our justification for the selection of these three approaches is as follows. We consider that aggregate analysis represents the "conventional" approach to integration, emphasizing integration of levels rather than concepts, largely through *measurement* inference. That is, aggregate analysis assumes that inferences can be made about one level of analysis from data collected and measured at a different level. In contrast, the ethogenic approach, combined with structural analysis, focuses on the integration of (i) concepts, and (ii) disciplinary and theoretical perspectives relevant to the research problem. Consequently, it emphasizes the need to integrate a range of data drawn from different levels through an "integrative" *theory* (Burrell and Morgan, 1979; Ransom *et al.* 1980). Finally, strategies of multiple triangulation emphasize the role different theoretical perspectives and their associated data-collection *methods* may play, through their juxtaposition, in achieving a "holistic" non-biased view of a research problem, spanning disciplines and organizational levels. None of these approaches, we consider, is without serious limitations but each can provide some leverage on this complex problem.

3.   Aggregate analysis—opportunities and problems

As defined by Roberts *et al.*, "aggregate analysis" is

... the use of some combination of responses (R's) or unit characteristics (U's) to reflect something about the immediately more macro unit of analysis (E's). .... Equally common, we find aggregated data used to make inferences about R's at a more micro level of analysis, without disaggregation.   (1978, p. 82)

Such an approach to combining different levels of analysis is frequently used in organizational research, such as when individual assessments of job satisfaction are aggregated to represent group morale, rather than such morale being assessed by measures taken at group level, for example, by observation (such as by sociometric analysis) or by the collection of material symbolizing collective sentiments (such as group songs, jokes, jargon, distinctive styles of dress and address and so on). A typical example of this "conventional" approach may be found in a recent paper by Wall (1980) in which group autonomy and task identity are measured in terms of individual perceptions of these group-level characteristics. Similarly this "conventional" approach has been applied to other properties of collectives, e.g. organizational climate, structure and technology are frequently measured by the use of individual perceptions (e.g. Hage and Aiken, 1969; Mohr, 1971; Payne and Pugh, 1976).

The advantages of this approach are largely two-fold. First, aggregate data at one level may be all that there is from which to seek explanations about responses at another. For example, where individual data cannot be obtained (say, on how each employee in a multi-plant organization balloted on a management pay offer), aggregate data (say, on balloting patterns in a particular area, such as the "Nottingham coalfields") may have to be used in seeking to explain individual behaviour, often in conjunction with other data (e.g. a colliery's strike record, productivity, overtime and absence records). Secondly, it is often cheaper, quicker and easier to integrate different levels of analysis by the use of aggregate data derived, for example, from company records or through questionnaire surveys, than by attempting to derive data unique to each level, perhaps involving a range of data-collection methods. Such constraints of time and research budget are particularly relevant if the research aims at large samples and/or inter-organizational comparisons.

In spite of these pragmatic advantages, aggregate analysis has to be treated with caution as it involves problems relating to conceptual development, sampling, time dimensions, measurement, data analysis and interpretation. Before embarking on a discussion of these issues, it should be noted that the arguments used here draw heavily on the work of Roberts *et al.* (1978, Ch. 4).

Conceptual aggregation occurs when the theory explaining a set of behaviours is relatively distant from the observations of them. Roberts *et al.* (1978) quote the following example. Organizational members, to varying degrees, follow rules. Some researchers, say social psychologists, observing this behaviour, might develop theories of control and conformity to explain it, such theories being closely tied to observations of individual rule-following. In these circumstances, theory and observations are located at the same levels of analysis (individual or small group). But other researchers, say sociologically orientated organization theorists, *when observing the same behaviour*, might utilize the concept of "formalization", i.e. the degree to which job descriptions are specified and to which job occupants are supervised in conforming to the standards and performance indicated by the formal job requirements (Dewar *et al.*, 1980). Obviously, in this case, the causal theory is not located at the same level of analysis as the observations. Thus, as Roberts *et al.* comment,

> If the paradigm used to explain rule following emphasizes conceptualization and measurement at the organizational level, individual rule-following behavior is neatly dealt with by developing an organizational construct to describe that response in its aggregate form. (1978, p. 88)

However, where *level in theory* is not closely linked with *level in observation*, misinterpretation can readily occur. This can happen, for example, when a construct, such as "organizational goals", which is essentially an abstraction from lower level behaviours, becomes reified. This sort of fallacy may contribute to, and indeed mirrors, another: that of "abstracted empiricism". This may be said to occur when the research methods used are inconsistent with the underlying theories upon which the research is based (Burrell and Morgan, 1979, p. 105). Examples of "abstracted empiricism" are perpetrated by

> Systems theorists who spend their energies measuring "structures"; interactionists who utilize static measurements of "attitudes" and "role situations"; integrative theorists who attempt to produce quantitative indices of "power", "conflict", "deviancy" and the like—all provide illustrations of abstracted empiricism, in that they engage in empirical research which violates the assumptions of their theoretical perspective.
> (1979, pp. 104–105)

To return, however, to the theory-at-one-level-and-data-at-another issue, Roberts *et al.* suggest that one way of avoiding this error is to develop

> ... composition theories (specifying relations among forms of one construct represented at different levels of analysis) to supplement and enrich content theories (describing relations among distinct constructs within a single level of aggregation or across levels)

and process theories (describing how different constructs are combined to produce response tendencies). (1978, p. 84)

However, as they comment, this approach also poses an argument against aggregation, but, given the length and complexity of this consideration, readers are referred to the Roberts *et al.* text.

The problems associated with conceptual aggregation suggest that the appropriate *unit to select* for observation in research should be consistent with its conceptual base. For example, if one is interested in the relationship between organizational control systems and the development of individual or group deviancy, the appropriate units of analysis are organizations and roles, not industries and employees classified by industry. Problems also arise when inferences are made about one level of analysis based on data from units at a more macro level. Thus, in ecological analysis, where individual data cannot be obtained (for example, each employee's daily output figures in a multi-plant manufacturing concern) aggregate distributions are established for, say, administratively defined units (for example, weekly output figures for a plant, possibly for departments within a plant) from which inferences about individual behaviour are drawn. This practice presents two potential difficulties. First, the aggregate unit selected may represent pre-existing administrative or geographical convenience in data collection, and have little relevance to the constructs under investigation. Secondly, using aggregate units, the researcher must be on his guard not to succumb to the dangers of the "ecological fallacy" (that is, the assumption that properties found to be correlated at the higher level are also correlated at the lower level). We shall return to this issue when considering problems in data analysis and interpretation.

Aggregation over *time* presents further problems. As Roberts *et al.* (1978, p. 92) point out, organizational researchers, unlike natural scientists, often have difficulty in handling "notions about the way time mediates processes and responses" because they "generally do not have natural cycles to guide them". Although this difficulty can to some extent be overcome by close observation of data and situations before embarking on time-series studies, in order to identify unobtrusive "naturally occurring benchmarks" (Roberts *et al.*, 1978, p. 92) it has tended to result in researchers paying inadequate attention to the specification of the time dimensions relevant to their research. This may result in several questionable practices. First, data are sometimes combined from samples collected at different times. Secondly, studies often include the comparison of measurements taken on the same variables at apparently arbitrary intervals (Legge and Hilling, 1974). Thirdly, researchers frequently indulge in "correlations between assessments of variables that reflect different units of time — for example, an assessment at a particular time of organizational climate over an unspecified time period and turnover in the same organization for the preceding two weeks" (Roberts *et al.*, 1978, p. 93). These latter two instances of failing to achieve coincidence between measures presents particular difficulties in interpreting the results of cross-lagged panel analyses as Roberts *et al.* (1978) and Feldman (1975) point out. Fourthly, researchers are sometimes insufficiently aware of problems associated with the use of data collected through retrospection, i.e. when individuals are asked to recall events which occurred before their measurement. This is often combined with aggregation, as when supervisors are asked to rate subordinates' performance over a previous time period. And, as Roberts *et al.* (1978, p. 94) warn, "aggregation over time and retrospection measures both introduce ambiguity, because it becomes unclear when the response of interest occurred". Further, "when a time-aggregation datum is correlated with another measure, lack of synchronicity may result".

These problems involved in the choice of time dimensions are not the only *measurement* difficulties that arise through aggregation. Roberts *et al.* (1978) go on to list three further difficulties. First, there is the issue of "summary" variables, such as job satisfaction, which may contain implicitly, but not explicitly, a summary of many things. Unless composition rules are made explicit, the researcher may become ensnared in measurement artefacts. For example, Wall and Lischeron (1977, p. 22) point to the problems of evaluating the participation-satisfaction thesis, when many of the supposedly relevant studies, in attempting to correlate supervisory "consideration" (a surrogate for a participatory management) with "job satisfaction" produce artefactual correlations "since the joint variation of the two measures used stems, at least in part, from essentially identical items being included in both". Thus, many studies use the Smith *et al.* (1969) "Job Descriptive Index" to measure satisfaction, and Fleishman's (1957) "Supervisory Behavior Description" to measure the consideration of supervision, without realizing the degree of overlap between the "supervisor scale" of the one and the "consideration scale" of the other (Payne *et al.*, 1976).

Secondly, some variables, for example, labour turnover and job level are not exclusively attached to one level of analysis — being the property of individuals, groups and organizations. However, unless this is clearly understood and made explicit by the researcher, assumptions of independence between variables may be falsely made, with consequent measurement and interpretation difficulties. A related problem, which raises a third difficulty, is that variables, between or within levels of analysis, may be causally interactive. Organizational psychologists, methodologically speaking, have still to come to grips with this problem and Roberts *et al.* (1978, p. 98) quote James and others (1978, p. 27) as stating that:

while psychologists have addressed the concept of reciprocal causation theoretically, research, including that in climate, has focused primarily on (implicit) unidirectional causal models or has simply avoided the issue of causality by emphasizing descriptive rather than causal interpretations of results; . . . the ramifications of reciprocal causation for measurement, for interpreting what has been measured . . . and for the appropriateness of research design have not been recognized, resulting, in some instances, in the treatment of what appear to be pseudo issues.

Finally, aggregation may give rise to serious problems of *data analysis and interpretation*. The former, problems of data analysis, stem largely from the fact that the way in which data are grouped (for example, whether randomly, or to maximize variation in the independent variable, in the dependent variable, or by spatial or temporal proximity) may affect the value that statistics — in particular Pearson correlations and regression coefficients — take, following a shift in level of aggregation (Blalock, 1964; Hammond, 1973; Hannan, 1971). This can give rise to problems of interpretation, which may be compounded by an absence of composition theories (Roberts *et al.*, 1978). The most common interpretational errors are the fallacies of the wrong level, defined by Galtung (1967, p. 45) as "not in making inferences from one level of analysis to another, but in making direct translation of properties or relations from one level to another, i.e. making too simple inferences". The ecological fallacy, defined earlier, is an example of this kind of fallacy, when projecting downwards, but it may equally be committed by projecting upwards, from individuals to higher level units, such as groups or organizations. An example of this kind of fallacy in projecting downwards, suggested by Lazarsfeld and Menzel (1961), would be to infer that the indecision of a "hung" jury meant that its members were indecisive — on the contrary. The problem is that correlations between averages, as in Durkheim's (1897, 1952) classic research on the relationship between religion and suicide, are very difficult to interpret.

This finding [that Catholic communities, characterized by large numbers of Catholics, had a lower suicide rate, an aggregated variable, than Protestant communities] may be the result of some property of Catholic communities, some characteristics of individual Catholics and Protestants, or an interaction between community composition and individual characteristics . . . conclusions are difficult to draw.

(Roberts *et al.*, 1978, pp. 103–104)

Aggregate analysis, then, tackles the problem of integrating different levels of analysis by making the questionable assumption that data collected at one level can reflect or represent something at another. Of course, such an assumption may facilitate the collection of data, e.g. the use of social surveys to study the structure of social class, but at the expense of subsequent interpretation.

Aggregated data, being frequently weakened by the problems discussed above, is then prone to gross misinterpretations. However, by way of comparison, we shall now discuss two alternative perspectives, i.e. ethogenic analysis and multiple triangulation, which have been selected because they may be seen to represent attempts to avoid some of the difficulties created by the conventional and essentially positivist approach.

4.   The integration of theory: ethogenic analysis

As suggested above, a useful way to combine different levels of analysis and disciplinary perspectives is to seek a method that places individual perceptions and interactions, whether dyadic or within groups, into an inter-group and organizational context, while showing the relationships between perceptions, interactions and context. One way of attempting this is to combine some form of reflexive or hermeneutic analysis, at the individual and group level, with some form of structural analysis at the organizational, institutional and societal levels. Such an approach has been illustrated, for example, by Gowler and Legge (1980) in reference to empirical data, and by Giddens (1976, 1979) and Ransom *et al.* (1980) in conceptual work. Gowler and Legge's method, which we shall discuss in detail below, is to juxtapose ethogenic analysis, with that of synchronic ("the analysis of social practices and institutions as they exist at any one time") and diachronic analysis ("the investigation of the stages and process by which these practices are created and abandoned, change and are changed") (Harré, 1978), but, in reference to the latter two, from a structural functionalist perspective.

Ethogenic analysis, according to our interpretation of Harré's (1978, 1979) position, consists, essentially, of the following steps. First, the researcher undertakes "episode analysis". That is, he or she observes action sequences, basing his or her analysis upon "the dramaturgical metaphor of scene (setting and situation) action and actor", using "externally attributed meanings and presently existing, consciously formulated social theories" to guide his or her analysis. In doing so the researcher differentiates between elements of the action sequence which may be seen in terms of "practical projects", directed at achieving some form of instrumental outcome and "expressive projects", directed at achieving "some self-presentational good" (Harré, 1979, pp. 123, 126). Secondly, the researcher seeks to analyse the "accounts" individuals present of their actions. Such accounts are of two kinds: "first-stage accounts which members use to provide interpretations of act/action episodes and which can figure as part of the action" and "second-stage (often negotiated) accounts in which members theorize about the action and the first-stage accounts, developing hypotheses in both folk sociology and folk psychology" (Harré, 1979, p. 123). The relationship between action and accounts is then explored, for the basic premise of this approach is that both the action and accounts an individual produces derive from his stock of "social knowledge". Thus,

Since the basic hypothesis of the ethogenic approach to the understanding of social action is that the very same social knowledge and skill is involved in the genesis of action and of accounts, by recording and analysing each separately, we have two mutually supporting and reciprocally checking ways of discovering the underlying system of social knowledge and belief. (Marsh *et al.*, 1978, p. 21)

Harré argues that a "central preoccupation" of this approach is to establish "fruitful connections" between the disciplinary perspectives of social psychology, "micro-sociology" (that is, the sociological perspective of symbolic interactionists and ethnomethodologists) and linguistic analysis. Thus the theories of micro-sociologists inform his episode analysis, those of linguistic philosophers, his account analysis, while both perspectives cast light on such social psychological issues as how individuals cope with threats to the social order, show themselves to be socially worthy as people, how they gain and maintain social knowledge, and so on (Harré, 1978, pp. 45–46).

However, as may be seen from this brief summary, the broader context (for example, the organization) in which action and accounts take place, is viewed largely in terms of individuals' social constructions of reality, as contained in their actions and accounts. As Harré's model is of "autonomous" rather than "plastic" man (Hollis, 1977), his view of the environment of action and accounts is as

a complex product of interaction between persons as active agents and the environment as a plastic construction than can be endowed with causal powers through the meaning-giving act of agents. Environments do not exist in their fullness independent of the agents who enter them. They are part created by the way the individuals who enter them assign meanings to the people, activities, settings and social situations they find within them and even actively create. Then they are themselves affected by that which they have created.   (Harré, 1979, p. 143)

The environment then is viewed less as causative of individual action and more as a source of "templates", which, being recognized by the individual, will shape the form such action takes.

While accepting the validity of this approach to context, we feel that Harré's perspective may be usefully supplemented by a parallel analysis from a contrasting position. In other words, environment or organizational context may, at the same time, be analysed from a macro-sociological perspective such as a structural functionalist or systems position and viewed as acting upon "plastic" man, constraining or even determining his actions. Given the different models of man implied in these different orientations to organizational context, however, true integration is hardly possible, but juxtaposing the findings of the two radically different perspectives and mapping the points of similarity and difference (as in analysing "deviant" cases) is likely to prove fruitful. (This point will be further developed in our subsequent discussion of "multiple triangulation" strategies.) Moreover, both perspectives may be usefully developed and contained within the framework of extended case analysis.

An example of the use of ethogenic analysis, to tape individual and group levels, but with a parallel analysis of organizational-level variables (such as markets, control systems, management structure, organizational "culture") from a structural functionalist perspective may be found in an extended case study reported by Gowler (1970) and Gowler and Legge (1980). In the first stage of the analysis, Gowler (1970) identified the organizational context or, as he termed it, "structural imperatives" such as market competition, product change and workflow administration that constrained supervisory style and the operation of control systems (such as the wage-payment system) in an electronics factory employing female assemblers. The structural imperatives acted:

(1) to pressure male supervisors—as "plastic" men—to increase and maintain productivity in the face of growing uncertainty; (2) to pressure operators—also as "plastic" men, or rather women—to reduce productivity in order to reduce uncertainty.

However, in order to analyse the form such behaviours took and their meaning to the actors involved, and through such an analysis to tap "the underlying systems of social knowledge and belief" (to reiterate Harré), Gowler and Legge (1980) turned to an ethogenic analysis of the actions and accounts of the participants within the researcher-defined context of the structural imperatives. The unit of analysis in terms of action was operators' and supervisors' interactions concerning and reactions to the measured daywork payment system through which the operators were rewarded. Briefly, the relationships between operators and supervisors were poor, supervisors demanding levels of output which operators either could not, or would not, produce, operators showing supervisors "no respect" and even challenging their authority.

The first-level accounts of these actions took the following form. As perceived by the supervisors, the payment system forced them to maintain given quantities and qualities of output purely through "human relations" skills, in which they had not been trained, without the sanction of a "carrot and stick" incentive payment system. As perceived by the operators, the payment system obliged them to "contract" to maintain a certain standard of performance in return for a guaranteed wage, without the freedom to fall back to lower levels of performance, according to inclination, once the contract was made. Their only "freedom" was to contract to maintain even higher levels of performance (with higher wages). If the operator did "fall back" the sanction was retraining and, if the contracted level of performance was still not regained, dismissal. (The managerial justifications for these rigid regulations are presented and discussed in Gowler and Legge, 1980.)

Following Harré's injunction that action and account analysis should form an iterative process, Gowler and Legge (1980), in the light of this first-level account analysis, returned to analyse and re-analyse action sequences. In doing so, it was observed that operators tended to "contract" for levels of performance well below their ability to achieve them, with the result that many operators had either a considerable amount of spare time (having completed their contractual obligations) or continued to produce extra components for which they would not be paid.

These behaviours then gave rise to a second rule that any operator discovered giving completed components to another would be dismissed. Management's rationale (account) for this rule was that such a practice not only undermined the "individual contract" basis of the wage-payment system, but created difficulties in workflow administration and quality control.

Relationships between supervisors and operators further deteriorated in the light of this second rule. If the supervisors pressed operators to contract for levels of performance which the latter could not maintain, they were then faced with the probability that they would have to dismiss them. If they left assemblers to contract low levels of performance, they had either to tolerate the latter conspicuously "wasting time", or producing components that might be "illegitimately distributed" to workmates who could not fulfil their contractual obligations, or *to meet other reciprocal obligations*. In either case, supervisors realized that this course of action could also incur management sanctions directed at themselves. Similarly, the operators' response to the supervisors' ambiguous position of power (i.e. to dismiss) but non-power (i.e. to force them to produce, to check "time-wasting") and undermined power (i.e. management were just as likely to sanction them for poor/illegal operator performance as the operators themselves) was to develop a contemptuous posture. This was expressed in such first-level accounts as the comment that "what sort of man would do a job like that—standing watching a bunch of women all day" or, as in the lines of their publicly chanted work song:

The chargehand and foreman and manager too,
Stand with their hands in their pockets,
    with nothing to do.
They stand on the floor and they bump and they shout;
They shout about things they know nothing about:
For all that they're doing they might as well be
Shovelling coal on the Isle of Capri.
(Part of work song, sun to the traditional tune of the "Mountains of Mourne", and recorded at the firm's annual dance.)

However, ethogenic analysis also contains the second-level analysis of accounts where surface data (overt accounts/justifications) are analysed for their deep structure and fundamental meanings. Gowler and Legge (1980) consequently applied second-level analysis to two stories recounted by supervisors during casual conversations. The stories were as follows:

(A) A girl subject to fits, an epileptic, who was said to have been "spoilt by her mother", took advantage of her condition and received an unusual amount of help from her workmates. This help consisted of the gift of completed assemblies and enabled her to meet her production targets. Later, a supervisor noticed that the operator concerned began to fall short of her quota but, before he could take action, the girl had left the firm. The supervisor was subsequently informed that other workers in this girl's group had refused to continue their support. The reason given for this withdrawal of help was that the girl gave nothing in return.

(B) A girl with a crippled leg became very friendly with the worker sitting next to her. Their relationship was so close that they were known as "a couple of lesbians". Their supervisor believed that the crippled girl was helping her friend, who made little or no attempt to improve her performance or to repay this assistance. Eventually, the supervisor confronted the girls with this and threatened to separate them. This resulted in both girls giving notice and each actually left the factory. However, the crippled girl returned to the firm, having found difficulty in finding suitable employment elsewhere.

In the context of the analysis of structural imperatives (synchronic analysis) and of action (episode) and first-level accounts analysis, viewing these stories functionally, at the second level of analysis, they may be said to be either:

(i) attributions made by "leaders" in conditions of extreme uncertainty (Green and Mitchell, 1979);

(ii) cautionary tales used to socialize new personnel (and researchers);

(iii) myths that permit the statement of what "would be difficult to admit openly and yet what is patently clear to all and sundry is that the ideal is not attainable" (Douglas, 1967, p. 52); or

(iv) rhetorics (Gowler and Legge, 1980) that combine the three functions identified above.

Developing these themes, Gowler and Legge use "structuralist" analysis, drawing on the work of Lévi-Strauss (1978) and Douglas (1975) to analyse these stories in terms of contextually based linguistic analysis.

Readers are referred to the original paper (Gowler and Legge, 1980) for a full explication and elaboration of this form of analysis. To give a flavour of the approach, however, two points may be made in reference to Fig. 1, which analyses the stories as "myths".

TABLE 1

The structural analysis of myth (from Gowler and Legge, 1980)

Text	Column 1	Column 2	Column 3	Column 4
A	Girl assembler crippled mentally (an epileptic–head?)	Spoilt by mother	Receives help from group	Leaves firm, result of workers' action
B	Girl assembler crippled physically (leg)	Very close relation-ship with friend ("lesbians")	Gives help to friend	Leaves firm, result of supervisor action, but returns

In Table 1, column 4, it may be observed how different meanings emerge when contrasts within the stories are complemented by contrasts (as oppositions) between stories. Thus story (A) indicates that, although the "problem" was removed, i.e. the "delinquent" operative left the firm, this was the result of the operators taking independent action, effectively usurping the supervisor's powers. Story (B), in contrast, reverses this situation, since the supervisor exercises his powers only to find that the "problem" (i.e. the crippled girl) returns. Consequently, if these are analysed as a single story, these two "causal" accounts are transformed into a single "correlation". This is that supervisory power is inversely related to supervisory problem-solving, which thereby changes diachronic cause-and-effect into synchronic correlation.

Further, following Lévi-Strauss' (1963, p. 211) injunction to break down accounts (stories) into "their gross constituent units or mythemes", then to treat the mythemes as counters to be arranged in such a way as to produce, both vertically (top to bottom) and horizontally (reading left to right) data-orderings (columns and rows) of items that exhibit common features, the stories are analysed at the level of their deep structures. To quote from Gowler and Legge (1980):

[Table 1] column 1 may be said to represent the common feature of extreme forms of *physical disability* and column 2 extreme forms of *inter-personal behaviour*. Column 3 represents (asymmetrical) forms of reciprocity . . . and column 4 extreme *social sanctions*. Then, to reduce this further by compressing columns 1 and 2 into extreme behaviour (physical handicaps are *socially* defined and managed, Goffman, 1964), and columns 3 and 4 into extreme retributions, we have the propositions *that excessive behaviour is related to excessive sanctions*.

There are, however, deeper levels of meaning revealed when each column is viewed in terms of its internal contrasts, and again the themes of extremes and excesses emerge. For example, column 1 internally contrasts extreme forms of physical disability, i.e. one "end" of the body against the other (hand/leg) . . . column 2, on the other hand, internally contrasts extreme forms of "affection", between kin and non-kin, and in column 3 there emerges the opposition between individual and group reciprocity. Finally, column 4 contrasts *workers-and-leaving with supervisors-and-returning*.

(A similar example of linguistic analysis applied to organizational research may be found in Manning, 1974.)

Gowler and Legge (1980) proceed to combine the analysis of deep structures with Marxist analysis, by relating ideas of excess, translated into "surplus", to an examination of "a manifestation of a major contradiction of capitalism, whereby the surplus value of labour is not available to either workers or employers".

By analysing an organization in this way, Gowler (1970) and Gowler and Legge (1980) attempt:

(1) to integrate, or rather, hold in parallel, individual and group-level analysis (actions and accounts);

(2) organizational analysis (functional analysis of "structural imperatives");

(3) within the framework of a longitudinal investigation, to conduct an extended case study which allows diachronic and synchronic analysis.

Moreover, by combining ethogenic analysis with a functionalist extended case, they attempt to combine analyses from several disciplinary perspectives (economic, sociological, social psychological and linguistic), and from several theoretical orientations (e.g. symbolic interactionist and structural functionalist) within one discipline (sociological). And, in an oblique fashion, they indicate how *exchange theory* (e.g. the transfer of completed components between workmates) may be used to relate *functionalism* (e.g. the model of the workplace as a social structure and system) with phenomenology (e.g. the model of textures of meaning embedded in accounts). Thus, in this integrated approach, structure, perception (including meaning) and behaviour simultaneously constitute relatively stable surface and submerged realities (Giddens, 1979).

This distinction between "surface and submerged realities" introduces another way of looking at levels of analysis, quite different from the conventional individual, group and organizational levels. An example of such an approach, quite apart from Gowler and Legge's (1980) attempt to move from an analysis conducted at the "surface" level to one at the "deep-structure" level, may be found in Light's (1979) examination of the socialization of psychiatric residents.

Obviously, such approaches are not without their difficulties. At a conceptual level there is the problem raised earlier of whether it is logically coherent to combine structural with reflexive analysis, given the very *different models of man implied by the two perspectives.* Certainly, this is a problem if structure is analysed from a purely functionalist perspective, with an acceptance of its heavily criticized teleological assumptions. Nevertheless, Giddens (1976, 1979) goes some way to meet this difficulty by arguing that, at the organizational and institutional levels, structural analysis may be more validly juxtaposed with reflexive analysis if the "duality of structure" is recognized. That is if

the structural properties of systems are [perceived to be] both the medium and outcome of the practices that constitute those systems . . . structure thus is not to be conceptualised as a barrier to action, but as essentially involved in its production . . . [as not] simply placing constraints upon human agency, but as enabling.

(Giddens, 1979, pp. 69–70; 1976, p. 161)

This approach, in reference to empirical data, has, in fact, been implicitly adopted by Gowler (1969) in his analysis of the "structuration" (to use Giddens' term) of an internal labour market (see also Doreian and Hummon, 1976, Ch. 2).

Giddens' position and our own is endorsed by Ransom *et al.* who, summarizing their approach, explicitly argue that

. . . a theoretical framework for the analysis of organizational structures should be underpinned by modes of analysis that are adequate at the levels of meaning and causation, and that seek to understand the purposes which actors attach to their conduct yet preserve the necessity of explaining the complex outcome of events intended and unintended. Such an integration at the methodological level permits the elaboration of a theoretical model that accommodates the conceptual categories of provinces of meaning, power dependencies, and contextual constraints, whose interconnection can explain the constitutive structuring of organizational structures over time. This more unified methodological and theoretical framework allows us to incorporate a number of ostensibly disparate perspectives: phenomenological perspectives, which typically focus at the micro level upon the intersubjective construction of meanings;

conditional, ahistorical organizational analyses of structural regularities; and broader sociohistorical perspectives of economy and culture.   (1980, p. 14)

However, it should be borne in mind that the greater the degree to which this mode of analysis eschews the conventional, positivist model of corporate life, the more difficulty those espousing such unconventional views will experience with those who control access to organizations and resources. As two sociologists, Bell and Newby, observe

A loss of confidence in positivism will almost certainly make consultancies harder to obtain, make sociology less demonstrably "useful", and make the information thus obtained less amenable to forming a basis for social control by élite groups. (1977, p. 29)

And organizational psychologists are, like other social scientists, equally subject to exclusion from the marketplace on the grounds of epistemological heresy, subversion, or just "ivory tower" nonsense.

Such attempts at combining reflexive analysis, at the individual and group levels, and structural analysis at organizational and institutional levels, raises the question of the use of strategies of multiple triangulation in integrating disciplinary perspectives and levels of analysis. Gowler and Legge's (1980) approach moves pragmatically in this direction. It might now be appropriate, therefore, to consider this approach more systematically.

5. Strategies of multiple triangulation

Triangulation has been defined by Denzin (1970, p. 301) as "the use of multiple methods in the study of the same object", and as such closely resembles Campbell and Fiske's (1959) advocacy of multi-method/multi-trait research. Denzin suggests that *triangulation involves varieties of data, investigators, and theories as well as methodologies:*

The four basic types of triangulation are: data, with these types (1) time, (2) space, (3) person, and these levels (1) aggregate (person), (2) interactive (person), (3) collective (person); investigator (multiple vs. single observers of the same object); theory (multiple vs. single perspectives in relation to the same set of objects); and methodological (within-method triangulation and between-method triangulation).
(Denzin, 1970, p. 301)

Multiple triangulation, according to Denzin, occurs when researchers "combine in one investigation multiple observers, theoretical perspectives, sources of data and methodologies". The example he uses for illustration is a research design directed at generating a grounded theory

(Glaser and Strauss, 1967) of interaction in face-to-face settings. Denzin suggests that to do this he would triangulate data sources by examining encounters in a variety of different settings and situations. Interactions in the different settings would then be sampled by time of day, number of persons present and location at the time of observation. Methodologies might include interviews, participant observation, unobtrusive measures and life histories of the persons interviewed. The perspectives of Goffman (1969), Homans (1961) and Blumer (1969) might be adopted, and specific propositions from each theorist would be derived and tested in terms of the above strategies. The "collectivity" level of data would be examined "only as it impinges on interaction in these settings" and "through the use of survey interviews, contextual analysis, and participant observation" (Denzin, 1970, p. 311). Finally, multiple observers would be used to avoid bias in favour of any one perspective or method, but also to increase the reliability of unobtrusive observations.

For researchers primarily interested in analysis at one level in the organization, from one perspective, and in hypothesis-testing rather than in generation, triangulation of data and method is chiefly employed as a means of establishing the reliability and external validity of findings. For those, however, who are more interested in integrating different levels of analysis, disciplinary perspectives and in generating hypotheses (and, as we suggested earlier, these orientations tend to go together) multiple triangulation "can capture a more complete, *holistic* and contextual portrayal of the unit(s) under study" (Jick, 1979, p. 603). In particular, multiple triangulation allows the researcher to "match the variety of the sources with variety in the sensing device that is applied to it" (Webb and Weick, 1979, p. 651). As illustrated in Gowler and Legge's (1980) implicit use of triangulation, different methods and data sources may be matched appropriately with the different theoretical perspectives and levels of analysis involved in each stage of the study to move towards holistic description. Such an approach encourages the researcher to avoid the trap of assuming that different levels of analysis may be satisfactorily integrated through aggregation — regardless of the potential pitfalls outlined earlier. Thus, use of multiple triangulation should alert the researcher to select collectively generated data when analysing at collective levels (group or organizational) — for example, to use observations of interaction at group level, to collect actual documents and other unobtrusive data at organizational level and so on. Over-reliance on questionnaire surveys as *the* instrument for the generation of "hard" data irrespective of its appropriateness to the level of analysis or the dynamic nature of the research question may hopefully be avoided.

One advantage of triangulation, apart from convergent validation and the "matching" facility mentioned above, is that when different methods yield dissimilar results the researcher, after conventional checks, is encouraged to enrich his analysis and to develop new explanations to reconcile the divergence. Furthermore, triangulation may help to uncover deviant cases or the off-quadrant dimension of a phenomenon (Jick, 1979), again encouraging the reassessment of old theories and the development of new ones. Triangulation may thus enhance the value of negative results.

Obviously though, a strategy of multiple triangulation is not without problems. First, as Jick (1979, p. 607) points out:

It is a delicate exercise to decide whether or not results have converged. In practice, there are few guidelines for systematically ordering eclectic data in order to determine congruence or validity. For example, should all components of a multi-method approach be weighted equally, that is, is all the evidence equally useful? If not, then it is not clear on what basis the data should be weighted, aside from personal preference. . . . While statistical tests can be applied to a particular method, there are no formal tests to discriminate between methods to judge their applicability. The concept of "significant differences" when applied to qualitatively judged differences does not readily compare with the statistical tests which also demonstrate "significant differences".

Secondly, as suggested earlier, this strategy can be expensive in time and other costs, particularly the more facets of triangulation are pursued. This raises a dilemma for the problem-oriented organizational psychologists. In return for access, the host organization(s) may demand relatively speedy feedback of results on a problem that requires, in management's eyes, instant solution. But precisely because problems do transcend different levels in the organization and require analysis from a range of relevant perspectives, it is difficult to see how genuinely useful "findings" can be produced speedily. One answer in gaining acceptance of a triangulated strategy may be, of course, to have it developed in the context of some modified form of action research, where the research process may be accepted by the "powers that be" as a worthwhile outcome, in the short term, encouraging a preparedness to wait for "findings" and "solutions" in the longer term.

6. Conclusions

From the foregoing discussions, what conclusions may be drawn for the organizational psychologist in particular, and for organizational research in general? We would suggest the following:

(1) Organizational psychology, from our perspective at least, seems conventionally, and overly, wedded to a positivistic, survey-oriented paradigm (Dunnette, 1976; or see any recent issue of *Journal of Applied Psychology* or *Organizational Behavior and Human Performance*). We consider, as may be evident from the foregoing arguments, that this stems from a worthy, if disproportionate, concern with hypothesis-testing, to the exclusion of hypothesis generation, and even at times, data interpretation. Such research, to quote Phillips (1971, p. 175), has frequently constituted "the same kinds of sterile, unproductive, unimaginative investigations which have long characterized most . . . research". In other words, masses of uninterpretable yet "hard" data have been generated, of little relevance to the problem-oriented world to which multi-level and multi-disciplinary research is addressed. Furthermore, we suggest that such an approach, in any attempt to integrate different levels of analysis and disciplinary perspectives (if such an attempt is considered respectable at all) is incapable of achieving its objectives and, at worst, may delude the researcher into thinking that integration has been achieved, when all that has resulted are various forms of aggregation fallacy. The "hard" data generated by such surveys, we feel, are no substitute for "soft" but interpretable data.

(2) In this paper, however, and particularly in our discussion of Gowler and Legge's (1980), Gidden's (1976, 1979) and Harré's (1976, 1979) approaches, we have attempted to suggest how individual, group and organizational levels of analysis and different disciplinary perspectives may be integrated. But we feel this attempt is, at best, a pale approximation, given the fact that different levels and perspectives in analysis would appear more easily *juxtaposed* than truly integrated. Perhaps true integration can only exist where analysis can accept one, either reactive or proactive, model of man or, alternatively, specify the conditions and circumstances when either model prevails. Although Giddens has proposed a way round this dilemma, it remains for his approach to be properly applied and operationalized in relation to

empirical studies. Researchers at Manchester Business School (Bowey, 1976; Gowler, 1969; Legge, 1970; Mumford, 1972) have implicitly made some attempts in this area, through the use of the mediating concept of role, as applied both to structure and constraint (job requirements), structure and orientations (job expectations), structure and meaning (job experience), and structure and action (job performance), but such work needs to be further developed. We should note too the lack of guidelines, in strategies of multiple triangulation, for comparing and weighting data elicited from different research perspectives in relation to different disciplinary perspectives (Jick, 1979).

(3) If organizational psychology is to break free from some of the limitations discussed here, and become part of a multi-disciplinary, multi-level approach to organizational analysis and problem-solving, questions may arise as to the nature of its unique contribution to such an exercise. However, it seems reasonable to suggest that organizational psychologists are well-placed to attempt a synthesis between, say, theories of perception, motivation and attribution and current developments in micro-sociology and social anthropology (Wallman, 1979). Given this view, we have suggested the "symbolic interactionist" position offers one way to bridge the gap between certain sociological and psychological perspectives. Furthermore, the "interactionist" position also offers opportunities for some intra-disciplinary integration and/or juxtapositions, e.g. a cognitive social psychology, where, as Zavolloni and Louis-Guerin (1979) put it, human-information-processing is seen to interact with the sociophysical environment to construct reality. Moreover, if theoretical and methodological integration is not forthcoming, organizational psychologists might utilize "organization development" (OD) skills to help orchestrate and translate different disciplinary perspectives. In other words, they might lead to an attempt to achieve a peaceful, and possibly fruitful coexistence of disciplines through OD.

(4) Of course, as implied in all that has been said here, we accept that organizational psychologists should be attempting to define and solve problems in all sorts of social collectives. However, this is not to accept that organizational psychologists are or should be the servants of any power élite. Indeed, we suggest that, if organizational psychologists present and negotiate "alternative realities" through the use of

"integrated theories", "methodological pluralism" and so on, they are likely to challenge the "taken for granted" views of the world and inevitably threaten those with a vested interest in the *status quo*.

(5) Organizational "problem-solving" research and interventions make it imperative that many of the difficulties outlined in this discussion are recognized, negotiated and, if possible, overcome. But, if it is accepted that a corollary of multi-level analysis inevitably involves multi-disciplinary approaches, we have also to recognize, regretfully, that it is doubtful whether academic institutions and funding agencies will respond with appropriate forms and levels of support. Moreover, as alternative paradigms and realities are explored, those involved not only become vulnerable to the standard criticisms, e.g. the inability to verify and predict, but also to charges of intellectual anarchy or dilletantism. And, certainly, those who attempt to move between the disciplines or deny the conventional approaches to the levels-of-analysis issue are likely to put their reputations and careers at risk. As Bailey (1977), when discussing these matters, observes, "The rate of survival for those who leave the trenches and venture into no-man's land is not high". But battles are not won unless the victors first venture out of the entrenchments and occupy no-man's land.

References

ALLARDT, E. (1969). Aggregate analysis: the problem of its informative value. In M. Dogan and S. Rokkan (eds), *Social Ecology*. Cambridge: Massachusetts Institute of Technology Press.

BAILEY, F. G. (1977). *Morality and Expediency*. Oxford: Blackwell.

BELL, C. AND NEWBY, H. (1977). Introduction: the rise of methodological pluralism. In C. Bell and H. Newby (eds), *Doing Sociological Research*. London: George Allen and Unwin.

BLALOCK, H. M. (1964). *Causal Inferences in Non-Experimental Research*. Chapel Hill: University of North Carolina Press.

BLUMER, H. (1969). *Symbolic Interactionism*. Englewood Cliffs: Prentice-Hall.

BOWEY, A. M. (1976). *The Sociology of Organisations*. London: Hodder and Stoughton.

BRAYFIELD, A. H. AND ROTHE, H. F. (1951). An index of job satisfaction. *Journal of Applied Psychology*, **35,** 307–311.

BURRELL, G. AND MORGAN, G. (1979). *Sociological Paradigms and Organisational Analysis*. London: Heinemann.

CAMPBELL, D. T. AND FISKE, D. W. (1959). Convergent and discriminant validation by the multitrait–multimethod matrix. *Psychological Bulletin*, **56,** 81–105.

DENZIN, N. K. (1970). *The Research Act*. Chicago: Aldine.

DEWAR, R. D., WHETTEN, D. A. AND BOJE, D. (1980). An examination of the reliability and validity of the Aiken and Hage scales of centralization, formalization and task routine. *Administrative Science Quarterly*, **25,** 120–128.

DOREIAN, P. AND HUMMON, N. P. (1976). *Modeling Social Processes*. New York: Elsevier.

DOUGLAS, M. (1967). The meaning of myth, with special reference to "La Geste d'Asdiwal". In E. Leach (ed.), *The Structural Study of Myth and Totemism*. London: Tavistock.

DOUGLAS, M. (1975). *Implicit Meanings*. London: Routledge and Kegan Paul.

DUNNETTE, M. D. (ed.) (1976). *Handbook of Industrial and Organizational Psychology*. Chicago: Rand McNally.

DURKHEIM, E. (1952). *Suicide: A Study in Sociology* (translated by J. A. Spaulding and G. Simpson). First published in French in 1897. New York: Free Press.

FELDMAN, J. (1975). Considerations in the use of causal–correlational techniques in applied psychology. *Journal of Applied Psychology*, **60,** 663–670.

FLEISHMAN, E. A. (1957). A leader behavior description for industry. In R. M. Stogdill and A. E. Coons (eds), *Leader Behavior: Its Description and Measurement*. Columbus: Ohio State University Bureau of Business Research.

GALTUNG, J. (1967). *Theory and Methods of Social Research*. New York: Columbia University Press.

GIDDENS, A. (1976). *New Rules of Sociological Method*. London: Hutchinson.

GIDDENS, A. (1979). *Central Problems in Social Theory*. London: Macmillan.

GLASER, B. G. AND STRAUSS, A. L. (1967). *The Discovery of Grounded Theory*. Chicago: Aldine.

GOFFMAN, E. (1964). *Stigma: Notes on the Management of Spoiled Identity*. Englewood Cliffs: Prentice-Hall.

GOFFMAN, E. (1969). *Strategic Interaction*. New York: Ballantine Books.

GOWLER, D. (1969). Determinants of the supply of labour to the firm. *Journal of Management Studies*, **6,** 73–95.

GOWLER, D. (1970). Socio-cultural influences on the operation of a wage payment system: an explanatory case study. In D. Robinson (ed.), *Local Labour Markets and Wage Structures*. Epping: Gower Press.

GOWLER, D. AND LEGGE, K. (1980). Negation, synthesis and abomination in rhetoric. In C. Antaki (ed.), *The Psychology of Ordinary Explanations of Social Behaviour*. London and New York: Academic Press.

GREEN, S. F. AND MITCHELL, T. R. (1979). Attributional processes of leaders in leader-member interaction. *Organizational Behavior and Human Performance*, **23,** 429–458.

HACKMAN, J. R. AND OLDHAM, G. R. (1974). *The Job Diagnostic Survey: An instrument for the diagnosis of jobs and the evaluation of job design projects*. York University, Department of Administrative Science. Technical Report No. 4.

HAGE, J. AND AIKEN, M. (1969). Routine technology, social structure, and organizational goals. *Administrative Science Quarterly*, **14**, 366–377.

HAMMOND, J. H. (1973). Two sources of error in ecological correlations. *American Sociological Review*, **38**, 764–777.

HANNAN, M. T. (1971). Problems of aggregation. In H. M. Blalock (ed.), *Causal Models in the Social Sciences*. Lexington: Heath.

HARRÉ, R. (1978). Accounts, actions and meanings—the practice of participatory psychology. In P. Marsh and M. Brenner (eds), *The Social Context of Method*. London: Croom Helm.

HARRÉ, R. (1979). *Social Being*. Oxford: Blackwell.

HOLLIS, M. (1977). *Models of Man*. Cambridge: Cambridge University Press.

HOMANS, G. (1961). *Social Behavior: Its Elementary Forms*. New York: Harcourt Brace.

JAMES, L. R. *et al.* (1978). *Psychological Climate: Implications from Cognitive Social Learning Theory and Interactional Psychology*. Fort Worth: Institute of Behavioral Research, Texas Christian University.

JICK, T. D. (1979). Mixing qualitative and quantitative methods: triangulation in action. *Administrative Science Quarterly*, **24**, 602–611.

LAZARSFELD, P. F. AND MENZEL, H. (1961). On the relation between individual and collective properties. In A. Etzioni (ed.), *Complex Organizations: A Sociological Reader*. New York: Holt, Rinehart and Winston.

LEGGE, K. (1970). The operation of the "regressive spiral" in the labour market. *Journal of Management Studies*, **7**, 1–22.

LEGGE, K. AND HILLING, S. (1974). Absence, overtime and the structure of the pay packet: some methodological points. Part 1. *Journal of Management Studies*, **11**, 205–223.

LÉVI-STRAUSS, C. (1963). *Structural Anthropology*. New York: Basic Books.

LÉVI-STRAUSS, C. (1978). *Myth and Meaning*. London: Routledge and Kegan Paul; Toronto: University of Toronto Press.

LIGHT, D. (1979). Surface data and deep structure: observing the organization of professional training. *Administrative Science Quarterly*, **24**, 551–559.

MANNING, P. K. (1979). Metaphors of the field: varieties of organizational discourse. *Administrative Science Quarterly*, **24**, 660–671.

MARSH, P., ROSSER, E. AND HARRÉ, R. (1978). *The Rules of Disorder*. London: Routledge and Kegan Paul.

McCLINTOCK, C. C., BRANNON, D. AND MAYNARD-MOODY, S. (1979). Applying the logic of sample surveys to qualitative case studies: the case cluster method. *Administrative Science Quarterly*, **24**, 612–629.

MILLER, G. A. (1967). Professionals in bureaucracy: alienation among industrial scientists and engineers. *American Sociological Review*, **32**, 755–768.

MOHR, L. B. (1971). Organizational technology and organizational structure. *Administrative Science Quarterly*, **16**, 444–459.

MUMFORD, E. (1972). *Job Satisfaction: A Study of Computer Specialists*. London: Longman.

MURRAY, C. (1979). Football hooliganism as a reactional activity? Paper presented at the Annual Conference of the B.P.S., Social Psychology Section, University of Surrey.

PATCHEN, M. (1965). *Some Questionnaire Measures of Employee Motivation and Morale*. Ann Arbor: Survey Research Center, University of Michigan.

PAYNE, R. L. AND PUGH, D. S. (1976). Organization structure and organization climate. In M. D. Dunnette (ed.), *Handbook of Industrial and Organizational Psychology*. Chicago: Rand McNally.

PAYNE, R. L., FINEMAN, S. AND WALL, T. D. (1976). Organizational climate and job satisfaction: a conceptual synthesis. *Organizational Behavior and Human Performance*, **16**, 45–62.

PHILLIPS, D. L. (1971). *Knowledge from What? Theories and Methods in Social Research*. Chicago: Rand McNally.

PLATT, JENNIFER (1976). *Realities of Social Research: An Empirical Study of British Sociologists*. London: Sussex University Press and Chatto and Windus.

PLATT, JOHN (1966). Strong Inference. In *The Step to Man*. New York: Wiley.

POPPER, K. R. (1959). *The Logic of Scientific Discovery*. London: Hutchinson.

PRICE, J. (1977). *The Study of Turnover*. Ames: Iowa State University Press.

RANSOM, S., HININGS, B. AND GREENWOOD, R. (1980). The structuring of organizational structures. *Administrative Science Quarterly*, **25**, 1–17.

RILEY, M. W. (1964). Sources and types of sociological data. In R. L. Faris (ed.), *Handbook of Modern Sociology*. Chicago: Rand McNally.

ROBERTS, K. H., HULIN, C. L. AND ROUSSEAU, D. M. (1978). *Developing an Interdisciplinary Science of Organizations*. San Francisco: Jossey-Bass.

ROUSSEAU, D. M. (1977). Technological differences in job characteristics, employee satisfaction and motivation: a synthesis of job design research and socio-technical systems theory. *Organizational Behavior and Human Performance*, **19**, 18–42.

SMITH, P. C., KENDALL, L. M. AND HULIN, C. L. (1969). *The Measurement of Satisfaction in Work and Retirement*. Chicago: Rand McNally.

SPECTOR, M. AND KITSUSE, J. I. (1977). *Constructing Social Problems*. Menlo Park: Cummings.

THOMPSON, J. D. (1967). *Organizations in Action*. New York: McGraw-Hill.

WALL, T. D. (1980). Group work design in context: a two phase model. In K. Duncan, M. Gruneberg and D. Walker (eds), *Changes in Working Life: Proceedings of the NATO International Conference*. London: Wiley.

WALL, T. D. AND LISCHERON, J. A. (1977). *Worker Participation*. London: McGraw-Hill.

WALLMAN, S. (ed.) (1979). *Social Anthropology of Work*. London and New York: Academic Press.

WEBB, E. AND WEICK, K. E. (1979). Unobtrusive measures in organizational theory: a reminder. *Administrative Science Quarterly*, **24**, 650–659.

ZAVOLLONI, M. AND LOUIS-GUERIN, C. (1979). Social psychology at the crossroads: its encounter with cognitive and ecological psychology and the interactive perspective. *European Journal of Social Psychology*, **9**, 307–321.

5 Models of Man:
Assumptions of Theorists[1]

FRANK LANDY

The past few decades have been turbulent for the sciences generally. It has become apparent that Humean empiricism and the Vienna Circle brand of logical positivism have been transcended. Gradually, physical scientists have come to a realization that research is not carried out in a vacuum. Motivations, values, habits, and human frailties often play a significant role in the direction of substantive research. Watson's description of the evolution of DNA research is dramatic testimony to this condition (Watson, 1968). The behavioural sciences have been somewhat slower to accept this point of view.

Often, the argument concerning values in behavioural science has been cast in unforgiving political debate. Thus, we have the arguments of the capitalists, the Marxists, the socialists, etc. While political concepts certainly capture some of the flavour of the argument, they break down rather seriously when one attempts to understand the process of science *within* political, social, and socioethical environments. As an example, it is useless to characterize the debate between the "nature" and "nurture" schools of intelligence by using terms such as "capitalist" or "socialist". Nevertheless, one might distinguish the two approaches in terms of "equity" v. "equality" orientations. Similarly, the debate might be structured around the distinction between an "individual differences" and a "group differences" orientation.

The role of individual values in research and theory-building is readily apparent in industrial and organizational (IO) psychology. In

the past decade, we have witnessed an ideological backlash to behaviourism, laws against sensitivity training, the elimination of individualized
testing, the infusion of humanistic principles in the workplace, the
minimization of productivity goals, the maximization of productivity
goals, etc. Not only can we detect these movements in a comparative
examination of cultures, but we can even see them *within* cultures. The
thrust of this essay will be to examine some general underlying influences
which may be seen in theory and research in IO psychology. The general
theme of the essay is the redefinition of the researcher/theorist as subject
and the research/theory as behaviour. It will be my task to identify
influences on this target behaviour. As may be seen from the examples
above, this is not a traditional examination of the philosophy of science;
it might be more appropriately labelled the *"sociology of science"* — an
examination of the social and individual context in which research and
theory-building is carried out.

For such an examination to be suitably balanced, it will be necessary
to examine the issues from several different perspectives. The first perspective might be thought of as cultural. It is related to the types of
variables chosen for study, the ideological anchors of the society in
which the research is carried out, and the interaction between these
components. A second perspective might be the orientation of the individual scientist — a much more molecular examination. This would
include the manner by which the particular researcher carries out the
research activities as well as how these activities influence theory-
building.

There is, in addition, a third perspective which is inextricably bound
with the first two. It is neither completely cultural nor completely idiosyncratic. It is addressed in other chapters of this volume (e.g. Chapters
1, 2 and 9) but for the sake of coherence, I must also deal with it. It
might be thought of as the distinction between "Old Science" and "New
Science".

1.   The cultural perspective

The dependent variable. The range of independent[2] or antecedent variables
available to the IO researchers is enormous. Some popular ones have
been supervisory characteristics, work environment, reward structures
and processes, work design, machine design, or individual worker

differences in traits or abilities. These simple generic terms mask a larger domain consisting of hundreds of variables which have been thought to exert some controlling influence on industrial behaviour. The range of dependent or consequent variables has been somewhat more limited. We shall typically examine one of three variable classes: emotions, intentions, or performance.

Industrial and organizational psychology has a long history of obsession with cost-effective aspects of behaviour. This is true not only of the North American brand of psychology, but generally of IO research in most industrialized countries. Recently, there has been schism between the traditional approach and alternative approaches. While certain exceptions might be noted, this schism is more obvious when comparing the research effort in different countries than it is when examining national or intramural research efforts. Thus, in the United States, theories of leadership and motivation are directed towards understanding work-group or individual "effectiveness". It is highly unlikely that a study would be conducted or a theory suggested which ignored the issue of "effectiveness". As I have pointed out elsewhere (Landy, 1978) this concern for effectiveness is at the root of many theories of job satisfaction. Thus, I would argue that even the research which is not directly concerned with profit maximization is done in service of the concept.[3]

In contrast, many European IO psychologists have minimized the role of performance in their research and theory-building. As an example, the most common class of dependent variable in Swedish research is emotion. While this is operationalized typically as job satisfaction, it also encompasses mental health, non-work adjustment, psychophysiological approaches to stress, and the quality of life as related to the quality of work.

The third class of dependent variable, intention, is usually represented conceptually as motivation. Interestingly, studies of motivation are conducted in support of either the performance approach (i.e. the intensity and direction of effort affects performance) or the emotional approach (i.e. need structures provide hints to "improving" emotional states). In this latter role, motivation appears similar to classical "personality" theory; it addresses fixed or parametric characteristics of the individual. In the former role, motivation appears much more like classical experimental psychology. Thus, it would seem that motivation is an important concept in most approaches, but for different reasons.

It seems obvious to me that the examination of one class of variables to the exclusion of another set has not produced dramatic advances in understanding the relationship between work and the worker. As an example, the reinforcement-oriented researchers and theorists can effectively describe the influences of rewards on performance only when the behaviour of interest has been made trivial or unduly specific. Such activity often reduces to nothing more or less than a training programme in which the "subject" attempts to learn and behave in accordance with "salient" influences as provided by the researcher.

Another example is the unswerving belief that emotions are stable, long-lasting, and pervasive in their influence on behaviour. A corollary to this assumption in IO research is that job-related factors are capable of producing such emotions. There has been an enormous amount of research in the area of job satisfaction which, at least implicitly, has been based on these assumptions about the stability, intensity and generality of job-related emotions. It would be considered barbaric in some circles to even *question* these assumptions in spite of the fact that the emotional basis of job-satisfaction theories has been only infrequently examined (Landy, 1978). Nevertheless, there may be good reason to question these assumptions. In the first place, emotions would seem to be much more dynamic than the current theories of satisfaction suggest. In addition, there seem to be substantial individual differences in emotional reactions to "objectively" similar situations. Finally, some studies of the quality of life assign little importance to the impact of work quality on life quality when work quality is compared to satisfaction with health, family, leisure, and religion (London *et al.*, 1977).

But how can it be that thoughtful and clever researchers have spent so much time considering a class of variables which may turn out to be trivial? The answer may lie in some assumptions about the nature of consciousness. The mind–body problem has been a major obstacle for the behavioural sciences from its earliest beginnings. Job satisfaction may be a manifestation of this problem. Books on the nature and importance of work often begin with some statement regarding the time which the typical adult spends at the work place. The implication of this type of statement is that by virtue of time spent, work must be, *by definition*, an important source of emotional variation. This, in turn, implies that the mind must be occupied with the context supplied by the body. The assumption is that there is an isomorphic relationship between "body time" and "mind time". I think someone must seriously question this assumption. The early capitalist model of Taylor (1947) implied no functional relationships between mind and body; the current humanist movement assumes a power[4] relationship between mind and body which suggests that emotions generated at work have a super-additive or geometric impact on non-work behaviour and adaptation. The neo-capitalist model implied by most path-goal theories implies that there is a vague ancillary (yet linear) relationship between mind and body which allows for a "poor man's" dualism, i.e. work context certainly affects emotions and work structure certainly affects performance and the two must certainly, somehow, interact.

On the basis of the argument which I have outlined above, I would contend that researchers often beg some important questions in their research efforts when choosing the dependent or consequent variable. I would further argue that political, social, and ideological influences are substantial in that choice of variables. Thus, I would suggest that the architects of theories in IO psychology must give more explicit attention to the role of *consciousness* in their work as well as the ideological environment from which these assumptions about consciousness derive.

2.   The role of individual differences

The distinction between the "experimentalists" and the "correlationists"[5] has been well articulated by Cronbach (1957). At the heart of the argument is the view which the particular researcher holds towards individual differences. Some researchers are appalled by the fact that the "treatment" which they applied to a sample of subjects did not have a uniform effect; other researchers are not at all upset by these circumstances, they occasionally even enjoy it. In the first instance, the researcher (who would most likely be classified as an "experimentalist") defines individual-differences variation as "error" and goes through a number of gyrations to reduce it. These gyrations might include redefinition of the sample, tightening experimental control, or transforming the data. In contrast, the second type of researcher (the "correlationist") is inclined to label this variance "true" variance and sets out to capture or account for it.

It is not my intention to re-evaluate the two approaches. Nevertheless, it must be obvious that the theories suggested by the two different types of researchers will vary substantially. As a simple example, consider the prescriptive motivational model of Herzberg *et al.* (1959) or

Maslow (1943) and contrast it with the individual-differences approach of VIE theorists (e.g. Porter and Lawler, 1967). They clearly hold different beliefs about the nature of man. On a much broader scale, research traditions can be identified in different countries. As an example, American IO behavioural research is currently in the grip of the "individual-differences" approach, while much of West European IO research considers these individual differences to be unfortunate anomalies, created and sustained by aberrant social, administrative, or organizational mechanisms.

The issue might be framed in a slightly different way. We could consider the unit of analysis thought to be appropriate in various research approaches. Thus, on the American IO scene, this unit is clearly the individual worker—at least *historically* that has been the tradition. On the other hand, in many countries with a strong social democratic or socialist movement, the nuclear work group is the smallest unit which is considered to be salient. (To be sure, many American researchers examine group effectiveness and many European researchers look for individual-difference moderator-variables of weak relationships, but these represent exceptions rather than the rule.)

Given these contexts, it is not surprising that American researchers go inside the organism to look for answers to the riddle of behaviour while their European colleagues look to general environmental (organizational or physical) issues. These differences in approach would not be so serious if theorists of the respective camps admitted to the credibility of the research line taken by those of the other camp. In that case, there would be a truly international community of scientists working on pressing areas of ignorance from different perspectives. At some point, it would be appropriate for the scientists to share information in a supplementary fashion. Consider the following proposition:

$$B = f[S, E, G, A, I]$$

where B = behaviour under consideration; S = a species specific parameter common to all *Homo sapiens* but non-zero in value[6]; E = the effect of an environmental variable; G = a series of variables roughly labelled "experience" which could be used to group individuals with common backgrounds; A = intra-species individual differences in organismic capabilities and limitations; and I = individual differences resulting from the interaction of $E, G,$ and A.

Using this framework, the task of the behavioural scientist becomes one of describing the functional relationship among the parameters and estimating the weights to be applied to each of them — i.e. their relative importance in understanding behaviour. Unfortunately, many theorists and researchers have begged the question with respect to the parametric determinants of behaviour.

The framework suggested above allows for the examination of a wide range of influences. Further, it allows for a more exact consideration of the relative weights or importance of environmental, group, and individual differences. If the individual is an inappropriate unit of analysis, parameters E and/or G should receive substantial weight; if individual differences are critically important in understanding behaviour, parameters A and/or I will emerge as major parameters. I would argue that researchers and theorists are currently constrained in their work by a most basic assumption — the one which they hold with respect to the importance of individual differences.

3. Process considerations

In the previous section we considered some rather broad influences on the types of theories which IO psychologists construct and examine. As exemplars of these influences I chose the issues of dependent-variable choice and the role of individual differences. It was suggested that social, political and cultural factors might help us understand the dynamics of these influences. I would now like to consider a completely different issue — the way scientists *think*.

One manifestation of the scientific thought-process might be the approach which the individual scientist takes to investigating the phenomenon in question. There are two basic methods of investigation (and ultimately theory construction) — the inductive and the deductive. It is not necessary here to fully examine the history and parametric characteristics of these approaches. For our purposes, it is sufficient to accept the following descriptions: *induction* — the derivation of a general principle of behaviour from a collection of specific instances of behaviour; *deduction* — the testing of a previously derived (logically or empirically) general principle of behaviour in a specific setting; an attempt to identify a specific instance of a general principle. While it should be obvious that these are not the classic definitions of induction and deduction, in order to make my point it is necessary for me to re-cast the definition in "investigative" terms. Strictly speaking, since both of these activities as defined imply probabilistic events, they must both be somehow inductive. Deduction is based on *a priori* propositions and has no probabilistic flavour. Some philosophers/scientists distinguish these two activities as *event-predictive* and *rule-derivative*, respectively (Munoz-Colberg, 1980). It is the probabilistic versus the universal premise which separates *event-predictive* induction from deduction. Since it is unlikely that many "deductive" theories flow solely from *a priori* premises (universals) and it is likely that these theories have been influenced by previous empirical investigations (probabilistic episodes), strictly speaking these theories are instances of *event-predictive* induction. With this qualification in mind, I will use the term "deduction" in its looser sense in the rest of this essay. If the reader feels more comfortable substituting the term *"event-predictive"* whenever the word "deductive" occurs, he or she is encouraged to do so.

4. Simple theories or simple theoreticians?

Industrial psychologists have been perpetually accused of "knee-jerk" or "dust-bowl" empiricism. While the charge has been most often levelled at personnel psychologists for mindless adherence to predictor/criterion correlations, our industrial and social brethren have not escaped a similar indictment. Locke (1976) is quite articulate in his condemnation of the "correlate-it-with-anything-that-moves" camp in job-satisfaction research. This type of argument is also central to the current attack on "positivism" by the enemies of empiricism. Most of these criticisms have been legitimate. But the problem has not been that induction is inappropriate; it has been that induction has never occurred. By definition, unless a general principle is derived from a set of observed relationships, the logical strategy has not been completed. Nevertheless, since the method involves gathering data *in order to* derive such a principle, the critics of the empirical approach cite the *operations* of induction as the villain rather than the resulting (or missing) theoretical structure or statements.

There are additional problems with the inductive process. For example, the generality of the inductive statement depends heavily on sampling procedures. The sampling of subjects, occasions, and variables critically affects inference. Yet sampling is most often treated in a casual manner.[7] Once again, critics will often choose to ignore differences between the *characteristics* of the inductive method and the catholicity with which the method was *employed*.

The other side of the coin is equally depressing. Deductive researchers and theoreticians presumably develop sets of logically sound and internally consistent propositions based on abstract reasoning and encouraged by previous research in the general area of interest. On the basis of these propositions, instances are created or identified in which certain corollaries of the propositions can be tested. It is assumed that if a corollary is supported, the initial proposition was correct.

This approach has been criticized as "armchair theorizing". The implication is that reflection, reasoning and introspection are not sufficient for theory construction. As an example, it was many years before Maslow's (1943) propositions were put to any rigorous test. Similarly, Herzberg (1954, 1966) has been criticized for developing an elaborate network of prescriptive and descriptive propositions covering work motivation and job satisfaction on the slimmest of data bases (a few hundred engineers and accountants). Once again, however, the problem may be less with the deductive *method* than with the scientist attempting to behave deductively. The statement of the theoretical propositions is merely one stage in the deductive process. The next stage might be the elaboration of those propositions in the form of corollaries, and the choice of subjects, occasions, and variables for tests of these corollaries. In the case of Herzberg's two-factor theory, the elaboration stage was poorly carried out, as demonstrated by King (1970) in his revealing reconstruction of the many "alternative" two-factor theories. In addition, attempts to support and refute Herzberg's propositions empirically (i.e. test instances for generalizability) seldom adhered to common sampling constraints (particularly with respect to subject selection). As a sequence of events, Herzberg's initial propositions, King's elaboration of them and the subsequent tests of that elaboration, provide an excellent example of how the deductive process *might* work if carried out properly.

If one accepts my representation of induction and deduction, then it follows that little of either is currently being carried out by IO psychologists. The "inductive" school seems unwilling to take the time to *collect and synthesize* the results of various studies. The "deductive" school is unwilling to co-ordinate *a priori* propositions with empirical information supplied by their positivist colleagues. The problem seems to be that the very activities which complete the inductive and deductive chains (synthesis and theoretical inference, respectively) are seldom undertaken. Thus, while traditional science depends on one or the other of these approaches for progress, neither of them are effectively represented in the research and theory construction of IO psychologists. It is small wonder that there is a clamour for a "new science"; nevertheless, it might not be a bad idea to give the "old science" a fair test.

5. The development of the behavioural scientist

For the sake of discussion, let us assume that we are capable of and willing to carry out genuine inductive or deductive operations. Is it likely that we will carry out one type rather than the other? Before answering that question, let me begin by contrasting the creative contributions of mathematicians and psychologists. It is common for mathematicians to make their substantial creative contributions while they are quite young, i.e. younger than 30. In fact, some have gone so far as to suggest that if the contribution has not been made by that time, it probably never will be. Mathematics is, of course, a language. It has a set of fixed rules which govern its use. These rules might also be thought of as concepts. The mathematician is often engaged in searching out instances of these rules—i.e. deductive activity. His experiments are the "instances" and the experimentation is less data-gathering than matching. The mathematician can carry his experiments with him wherever he goes as long as he has come to an understanding of the concepts or rules which govern the combination of variables. The fact that age seems to play a role in efficacy of mathematical reasoning may be due in part to developmental changes in thought-processes, intrusion of irrelevant mental activities into the thought-process (e.g. occupational, social, or leisure pursuits), or a combination of these factors.

In psychology, contributions of a significant nature seem to occur considerably later in the individual's professional career. Seldom does the new Ph.D. make dramatic breakthroughs in theory, method, or inference. Often, it appears that the younger scientists have a difficult time separating the substantial from the trivial.

As the career of the behavioural scientist progresses, he finds himself less overwhelmed with results from single studies, and more interested in general themes which might be extracted from studies in several different areas. He does much more "reviewing" and tends to leave the empirical studies to less experienced colleagues and students. In short, he stops gathering data and starts thinking about it. This would be a manifestation of the inductive process, but stretched over a career stage rather than a period of study.

In contrasting the activities of the mathematician and the psychologist, it almost seems inevitable that they would choose different initial methods of investigation. If all of the rules exist, it is the task of the investigator to become proficient in the manipulation and application of those rules. If the rules are absent, one must somehow set about deriving them. Since the subject-matter of psychology is behaviour, psychologists find themselves confronted with opportunities for inducing the rules at every turn. The stylized form of this activity is the "study" whether it be conducted in the laboratory or the field. Thus, I am suggesting that data collection plays a critical role in the construction of theories. But contrary to traditional propositions, these data do not answer the initial questions posed, rather they play a central role in the "education" of the experimenter. They teach him the *meaning* of the antecedent and consequent variables. It is only through this deeper understanding of the variables in question that the researcher can hope to form a theory which accounts for their observed relationship. Data do not construct theories, people do.

Now, to get back to the question which was used to introduce this section, it is likely that behavioural scientists are more inclined or better suited to constructing theories using one approach rather than the other. But this question implies that one must choose *between* inductive and deductive strategies. I believe that the two are sequentially[8] related rather than mutually exclusive. Further, I would suggest that the sequence progresses from inductive to deductive rather than in the opposite direction.

The young researcher must come to a firm conceptual and operational understanding of the variables in question (and through those variables the underlying constructs for which they stand) before a good deal of the research conducted by other scientists can be of any use to him in forming theories or frameworks. This understanding can be best achieved through empirical investigation. Through such investigation the researcher is able to form more abstract concepts which eventually free him from the shackles of his own data and allow him the luxury of inference from the data of others.

I am arguing that the pre-condition for effective theoretical inference in the behavioural sciences is extensive first-hand experience with the variables in question. This suggests that before one is capable of constructing a theory of work motivation, job satisfaction, leadership, etc., one must have broad research exposure to the critical elements of that theory. As behavioural principles become more fully developed within IO psychology, this "apprenticeship" will become less crucial; like the mathematician, the psychologist will be expected to make his contribution early in his career. Nevertheless, the progress in the behavioural sciences to date suggests that we have a few centuries ahead of us before this comes to pass.

Above and beyond the fact that the processes of induction and deduction are inextricably bound to the development of the scientist and his theories, theories themselves imply beliefs about the cognitive activities of subjects addressed by those theories. Some theories imply that man is basically deductive, while others assume a basically inductive approach by man to his world. Theories of work motivation provide nice examples of this difference. Most "need" theories of motivation (e.g. Maslow's hierarchical theory and Herzberg's two-factor theory) imply that individuals have "rules" (needs) which are built into them and that these individuals seek to identify situations which meet or satisfy those rules. Epistemologically, man's task is to identify certain instances of more general rules. In contrast, most "instrumentality" approaches (e.g. Porter and Lawler, 1967) imply that man derives situational principles as a function of experience; individuals are thought to learn the rules of their environment as a function of interacting with it. Epistemologically, man's task is to formulate the rules from the instances of those rules in operation.

It is common to distinguish among theories of motivation on the basis of process or content (Campbell *et al.*, 1970). Process theories emphasize the "how" of motivation; content theories emphasize the "why" of motivation. The distinction which I have made above, however, is not commonly made. Curiously, most theories which lean heavily towards the content side (e.g. Maslow's theory) also seem to assume deductive operations in man. The process theories (VIE), on the other hand, imply primarily inductive operations in subjects. Such a distinction can be made in other areas of IO research as well. Models of training (see Landy and Trumbo, 1980) mirror the distinction. Miller (1961) contrasts two models: one assumes that training proceeds most efficiently from the general to the specific—from learning general rules to the application of those rules. The other suggests that one should be exposed to many instances of those rules in order to incorporate them. The latter approach is also supported by much of Harlow's (1959) experimental research on "learning to learn".

The point I am trying to make with these examples is that many of the theories which guide research and practice in IO psychology assume either inductive or deductive approaches on the part of the subject. Unfortunately, these assumptions are seldom recognized. I would suggest that the epistemological assumptions concerning the subject represent the most basic "model of man" adopted by researchers and theoreticians. These assumptions deserve careful consideration.

6. Communication v. understanding

To the uninitiated, many psychological constructs seem relatively simple. As a result, the theories of the uninitiated are also simple. But, as topical ignorance gives way to immersion, the theories become more baroque. It is commonly observed that the more we read the less we know. The problem then becomes one of recognizing when the theory and the behaviour it purports to explain are in an appropriate scalar relationship to each other.

In a recent review of motivation theories (Landy and Trumbo, 1980), I suggested that most of these theories are more complicated than the behaviour of the subjects in question warrants. For example, there is reason to doubt that adults can make the subtle distinctions among schedules of reinforcement which are implied by the research of the behaviourists. This is not to say that adults are less subtle or clever than animals or children; simply that adults have more stimuli to attend to simultaneously. As a result, the major conclusion which one might draw concerning schedules of reinforcement in work settings is that contingent rewards have different effects to those of non-contingent rewards— a much less complicated statement than that implied by most traditional behaviourist approaches to the phenomenon of work behaviour. Similarly, there have been questions raised with respect to the major components of instrumentality approaches. Can people accurately assess expectancies, instrumentalities or valences? Several researchers have suggested that valences are much more critical to the cognitive approach than either instrumentalities or expectancies. In short, there is some reason to suspect that instrumentality theories may imply more complicated behaviour on the part of subjects than is warranted. Similar arguments may be made with respect to equity theory (see Landy and Trumbo, 1980, for a more complete review of this argument).

But why is it that theories are so complicated? Do psychologists have some deep "need to complicate" which manifests itself in their theoretical writings? I would suggest that this "complication" is the inevitable result of two distinct forces: (1) the increasingly elaborate cognitive structure demanded of the scientist by virtue of increasing exposure to an area of interest; and (2) the need to communicate with other scientists. I will deal with these two forces separately.

The Piagetian approach to cognitive development suggests that individuals assimilate information into existing cognitive structures (schemata or concepts) until this information exceeds the bounds of those structures. It is then necessary to accommodate — to form new concepts to deal with additional information. The process of accommodation is largely controlled by environmental demand. Assuming equal or sufficient physical maturation, individuals who are required to process greater amounts of information will have more elaborate conceptual networks than those processing lesser amounts of information. It is reasonable to assume that conceptual frameworks are related in some manner to environmental interaction. Thus the psychologist who has studied job satisfaction for fifteen years is likely to have a slightly more complicated view of the phenomenon than the postgraduate student being exposed to the topic for the first time. Unfortunately, if this is a correct representation of the developing conceptual network of the scientist, then it follows that the "theory" will become increasingly complex as a result of the behaviour of the psychologist — independent of the behaviour of the subject. The emergence of the "moderator variable" or "covariate" in the IO research of the last decade may be a symptom of this process. One seldom sees a theory or approach made *less* complex — "improvements" are generally defined by increasing complexity.

The second force leading to increasing complexity is more a function of the nature of the traditional scientific method than it is of the developmental characteristics of the scientist. A genotypic parameter of science is its "communicability". One scientist can *tell* another scientist about the results of a particular experiment. This enables the second scientist to build on the findings of the first and the "body of knowledge" grows in proportion to the number of scientists working in a problem area. If this were not possible, if everyone were required to conduct all salient research personally (i.e. *experience* all aspects of the phenomenon under consideration) the body of knowledge would be limited not by the number of scientists, but by the life-span of the oldest scientist (assuming that he/she was also the most clever).

This communication requirement is easier said than fulfilled.[9] As the conceptual network of the scientist becomes more elaborate, communication becomes more complicated. For example, it is much easier for two postgraduate students to discuss a topic of mutual interest without getting bogged down in unpleasant semantic skirmishes than it is for two professionals who have been actively engaged in research in the same area for ten years or so. Unfortunately, the nature of scientific communication is seldom "face to face", but rather occurs through the medium of journals and books. As a result, theoretical statements must be complex enough to efficiently foster both operational and conceptual information exchanges among and between scientists.

I am suggesting that theories play two distinct roles in scientific endeavour. On the one hand, they purport to explain the phenomenon under consideration; on the other hand, they represent a vehicle for communication in the scientific community. This communication demand may be in conflict with the explanatory demand. In other words, in order to communicate it may be necessary to create a more elaborate theory than justified by the phenomenon in question.

What is to be done to "save" theories from the joint influences of the cognitive development of the scientist and the tyranny of the written word? The second problem is easier to deal with than the first. In IO psychology there has been depressingly little taxonomic research. It is more popular to invent a new label or concept than to accept an old one. The same is true with the operational definitions of concepts, e.g. job-satisfaction questionnaires. This predilection has in the behavioural sciences led one observer to note that the physical sciences are distinct from the social sciences in that physical scientists climb on the shoulders of those who came before them while social scientists step in the faces of their predecessors. The work of Fleishman (1966) in developing a taxonomy of skills and abilities has had substantial influence on the study of skilled performance and is beginning to have an impact in the personnel selection area as well; the "Job Descriptive Index" of Smith *et al.* (1969) has had a substantial impact on the conduct of job-satisfaction research. These are two examples of the value of taxonomic research to the communication process. These taxonomies have allowed for more efficient communication among scientists. Similar efforts must be made in areas such as leadership, organizational climate and work motivation. It is only through this fundamental taxonomic research that communication will cease being a burden and start being an aid to investigation.

We are still left with the problem of the increasing conceptual complexity of the individual scientist. This is more difficult at a superficial level. Theoreticians may be urged to carefully consider the salience of components of their theories; they might be asked to distinguish between intervening variables (useful for heuristic purposes) and hypothetical constructs (necessary but not sufficient conditions for understanding the phenomenon). Another approach might be to encourage individual scientists to "simplify" the work of others.[10]

As you can see from the discussion above, it is considerably easier to point out potential problems than it is to solve them. Nevertheless, the goal of this essay is to articulate the influence of various factors on theory-building in industrial and organizational psychology. It is my contention that extant theories imply a complexity to behaviour which is not always warranted.

7.   Some concluding comments

In examining my own research career, I have discovered a trend. It seems to me that I have moved from a traditional positivist approach to a more moderate positivist position. I would not argue that empirical evidence is useless, confusing or trivial. Neither would I argue that self-reflection[11] plays no role in theory-building. I am proposing that theorists inevitably synthesize information which they have collected over long periods of time; this information is gathered both by "experimentation" and by reading the work of others. They subsequently develop concepts from that synthesis. These concepts then become the building-blocks of theories. The greater the direct experience and the wider the indirect exposure, the more elaborate and numerous the concepts. Thus, I am suggesting that the process of data collection is the necessary but not sufficient condition for theory-building. These data represent the attempt by the theorist to understand the limits and dynamics of the "problem"—it is an epistemological exercise on the part of the theorist. Nevertheless, these data do not answer the question at hand or solve the "problem". This is simply demonstrated by giving the same data set to an experienced and an inexperienced researcher in a given area for which the data are salient and asking each to "interpret" them. The interpretations (and implied theories) would be substantially different.

In its simplest form, my argument is of the *ad hominem* variety. The theory which we consider is inextricably bound to the level of development of the theorist who proposed it. But the theory does not exist independently of some "objective reality". It is here that I will attempt to set my arguments apart from those of traditional positivism as well as the more recent arguments of the anti-empiricists. By "objective reality" I mean to imply not only the behaviour of others and the situational constraints on that behaviour but also the cultural and societal constraints on the theorist. The traditional positivist in IO psychology would not accept this definition of objective reality.

Classical empirical operations are critically important to subjective reality—they represent the *sine qua non* for theory-building. The anti-empiricist in IO psychology would have difficulty in swallowing that proposition. I would hope that my articulation of this middle ground will allow for a more informed debate between the two opposing camps —an activity noticeably absent in the literature.

To return one final time to the theme of this essay, it is my feeling that the *models of man* which underlie current theories of organizational behaviour are as much dependent variables as the organizational behaviour which they purport to explain. Until and unless the behaviour of the theorist can be better understood, his theories remain mute.

Notes

1. I would like to thank Bob Guion and Magda Munoz-Colberg for comments on earlier drafts of this chapter.
2. The terms "independent" and "dependent" are used merely as conventions; they are not meant to beg the question of causal relationships. Thus, if the reader is more at ease accepting a temporal distinction such as antecedent-consequent, I have no objection. Similarly, the antecedent-consequent distinction is not meant to beg the question of reciprocal or multiple relationships.
3. For an interesting treatment of this issue, the reader is directed to the debate between Nord (1977) and Locke (1978).

4. The term "power" is borrowed from the classical psychophysics of S. S. Stevens and is used to imply the power to which a value must be raised before one can understand its direct influence on another variable of interest.

5. It should be noted that the use of this term is not meant to imply a particular statistical treatment of data, such as the use of correlation coefficients or the analysis of variance. Rather it is meant to imply a method of investigation. The "experimentalists" typically are active in changing levels of an independent variable, while the "correlationists" typically observe and record covariation in two or more variables.

6. An example of this parameter might be the level of cortical development, or the characteristics of sensory mechanisms typically found in humans.

7. Bob Guion has mocked the manner by which subjects are chosen in the prototypic IO study by referring to the sampling procedure as "scrounge-sampling".

8. Since in the strictest sense, deduction is based on *a priori* propositions, I would be willing to consider the relationship a co-ordinate rather than a sequential one. The term "sequential" is not meant to imply causal bonds.

9. This is not an *intended* play on words.

10. This may, in turn, require a substantial shift in values by those responsible for granting advanced degrees, assigning tenure and making promotions.

11. Introspection is a commonly understood and historically grounded concept; a colleague of mine (Martin, 1980) has written extensively on the topic and has introduced a term which is more appropriate to my present argument — "self-reflection". This more clearly highlights the procedural aspects of theory-building while at the same time it avoids the occasionally unfortunate connotative meaning of "introspection".

References

CAMPBELL, J. P., DUNNETTE, M. D., LAWLER, E. E. AND WEICK, K. E. (1970). *Managerial Behaviour, Performance and Effectiveness*. New York: McGraw-Hill.

CRONBACH, L. J. (1957). The two disciplines of scientific psychology. *American Psychologist*, **12,** 671–684.

FLEISHMAN, E. A. (1966). Human abilities and the acquisition of skill. In E. A. Bilodeau (ed.), *Acquisition of skill*. New York and London: Academic Press.

HARLOW, H. (1959). Learning to learn. In S. Koch (ed.), *Psychology: The Study of a Science* (Vol. II). New York: McGraw-Hill.

HERZBERG, F. (1966). *Work and the nature of man*. New York: World Publishing.

HERZBERG, F., MAUSNER, B. AND SNYDERMAN, B. (1959). *The Motivation to Work*. New York: Wiley.

KING, N. (1970). Clarification and evaluation of the two factor theory of job satisfaction. *Psychological Bulletin*, **74,** 18–31.

LANDY, F. J. (1978). An opponent process theory of job satisfaction. *Journal of Applied Psychology*, **63,** 533–547.

LANDY, F. J. AND TRUMBO, D. A. (1980). *The Psychology of Work Behaviour* (revised edition). Homewood: Dorsey Press.

5 MODELS OF MAN: ASSUMPTIONS OF THEORISTS   121

LOCKE, E. A. (1976). The nature and causes of job satisfaction. In M. D. Dunnette (ed.), *Handbook of Industrial and Organizational Psychology*. Chicago: Rand-McNally.
LOCKE, E. A. (1978). Job satisfaction reconsidered–reconsidered. *American Psychologist*, **33,** 854–855.
LONDON, M., CRANDALL, R. AND SEALS, G. W. (1977). The contribution of job and leisure satisfaction to the quality of life. *Journal of Applied Psychology*, **62,** 328–334.
MARTIN, J. E. (1980). Presentationalism: An essay towards self-reflexive psychological theory. Unpublished manuscript, Pennsylvania State University.
MASLOW, A. H. (1943). A theory of motivation. *Psychological Review*, **50,** 370–396.
MILLER, R. B. (1961). (Comments) in W. F. Grether (ed.), *The Training of Astronauts*. Washington, D.C.: National Academy of Sciences – National Research Council.
MUNOZ-Colberg, M. (1980). The measurement of inductive and deductive reasoning abilities in the deaf and blind. Conference on employing the handicapped. Personnel Testing Council and BNA Education Systems. Silver Spring, Maryland. 16–17 April.
NORD, W. R. (1977). Job satisfaction reconsidered. *American Psychologist*, **22,** 1026–1035.
PORTER, L. W. AND LAWLER, E. E. (1967). *Managerial Attributes and Performance*. Homewood: Dorsey Press.
SMITH, P. C., KENDALL, L. AND HULIN, C. L. (1969). *The Measurement of Satisfaction in Work and Retirement: A Strategy for the Study of Attitudes*. Chicago: Rand-McNally.
TAYLOR, F. W. (1947). *Principles of scientific management*. New York: Harper.
WATSON, J. D. (1968). *The Double Helix*. New York: Mentor.

6 Theory-building

JERALD HAGE

The purpose of this essay is to move beyond a linear and additive conception of organizational theory to a non-linear perspective that is more complex. To do so requires that we change our ways of thinking about organizations. And this is the objective of applying techniques of theory construction. They can channel our thought processes and guide us to discovery (see Hage, 1972). Most techniques of theory construction (see Zetterberg, 1963; Blalock, 1969; Hage, 1972) have encouraged the development of linear theories. We now need a new set of techniques for non-linear thinking.

Most organizational theories (see Zey-Ferrell, 1979, for a good review) have been essentially simple, linear and additive in nature. That is, we assume that as x increases, y increases or that as x and y are added together, z increases. For example, the larger the size, the greater the structural differentiation. A hypothesis such as this is simple and linear, not complex and non-linear.

Words like "complexity" and "non-linear" require some definition. They have many interpretations. Sometimes, as in Blau's work (1970), one sees size logarithmically transformed or statements that a particular variable has diminishing effects. This is still essentially linear thought. There is a transformation in the distribution so that we can proceed with our well-developed regression techniques (see Hage, 1965; Perrow, 1967; Thompson, 1967; Lawrence and Lorsch, 1967a, b; Price, 1968; Blau, 1970; Hickson et al., 1971; Hage, 1974; etc.). This mode of thought has been facilitated by modern regression techniques

(Blalock, 1969; Heise, 1975) which make the same basic assumptions. The analysis consists of adding more and more variables until there is no more gain in the amount of variance explained. Organizational research designs have been cross-sectional so that assumptions about causal ordering are usually made on the basis of the size of the zero-order correlation (much of the work of Blau, 1972, 1973 and the various Aston studies (Pugh *et al.*, 1968, 1969) have proceeded in this way). Thus linear hypotheses combined with a regression analysis lead to a ready acceptance of theory as consisting of the addition of more and more concepts. The logical format is:

$$A + B = C$$

Instead one should be more concerned with strategic concepts combined in non-linear ways as in:

$$AB = C$$

The equation $A + B = C$ is the basis for path analysis (Heise, 1975). Yet the organizational world is more complex than this, and more like $AB = C$.

My definition of non-linear theory requires hypotheses that are either curvilinear or contain complex polynomic functions. For example, in a recent publication (Hage, 1980) I suggested that conflict could be predicted with the following equation:

$$(X - Y)^P = \tan C$$

where $X =$ concentration of specialists; $Y =$ decentralization; and $C =$ conflict. This is a more complex model; it is not a simple, additive view of the world. The equation suggests that as the *difference* between two structural variables increases, its impact on conflict grows exponentially with the behavioural trajectory approximating a tangent function. In other words, there is a tendency for the conflict to explode. While there is some evidence to support this equation, it is still too soon to say how accurate it is. However, this formulation does represent an interesting example of how one can move into more complex models by building upon past work—even though that work is linear itself! Previous work is a first approximation—as linear models usually are. It is not wasted effort, but represents a starting point for constructing more complex theories. A very important kind of complex theory is one comprised of multivariate hypotheses in which conditions are specified. The logical form is:

> Given A, the greater the X, the greater the Y

or

> Given a high score on A and a low score on B, then the greater the X, the greater the Y

An illustration of the first hypothetical form might be: given routine technology, then the greater the centralization, the more conservative the managerial ideology (Perrow, 1967). This format would be particularly helpful for those who would like to combine qualitative and quantitative theory. In various areas of organizational analysis one sees the need for the combination of these two kinds of theory. In regression, qualitative analysis merges with quantitative and is called "covariance analysis". An illustration of the second hypothetical form is: given simple tasks, with many exceptions, and if the size of the work force is small, then the most efficient arrangement is low mechanization with a pooled work-flow housed in a moderately flat structure (Hage, 1980, Ch. 12).

Another model of more complex organizational theory is to specify that the hypotheses hold only within certain ranges of particular variables. Here the format is:

> Within a medium range of X, the greater the X, the great the Y

A classical example of this is the old argument about conflict facilitating social change. Essentially we have a curvilinear hypothesis with too much and too little conflict being negatively related. More complex formulations would be that the relationship only exists within a certain range rather than curvilinearity *per se*.

Social scientists forget that physical theories have much more complex statements than our simple linear-additive path-analytic models contain. Surely organizations are more complicated than physical matter. If so (and I am sure we are all in agreement about this) then we need to construct more complex theories.

It is also the case that just making a plea for more complex models does not ensure their creation. There is a question of timing. There comes a moment in the course of a speciality's development where it seems only natural to turn to non-linear equations. To jump immediately into sophisticated mathematical modelling does not appear advisable. There are advantages to starting with more simple theories and ideas and of moving only gradually towards much more complex ones.

Organizational theory would appear to have reached a stage of intellectual development where the historical moment is right for just this kind of qualitative advance. In the recent work of Mintzberg (1979) on organizational design, Aldrich (1979) on population models, Burrell and Morgan (1979) on four organizational paradigms that are quite disparate, as well as my own recent work (Hage, 1980), one sees a variety of attempts to break out of simple linear thinking. There is a parallel in some of the recent calls for more process studies whether of technology (Abernathy, 1978), adaptation (Starbuck and Derzhen, 1970; Freeman and Hannan, 1975) or of power (Abell, 1975). As one moves towards studies that emphasize a longitudinal perspective, one is led to non-linear theory almost automatically. Viewing organizations cross-sectionally encourages the use of standard regression techniques and thinking about causal variables as being additive in their impact rather than multiplicative. The longitudinal research of Freeman and Hannon (1975) and the Hage–Aiken panel study (Hage, 1980, Chs 3, 6 and 8) both indicate how one needs more complex analytical techniques. Viewed across time, organizational researchers find the necessity of searching for multiplicative and non-linear formulations.

So far, I have found four techniques for helping my students and myself construct non-linear and multivariate hypotheses. They can be arranged in order of increasing difficulty:

(1) the extreme- or deviant-case method;
(2) the typological method;
(3) the paradigmatic or theoretical perspective method;
(4) the multi-analytical-level method.

These techniques can be combined as well since in various ways they imply one another. Complete detailed examples are, of course, not possible in the space provided. My intention instead is to indicate ways in which others might develop more complex theories about organizations.

1.   The method of the extreme or deviant case

There are two common research strategies. One strategy is to focus on a single case. Frequently the abundance of detail prevents any generalization, whether linear or non-linear, from being perceived. The other strategy is to take a large number of cross-sectional cases as in the work of the Aston studies (Pugh *et al.*, 1968, 1969) and the studies by Blau and his students (Blau and Schoenherr, 1971; Blau *et al.*, 1976; Meyer, 1972). The analysis consists of standard regression techniques (factor, multivariate, and path analysis). However, neither is by itself satisfactory. We need instead some compromise between these two kinds of research design. This would appear to be the comparative longitudinal study of organizations.

There are some interesting theoretical examples in the literature. It is Weber's contrast between traditional and rational-legal organization that leads to his insights about the latter. Likewise we see the same contrast in Burns and Stalker's (1961) formulation of mechanical and organic organizations. However, both of these formulations – and especially the latter – are linear theories. Mechanical organizations have an hierarchy of authority while organic ones have a network, and there are a number of variations in between. How do we theoretically sample our cases so as to break out of this mode of thinking? The answer lies in the choice of either extreme cases or deviant cases. For example, in the equation of conflict cited above, conflict is found by an intensive analysis of the exceptions, that is, where the concentration of specialists and decentralization are *not* related. To a certain extent, we can do this with the present cross-sectional studies. Longitudinal analysis, if involving multiple cases, gives us much more confidence in the causal ordering.

Thus *our first rule is that wherever we have moderate-size correlations* (from 0.40 to 0.70) *we should examine carefully the exceptions or deviant cases.* The literature contains a large number of relatively consistent findings (see Zey-Ferrell, 1979; Hage, 1980). These findings can provide a rich treasure on which to build our more complex theories. Exceptions can occur in a variety of ways so that it is not possible to provide *a priori* solutions. Among many possibilities are those considered below.

The exceptions may involve the presence of another variable which must be specified as a condition. That is, the original linear hypothesis – the greater the X, the greater the Y – should be reformulated to say, given Z, then the greater the X, the greater the Y. Some of the following techniques suggest ways in which one might find the Z that is these conditions. Here longitudinal research helps us to determine the correct causal ordering and the most likely conditions.

The most brilliant example of this approach to theory construction comes out of Lipset *et al.*'s work *Union Democracy* (1956). Most labour unions in the United States are authoritarian and centralized. Lipset *et al.* selected an exception, the ITU, and then studied it longitudinally and intensively. From their analysis emerges a whole series of special conditions that specify when labour unions are likely to be centralized and when they are not. Since the ITU was the exception its characteristics, if absent in centralized unions, allowed for correct inference.

One of the consistent findings I have come across (Hage, 1980, Ch. 3) in a re-analysis of a number of studies is that the concentration of specialists is highly associated with decentralization. Despite the consistency of the finding there are still exceptions, most notably in the Azumi (personal communication) study of Japanese organizations. Having done some work on business organizations in France, and knowing that they are exceptions as well, I was led to the following conclusion: the concentration of specialists leads to decentralization only when generalists are *not* trained or available. This condition not only helps explain differences in findings by country but also differences within nation-states. The contrast of organizational studies across nation-state typically highlights these kinds of differences.

Many of the seemingly disparate findings in the literature could be reconciled in this way if we studied such differences more carefully. For example, some of the Aston findings have not been replicated in universities (Holdoway, *et al.*, 1975). What is it about this kind of organization that results in a different pattern of results? By selecting several universities and studying them across time, we might determine the reasons. Thus one approach to finding a condition is to contrast different kinds of organizations. Rather than just accept differences in findings and assume it is measurement error or managerial choice or whatever, it is better to isolate the specific factors that elucidate differences. The correct theoretical approach is to explain why by specifying a condition, that is, by identifying the condition as a new variable.

One could push this logic even farther and ask why we do not obtain exactly the same size-correlation or path-coefficient between two variables. Here, even more, one would be forced to take some detailed case studies of organizations of different kinds and attempt to specify the reasons why, for example, routine technology might have a stronger impact on centralization in automobile companies as opposed to computer manufacturers. A focus on the strength of the association rather than the sign alone would be a very healthy first step in the direction towards more complex theories.

A simple way of proceeding might be to start with the many cross-sectional studies in the literature and then to study the special characteristics of each group to see if they suggest some reasons for differences in findings. For example, there is the obvious difference of welfare agencies in the Hage and Aiken (1970) studies and business organizations in the Aston studies (Pugh *et al.*, 1968, 1969). But to leave it at this is not enough — one must look for the explanation, the variable or factor, that elucidates *why* there are these differences. Indeed, if there is one dominant intuition I have about the state of organizational theory it is this need to specify conditions as to when particular hypotheses are supported or "valid".

Exceptions to findings may be non-linear combinations of the variables that have been analysed linearly. Here is where longitudinal research becomes so important. Frequently small changes in variables appear to produce multiplicative effects in other variables. Thus, in the Hage–Aiken panel study, a doubling in the rate of innovation in welfare agencies produced a different impact on formalization and morale (see Dewar, 1976). Normally a welfare agency on the average adds about one new programme for its clients per year. Those agencies with higher rates of innovation had *higher* morale. The greater availability of funds starting in the mid-1960s led to the introduction of two new programmes. Those agencies that in fact increased their rate of innovation experienced a considerable drop in morale. Now those agencies with high rates of innovation had *lower* morale. Symbolically this may be expressed as:

$$-\Delta X^2 + \Delta X = \Delta Y$$

where $X =$ innovation rate and $Y =$ morale. Small amounts of change are not disruptive but large ones are, causing a reversal in the sign of the association. While this is an idea found in various descriptions of change, our theories have not included this kind of complexity as yet.

Economists have made much of marginal utility theory, which is of the same form, but as yet sociologists have not looked for this kind of curvilinearity. One fruitful area for doing so is in studies of morale and productivity. The confusion of findings in this area may be handled by observing whether small changes in job conditions produce small alterations in either productivity or morale while large changes have the reverse effect. Equally critical is the notion of some limits being exceeded. By examining some extreme cases, we are likely to find if these limits exist. This may help us understand when managerial succession makes a difference and when it doesn't. Productivity, morale, and the structural conditions that effect these two variables are likely to be related in very complex ways.

One whole area where one might expect marginal utility models or curvilinear equations to be especially relevant is in the association between structure and performance. Here one might expect small changes in the structural element to produce some major changes in the performance because of the operation of thresholds. This appears to be the meaning of both the Gouldner (1954) and Guest (1956) studies. Leaders change some of the structural characteristics of the organization and it is these changes that produce improvements in performance. But the relationships between structural variables and performance are anything but linear.[1]

One way of selecting extreme cases is to examine the ranges of variables and then choose those organizations that score at one or the other extreme. The size of an organization would be a trivial example. However, it can be an informative one. Most large-scale studies have been done in organizations of personnel size 250 or larger. The Hage–Aiken panel study was accomplished in organizations, most of which were less than 100 in personnel size. In particular, one might expect that in small organizations a very different interpersonal and bureaucratic dynamic might follow. Indeed, one suspects that each study should specify as relevant conditions to their findings both personnel size and technology. Under these circumstances the researchers would be encouraged to think in multivariate terms and about conditions that make their hypotheses — and thinking — more complex.

Examining the continuum of the variable encourages the search for curvilinear relationships. We might find that the range of personnel size 20 to 100 produces one pattern of findings but personnel size 2000 to 10 000 a very different one. One analytical technique that is quite helpful is the use of covariance path models where the control variable is a range along a particular continuum. One can test to see if particular ranges do have significantly different slopes. Since we seldom look for these differences we seldom find them.

Admittedly one can in effect see this in a scatter plot as long as there are only two variables. The perception of significant differences becomes much more difficult when there are a multitude of independent variables. In recent research that I have been doing — a comparative longitudinal study of nations — I have discovered that different size coefficients are important in different time periods even though the total impact of the independent variables remains the same. For example, one might imagine that the relative importance of particular causes of organizational conflict might be different in different eras. In times of expansion, economic factors might be most critical and in times of contraction, political variables might be the more potent cause. The search for changes in the parametric structure as a consequence of societal context is only possible if one undertakes panel studies of organizations.

How critical timing is in the determination of parametric structure is illustrated in the Hage–Aiken panel study (see Dewar, 1976) when President Kennedy's impetus to create the "Great Society" produced considerable changes in the second wave of interviews relative to the first and third waves. The infusion of funds from the federal government allowed welfare agencies to either expand their staff or to add new services. The speed and magnitude of these changes produced considerable internal strain. These changes were all essentially non-linear. As yet societal context, and its impact on parametric structure (whether across nations or across eras), has been largely ignored as a theoretical issue. More focus on it would lead to the specification of conditions, limits, and the formulation of polynomic functions.

A very special case of deviant case analysis concerns the boundaries where organizations may no longer be considered as organizations. At what point do groups become organizations? What is the difference between an organization and a project? When does an organization become a multi-organization? In chemical engineering this is called the "origin problem" and inevitably functions become very complex near the origin. We have tended to ignore the critical cutting points in our definitions of what constitutes an organization. I have discovered (Hage, 1980, Ch. 3) a fairly consistent relationship: when organizations are of personnel size 10 or less hypotheses are no longer supported. Likewise Chandler's (1962) work suggests another critical distinction, a difference in technology and/or product market. Again, we are led not only to the notion of technology and size as conditions — the essential insight of Lawrence and Lorsch (1967a, b) in their contingency theory — but to the observation that particular ranges along the quantitative continuum can produce qualitative changes in the associations between variables.

This use of continua and the examination of extremes can be applied to many other variables as well. Extremes in communication, centralization, complexity, formalization and the like, if intensively studied across time, might provide the recognition either of special conditions or of the need for non-linear combinations of variables, or both.

As one looks at extreme cases relative to some dimension one frequently finds that the initial insight or hypothesis must be corrected or amended. Generally, for extreme cases we find we must set limits to hypotheses, that is, they will not work except within a certain range or context. There is a measurable increase in the complexity of our understanding when we know where our hypotheses are invalid. If we systematically search for cases where our hypotheses do not work we will surely find them. One way of proceeding is to examine the extremes in any empirical distribution via covariance techniques. The control variable is the range — empirically specified — along some dimension. In the analysis, one would look at the interrelations between variables in each of three separate situations: low, medium and high. How many cases are placed in the middle category relative to the other two could be determined on theoretical grounds or on the basis of the empirical distribution. A normal distribution would be broken into 1·5 or 2·0 standard deviations depending upon the size of the sample. However, organizational scores frequently do not fit a normal curve — meso and macro properties are distributed differently from micro or individual properties. A typical distribution is a "Chi-square" or "*poisson*" distribution, that is, a large number of cases bunched together with a rapid falling off in frequency. This kind of distribution is worth exploring for extreme cases because one can anticipate that the extremes are indeed very different.

It is seldom that one sees reported in the literature the actual distributions of various variables. Yet, they contain a great deal of information. Not only do they sensitize us to the nature of the distribution and therefore raise fundamental questions about whether extremes might exist, but when we compute correlations we will always have exceptions, that is, some cases will fall a considerable distance from the regression line, and this distance is precisely measured by the computation of residuals.

Unfortunately, the thrust of regression analysis tends to discourage us from looking at the residuals, and hence we tend to ignore the deviant cases. Yet in the residuals are buried perhaps the most interesting findings. For example, in testing the hypothesis that the concentration of specialists and decentralization — when not related — produces conflict (Hage, 1980, Ch. 10) I found one extreme case. Close inspection indicated that it was a religious organization in which the professionals were struggling for secular autonomy. In fact, it was a special case of the hypothesis although the measures did not capture this complexity since the agency was low in the concentration of specialists, being a welfare agency.

In another analysis, I found cases where organizations that were centralized had high rates of change (Hage, 1980, Ch. 6) contrary to my previous thinking (Hage and Aiken, 1970). A close examination of these cases indicated that they were all sub-professional organizations and were in the process of catching up to the prevailing professional norms. The hypothesis about centralization and innovation must now be reformulated as follows: (a) if the innovations are simply to catch up with the general standard of the field, then the greater the centralization the greater the innovation; (b) if the innovations are to advance the general standard of the field, then the less the centralization, the greater the innovation. In the first example on conflict our exception proved our rule but did require a change in the quality of instrumentation so that the conflict of professional autonomy and bureaucratic control had to be extended to cover the case of religious control. In the second instance our exception required specification of a condition, one that considerably alters the original linear hypothesis.

It was relatively easy to explore these deviant cases and determine the reasons for the exceptions because the study involved panel research with a small number of organizations intensively analysed. This allows for a quicker recognition of exceptions and reasons for them. As one collects three waves of data on a sample of organizations over a six-year time period there is a considerable accumulation of knowledge about them.

In summary, deviant- or extreme-case analysis has much to offer us as a way of making our theories more complex. This is best done when several cases, carefully selected, are analysed across time. But, also, much can be done by re-analysing the large number of cross-sectional studies that have accumulated. Here there are three things that need to be done:

(1) Examine moderate or large correlations to see if the exceptions can be handled by more complex formulations.

(2) Examine the extremes of the empirical distributions to see if there are qualitative shifts in the interrelationships between variables.
(3) Examine the extreme residuals to see if new variables or formulations are necessary to handle these exceptions.

All of these approaches will help us to develop more complex hypotheses by establishing conditions and limits and by recognizing non-linear combinations of variables. Given the large amount of work that has been done with regression analysis one would not want to ignore this rich literature. It can be easily re-analysed with existing covariance analytical techniques.

2. The method of typology

It is my belief that we are ready for a combination of quantitative and qualitative theory in organizational analysis. One way of building this kind of theory is to combine typologies with existing empirical generalizations. The techniques suggested above can help us start by finding concepts inductively — either quantitative or qualitative — that specify conditions or limits. Then one tries to find a typology that summarizes the conditions that have been found empirically. Instead of seeing each hypothesis as isolated, one looks for some larger framework.

There are several typologies in the literature worth exploring. Our task is to focus on one that implies non-linear combinations of the same variables. A good illustration is Perrow's (1967) technology typology. A careful reading indicates that if one does look at the two main types off the main diagonal, then one is likely to find different patterns of association. Mintzberg (1979) and Hage (1980) in their recent formulations have been even more explicit about various non-linear combinations. Mintzberg's typology is built up from the micro level on the basis of the structuring of the organization, while Hage's starts with the macro or environmental level and, more specifically, the sophistication of the technology and the optimal size of the organization.

In selecting the typology, one wants critical dimensions or ideas that are likely to make a difference in a wide variety of areas. The ones selected will vary according to the nature of the problem. Thus it is difficult to assign specific criteria. Both Mintzberg and Hage justify their typologies on the basis of a large number of variables (see Mintzberg, 1979; and Hage, 1980, Chs 3, 6, 12, and 13). But each of them has a specific theoretical focus that, while broad, is not adaptable to every-one's needs.

What does one do if the existing typologies are not relevant? How does one build one's own typology? *One way (an empirical approach) is to select as axes of the typology variables that have little association among them-selves* (e.g. Pugh *et al.*, 1969). The cells in such a typology *are most likely to have these non-linear combinations* and to lead to quite striking effects. Thus, in one instance, I created a typology by using the two variables of "sophistication of technology in the production process" and "opti-mal size" precisely because they have little association. In fact, there is a rather consistent correlation between these two variables of about -0.10 across a number of studies in different countries and collected at different time points (Hage, 1980, Ch. 12).

Arguments in the literature also represent useful starting points for the contruction of a typology. A current one (see Hage in Warner, 1977) relating to the question of managerial choice versus structural determin-ism is a good example. One can take the values of the managers or administrators and the structural characteristics relative to the same problem. For example, take the problem of innovation. Elites might be pro- or anti-change and the structure might be pro- or anti-change. This provides the following typology:

		Attitudes of élite	
Structure		Anti-change	Pro-change
Concentration of specialists:	Low	Low rate of innovation	Catch-up innovation
	High	Moderate rate of innovation	Radical innovation

Here the point of the typology is to specify qualitatively different kinds of innovations in each of the four situations. Each of these has the following logical structure:

Given a high score on *A* and a low score on *B*, then there is. . . .

This becomes more interesting when the typology is employed to specify conditions in which the relationships between the *same* variables are different. Thus both Mintzberg (1979) and Hage (1980) employ their basic typologies to indicate how the number of departments/divisions and the number of levels can be combined. Mintzberg's work in particular is very rich and subtle relative to the problem of organizational design.

In this instance of the concentration of specialists and attitudes towards change one would go on to build various hypotheses relative to other variables. For example, in the case of low concentration of specialists and pro-change attitudes one would predict that the greater the centralization, the greater the innovation rate. However, in the exact opposite case, the hypothesis would be opposite, namely: given a high concentration of specialists and non-pro-change attitudes upon the part of the elite, then the less the centralization, the greater the innovation. Here we see how typology combined with existing literature, both theoretical and empirical, leads to the specification of opposing hypotheses. They also help elucidate an argument in the literature about the role of centralization in facilitating change. Sometimes it does and sometimes it doesn't. In this case the specific conditions and the kind of innovation both vary.

In this example of the combination of quantitative and qualitative theory the first two concepts, a high concentration of specialists and pro-change represent our qualitative concepts — that is, ranges of variables. We could use some quantative terms to describe these ranges, which are our conditions. In the case of pro-change the accent is more on an extreme end of the distribution that is pro-change versus all other attitudes. In constructing typologies, it is often useful to use more extreme ends of the continuum as a way of enhancing the probability that we will obtain both qualitatively different phenomena, as in the kinds of innovation, and more complex hypotheses, as in the multivariate ones relating centralization and innovation.

As a general rule, the combination of élite attitudes and some major structural variable represents a very useful way of building a typology. The presence of arguments about attitudes versus behaviour in the literature is a sign that one needs a more complex way of proceeding. Both are relevant.

Another area where typologies can be usefully employed is in the relationship between environmental conditions and human responses to them. This has been highlighted by the work of Hirschman (1970) on "exit" (turnover), "voice" (conflict) and "loyalty" (commitment). He notes that sometimes exit is employed and sometimes voice. March and Simon (1958) made much of the motivation to participate, which is another way of saying exit, but said nothing about conflict. Here we see the need for a typology to handle this kind of complexity. Or to take another example from the literature that is equally provocative, Kahn *et al.* (1964) in their work on organizational stress found it necessary to use a typology of personality as a way of building a theory of how different individuals respond to the same problem, in this instance role conflict. Typologies of individuals, and/or groups, and their responses would thus appear to be a strategic starting place for the construction of more complex theories.

Less obvious, but equally critical, are models of processes. The most famous one in the organizational literature is on the stages of change (Zaltman *et al.*, 1973). The theoretical argument is that each stage varies not only in the kind of phenomenon present but also in the interrelationships between variables. For example, conflict is most likely in the implementation stage. Also, the role of centralization is perceived as different in different stages.

We need much more theory-building like this. If constructing a theory about decision-making processes, we might create first a typology of decisions and then construct different hypotheses relative to these kinds of decisions. Or, if we are interested in innovation, we might establish a typology of innovations and construct different hypotheses for different kinds of innovations. Here the work of Kalunzy *et al.* (1974), on the differences between high- and low-risk innovation is suggestive. Again, once we have typologies relative to processes, and if there are data available, it is then possible to employ covariance as they did. This more complex analysis revealed that formalization and innovation are related in different ways depending upon whether the innovation is of high or of low risk.

In the analysis it is critical, however, that one looks for non-linear combinations of the variables as well as control for other specific kinds of phenomena or specific stages in some process. Then one tests to see if there are significant differences in the partial correlations or betas in a path-analytical model. Significant differences are suggestive of different combinations of the variables *across* the cells. Within each cell of the typology it would be important to explore the scatter plot to ascertain how linear the relationship in fact is.

3. The method of different paradigms

Perhaps the most common mistake that has been made is to assume that by adding more variables or more attributes we have a more complex understanding. This is the real error in the linear, additive model of regression analysis. We can easily add more variables but does this really mean that we know or understand more? I think not and for a variety of reasons. Given the interrelationships between variables, one is not extending the understanding by simply including more variables. Certainly we know that the amount of variance explained will not increase. Most researchers have learned that once one obtains 50% of the variance explained, it is hard to move beyond this barrier regardless of the number of variables included.

Sometimes when additional variables are added in a regression analysis, a major difference can occur. For example, Hage and Dewar (1973) found that adding more structural variables did not increase the amount of variance explained in the rate of innovation, but including the values of the elites did, as did the previous history of change. One variable from each of these areas was all that was necessary and together they accounted for 70% of the variance.

What distinguishes each of these variables is that they represent different paradigms. We have already noted that attitudes and structures can fruitfully be combined to form typologies. Part of the reason is empirical — low association; and part is theoretical — different perspective. *What is fruitful is the addition of separate paradigms or theoretical orientations in our regression analysis.* It is with each orientation that we see something different because it poses different questions. Most critically, each orientation sets limits or qualifications on the other — and this is true at all levels: assumptions as well as equations, variables as well as causal priorities.

One might ask in the example of the Hage and Dewar (1973) article what paradigm or orientation is represented by the previous history of change? Actually we frequently lose sight of the idea that organizations — for whatever reasons — develop distinctive patterns of growth and development. While there has been a call for more historical studies, there has not been a thinking-through of what this means. One implication is the use of past behaviour as the predictor of future behaviour. While it is boring to say that organizations keep on doing what they have previously done, it is a way of conceptualizing history. It does provide a distinctive orientation and a great deal of predictive power as well.

Some might be concerned that combining paradigms means that you are no longer remaining true to them. But this is not necessarily the case. In fact this technique is only successful if we maintain the integrity of each paradigm. This may sound impossible to do, especially when one considers the great extremes in paradigms that exist (Burrell and Morgan, 1979). How can one combine structural-functionalism and conflict theory? Simply by recognizing that one works in certain situations and within certain ranges of variables and that the other works in other situations and within other ranges. For example, in a recent book (Hage, 1980) I have argued that structural-functionalism works well with innovation rates, but cannot explain radical innovation. The latter necessitates a conflict perspective. The same can be said for the differences between typical or routine decisions and high-risk decisions. The examples are endless.

Or to take what is perhaps an even more interesting contrast, how can a phenomenological perspective and a structural-functional perspective be combined? Simply by looking for situations or problems where the former is more effective and other situations or problems where the latter is more telling. My own preference is to argue that a phenomenological perspective is most helpful in drawing the boundaries of units whether positions, departments, organizations or the like, whereas a structural perspective works well within the boundaries — once they are drawn. Each has a contribution to make but neither is sufficient by itself.

Our intellectual gains are most likely to be greater as we combine perspectives from other disciplines. For example, Cyert and March (1963) have suggested that we employ a political perspective. The problem is that they did not really borrow the interest-group model that has been developed in political science. How rich this is can be seen in the work of Baldridge (1971), a political scientist (and at Stanford University). Are there particular perspectives that are likely to have the best payoff?

My candidates would be the combination of occupational sociology or the sociology of work (Ritzer, 1977) with a structural perspective, and with general equilibrium theory from economics. With regard to the first perspective, one can imagine either dummy variables representing certain kinds of occupations or a typology of occupations being employed in regression analysis of the interrelations between any of the variables typically analysed. For example, does the concentration of specialists have more or less of a relationship with centralization if the specialists are social workers or engineers or "McNamara whizz-kids"? The amount of conflict may vary enormously depending upon how well organized the union is or even whether it is a professional association as distinct from a union. My intuition is that a large number of more complex ideas could be derived by systematically integrating these two isolated literatures.

Equally exciting is the potential for combining some of the micro-economic models with organizational models. There is a whole range of potential theories here. On the one hand, organizational theory suggests how costs can be lowered and on the other hand economic theory suggests how price is a function of supply and demand (Chandler, 1977). Organizational theory's concern with innovation versus efficiency is somewhat parallel to the economists' distinction between taste and price. Slack resources (Cyert and March, 1963) and economies of scale (Freeman, 1974) are again quite similar in meaning. A particularly interesting avenue of research is the role of organizations—both public and private—in the development of stagflation. I am currently working on a theory that explicates how organizations affect the rate of inflation, the balance of trade and kindred issues.

Production functions have played an important role in economics and they are a way of estimating the impact of technology. Organizational theory could be enriched by attempting to build production functions where technology is explicitly operationalized. It would be a first step in understanding how organizational *structure* affects cost. One cannot determine the precise impact of centralization and of other structural variables without holding constant technology's impact on the speed of throughput.

When synthesizing paradigms, one keeps both orientations and argues that each is an independent causal force. For example, organizations can retard or speed up the response of supply to demand. In this way one is not arguing against economic laws but instead indicating how they are influenced by another perspective. Inevitably, as one does this, conditions and limits are established and more complex functions are constructed. The combination of marginal utility theory with current structural ideas, as I have already suggested, would do much to enrich our thinking and move us beyond linear theory. Note that the combination of organizational thinking with the laws of supply and demand help us to specify the speed of response, a critical step in the construction of dynamic equations.

It is also useful to ask why perspectives, and especially paradigms, are *not* integrated. There are good reasons and these must be understood as barriers to the kind of model-building being advocated. The more well-developed a paradigm or orientation, the more difficult it is to see the utility of another perspective. Many times economists have avoided employing organizational variables and theories even though I have found it helpful to do the reverse (which they do understand!). This suggests that perhaps the only way an effective synthesis is possible is by having a team work on the problem, where each member represents a distinctive perspective. We are not used to thinking of teams constructing theories, but this approach to model-building should at least be tried.

4. The method of different analytical levels

Just as shifting theoretical orientations allow us to see in new ways what we are studying, so do integrating analytical levels. Most of us, myself included, focus on a particular analytical level. For me it has been the environment-organization. For some psychologists, it has been the environment-individual. For still others, the environment-community or environment-society or environment-group. I couple the environment with the analytical unit. But the pair environment-analytical unit does represent the limit of most individuals' work.

Although there is a perception that when one has shifted to the environment one has changed levels, there is in fact a continuum. The environment of a work group in an organization can be, and usually is conceptualized as something other than the organization, such as a department or a work climate in the immediate area (Homans, 1950; Lipset *et al.*, 1956). To shift to the organization would represent a more striking comparison.

The environment of the organization is usually thought of as the market situation (Lawrence and Lorsch, 1967). It is a much more radical shift in perspective to consider the society or culture as the environment. For example, are business organizations different in capitalist and socialist societies? Although the answer is obviously

"Yes", it is interesting that few have really explored this issue (see Tannenbaum *et al.*, 1974).

How an educational organization operates in a centralized system such as France is quite different from the operation in a more decentralized system. On the other hand, universities in the two systems are more similar, mainly because of the greater power of the faculty. As we think about these multiple levels we begin to discover automatically various conditions and limits to our hypotheses.

As soon as researchers start examining multiple levels, they quickly appreciate how multivariate hypotheses must be created to handle the obvious exceptions and qualifications. This has perhaps been appreciated more in political science and political sociology than in organizational sociology. But there are examples in our literature. Again *Union Democracy* stands out. Liberals voted differently when placed in conservative locals and vice versa. While perhaps obvious, it calls attention to the fact that every problem is located in a larger context.

If we start with a basic three-tier perspective on organizations— micro, meso, and macro—then we can begin to pose a number of theoretical questions about how these levels set limits or conditions on each other. Too often, sociologists and psychologists explain one level by another rather than argue for the unique contribution of each level.

The full potential of the macro level as a unit of analysis is perhaps only now being realized with the work of Azumi, Hickson and McMillan (personal communication) on the differences between Sweden, Britain and Canada. (Actually, their starting point is how similar organizations are rather than how different!) The current interest in a political-economy paradigm also offers rich promise as we begin to understand how the state and economic organizations are interrelated.

But this rich promise is unlikely to offer much in the way of more complex theory unless the insights of macro analysis are combined with those of the meso and micro analytical levels. There is a danger that in our desire to be on the frontiers of knowledge, we are unlikely to connect the new with the old. The macro focus becomes an analytical focus and an interest in itself rather than a way of deepening our understanding of other levels.

Just as with paradigms, so with analytical levels we find a specialization that is unfortunate. We become so used to thinking about one slice of reality that we ignore the other slices. Again, a team might be the best way of proceeding. However, we are beginning to see more and more attempts to integrate levels (Rousseau, 1978) and more and more recognition of their distinctive reality (Hage, 1980; Ritzer, 1976).

To successfully combine analytical levels, we will be forced to change our research designs so that we select societies to represent certain critical variables or categories. Again, we have something akin to a covariance model but now one employed in our research design. France and Britain might be selected because of the greater centralization of the State in the former case or the greater power of the unions in the latter instance. Regardless, some thought must be given to the conceptual reasons for having samples of organizations in different countries.

The specification of the causal connections between levels will be difficult because how one level sets the context for the other is not immediately clear. How does the power of unions in the larger society influence the choice of "exit" or "voice" (see Hirschman, 1970) given poor working conditions? How does the centralization of the State affect the centralization of business organizations in the same society? The chain of influences is not easy to specify. If we adopt the tolerant opinion that each level interacts with another, and we systematically search for how this occurs, then we shall perhaps begin to perceive connections that previously we have missed. This is as true for me as it is for most organizational sociologists who have systematically ignored the micro level in their theories. As we build three analytical levels into our analysis we shall surely develop more complex theories than we presently have.

5. Summary

The constant theme of why we have not developed more multivariate hypotheses is because we do not change our perspective. Once we do we immediately see new complexities that are translated into conditions, limits, or multiplicative hypotheses. Each of the suggested techniques is designed to break a pattern of thought about our work. Thus to examine moderate or large correlations to see if the exceptions have their own formulation, to examine extremes to see if these are qualitative shifts and to examine residuals to see if there is a need for new variables, are all ways of changing our perception. They build upon previous work and yet move us beyond it. Covariance analytical techniques are the regression counterpart.

The setting of conditions and limits are the easiest ways of moving from linear to non-linear thinking. They make one build multivariate hypotheses almost automatically. However, even more complex formulations can be built with the search for non-linear combinations of variables or polynomic functions.

The present stage in the development of organizational theory appears to beg for the merging of qualitative and quantitative theory. The use of typologies in combination with existing hypotheses and empirical generalizations appears to be one way of proceeding to achieve this objective. Another is the synthesis of different paradigms and of different analytical levels. Key concepts from other perspectives and analytical levels, which summarize a number of ideas, can be employed as the qualitative distinctions.

Alternative perspectives and analytical levels also establish limits and conditions on hypotheses and theories within a specific framework and level of analysis. Again, they represent ways of breaking our traditional perspective and lead us to new insights. Shifting levels of paradigms requires much more work and is harder to do. Regardless of the effort involved, the rewards would appear to be great: a more complex view of the organizational world.

Note

1. I suspect that this is the problem with most studies of the relationship between structure and morale. Morale, like productivity, can alter in large amounts given even minor adjustments in the nature of the working conditions. Woodward's (1965) finding relating average span for each of three technology patterns to success implies this kind of marginal utility. So does the research by Lawrence and Lorsch (1962), when they relate differentiation and integration to success. These kinds of studies are rare because organizational sociologists have tended to ignore the problems of bottom line, that is, how structure affects performance.

References

ABELL, P. (1975). *Organizations as Bargaining and Influence Systems*. London: Heineman.

ABERNATHY, W. (1978). *The Productivity Dilemma: Roadblock to Innovation in the Automobile Industry*. Baltimore: Johns Hopkins.

ALDRICH, H. (1979). *Organizations and Environments*. Englewood Cliffs: Prentice-Hall.

BALDRIDGE, V. (1971). *Power and Conflict in the University*. New York: Wiley.

BURNS, T. AND STALKER, G. M. (1961). *The Management of Innovation*. London: Tavistock.

BLALOCK, H. M. (1969). *Theory Construction: From Verbal to Mathematical Models*. Englewood Cliffs: Prentice-Hall.

BLAU, P. M. (1970). A formal theory of differentiation in organizations. *American Sociological Review*, **35**, 210–218.

BLAU, P. M. (1972). Interdependence and hierarchy in organizations. *Social Science Research*, **1**, 1–24.

BLAU, P. M. (1973). *The Organization of Academic Work*. New York: Wiley-Interscience.

BLAU, P. M. AND SCHOENHERR, R. (1971). *The Structure of Organizations*. New York: Basic Books.

BLAU, P. M., FALBE, C. M., McKINLEY, W. AND TRACY, D. K. (1976). Technology and organization in manufacturing. *Administrative Science Quarterly*, **21**, 20–40.

BURNS, T. AND STALKER, G. M. (1961). *The Management of Innovation*. London: Tavistock.

BURRELL, G. AND MORGAN, G. (1979). *Sociological Paradigms and Organizational Analysis*. London: Routledge and Kegan Paul.

CHANDLER, A. (1962). *Strategy and Structure: Chapters in the History of Industrial Enterprise*. Cambridge: M.I.T. Press.

CHANDLER, A. (1977). *The Visible Hand*. Cambridge: Harvard University Press.

CYERT, R. AND MARCH, J. (1963). *A Behavioral Theory of the Firm*. Englewood Cliffs: Prentice-Hall.

DEWAR, R. (1976). Shifts Toward More Mechanistic Styles of Social Co-ordination and Control as Consequences of Growth and Technological Innovation. Unpublished Ph.D., University of Wisconsin.

FREEMAN, C. (1974). *The Industrial Economics of Innovation*. Harmondsworth: Penguin.

FREEMAN, J. AND HANNON, M. (1975). Growth and decline processes in organizations. *American Sociological Review*, **40**, 215–218.

GOULDNER, A. W. (1954). *Patterns of Industrial Bureaucracy*. New York: The Free Press.

GUEST, R. H. (1956). Of time and foremen. *Personnel*, **32**, 478–496.

HAGE, J. (1965). An axiomatic theory of organizations. *Administrative Science Quarterly*, **10**, 289–320.

HAGE, J. (1972). *Techniques and Problems of Theory Construction in Sociology*. New York: Wiley-Interscience.

HAGE, J. (1974). *Communication and Organizational Control: Cybernetics in Health and Welfare Settings*. New York: Wiley-Interscience.

HAGE, J. (1980). *Theories of Organizations. Form, Process, and Transformation*. New York: Wiley-Interscience.

HAGE, J. AND AIKEN, M. (1970). *Social Change in Complex Organizations.* New York: Random House.

HAGE, J. AND DEWAR, R. (1973). Elite values versus organizational structure in predictory innovation. *Administrative Science Quarterly,* **18,** 279–290.

HEISE, D. (1975). *Causal Analysis.* New York: Wiley.

HICKSON, D. J., HININGS, C. R., LEE, C. A., SCHNECK, R. E. AND PENNINGS, J. M. (1971). A strategic contingencies theory of intraorganizational power. *Administrative Science Quarterly,* **16,** 216–229.

HIRSCHMAN, A. (1970). *Exit, Voice, and Loyalty: Responses to Decline in Firms, Organizations, and the State.* Cambridge: Harvard University Press.

HOLDOWAY, E. A., NEWBERRY, J. F., HICKSON, D. J. AND HERON, R. P. (1975). Dimensions of organization in complex societies: The educational sector. *Administrative Science Quarterly,* **20,** 30–58.

HOMANS, G. (1950). *The Human Group.* New York: Harcourt and Brace.

KAHN, R. L., WOLFE, D. M., QUINN, R. P., SNOEK, J. E. AND ROSENTHAL, R. A. (1964). *Organizational Stress: Studies in Role Conflict and Ambiguity.* New York: Wiley.

KALUNZY, A., VENEY, J. AND GENTRY, J. (1974). Innovations in Health Services. *Millbank Memorial Fund Quarterly,* **52,** 51–82.

LAMMERS, C. AND HICKSON, D. (1978). *Organizations Alike and Unalike.* London: Routledge and Kegan Paul.

LAWRENCE, P. AND LORSCH, J. (1967a). Differentiation and integration in complex organization. *Administrative Science Quarterly,* **12,** 1–47.

LAWRENCE, P. AND LORSCH, J. (1967b). *Organizations and Environment: Managing Differentiation and Integration.* Cambridge: Harvard Graduate School of Business.

LIPSET, S., TROW, M. AND COLEMAN, J. (1956). *Union Democracy.* Glencoe: Free Press.

MARCH, J. G. AND SIMON, H. A. (1958). *Organizations.* New York: Wiley.

MEYER, M. (1972). Size and the structure of organizations. *American Sociological Review,* **37,** 434–441.

MINTZBERG, H. (1979). *The Structuring of Organizations.* Englewood Cliffs: Prentice-Hall.

PERROW, C. (1967). A framework for the comparative analysis of organizations. *American Sociological Review,* **32,** 194–209.

PRICE, J. (1968). *Organizational Effectiveness: An Inventory of Propositions.* Homewood: Irwin.

PUGH, D. S., HICKSON, D. J., HININGS, C. R. AND TURNER, C. (1968). Dimensions of Organization Structure. *Administrative Science Quarterly,* **13,** 65–105.

PUGH, D. S., HICKSON, D. J., HININGS, C. R. AND TURNER, C. (1969). The Context of Organization Structure. *Administrative Science Quarterly,* **14,** 91–114; see also 115–125, An empirical taxonomy of structures of work organizations.

QUINNEY, R. (1979). *Capitalist Society: Readings for a Critical Sociology.* Homewood: Dorsey.

RITZER, G. (1976). *Sociology: A Multiple Paradigm Science*. Boston: Allyn and Bacon.

RITZER, G. (1977). *The Sociology of Work* (2nd edition). Englewood Cliffs: Prentice-Hall.

ROUSSEAU, D. M. (1978). Characteristics of departments, positions, and individuals: Contexts for attitudes and behavior. *Administrative Science Quarterly*, **23,** 521–540.

STARBUCK, W. AND DERTHEN, J. (1973). Designing adaptive organizations. *Journal of Business Policy*, **3,** 21–28.

TANNENBAUM, A., KAVCIC, B., ROSNER, M., VIANELLO, M. AND WIESER, G. (1974). *Hierarchy in Organizations*. San Francisco: Jossey Bass.

THOMPSON, J. D. (1967). *Organizations in Action*. New York: McGraw-Hill.

WARNER, M. (1977). *Choice and Constraint*. London: Halsted.

WOODWARD, J. (1965). *Industrial Organization*. London: Oxford University Press.

ZALTMAN, G., DUNCAN, R. AND HOLBECK, J. (1973). *Innovations and Organizations*. New York: Wiley.

ZETTERBERG, H. (1963). *On Theory and Verification in Sociology*. Totowa: Bedminster.

ZEY-FERREL, M. (1979). *Dimensions of Organizations: Environment, Context, Structure, Process, and Performance*. Santa Monica: Goodyear.

7 Issues in Research Design and Analysis

PAUL JACKSON

Is there any reader who has not changed his research question because he is unaware of a convenient statistical technique freely available to fit the appropriate conceptual model? To some degree we all of us define our research questions and underlying conceptual frameworks in terms of the analytical techniques with which we are familiar or feel at home. In other words, established research methods to a large extent drive the research process itself. It is rare for research questions in applied organizational psychology to lead to the development and application of novel methods either in research design or in procedures for statistical analysis. Rather, each discipline has its own set of orthodoxies of techniques for conducting research, and individuals make decisions about method by choosing from within the very restricted array of options in their "tool kit".

Needless to say, this state of affairs has adaptive value both in the evolution of individual careers and in the advancement of the discipline as a whole. The researcher who designs a study which cannot meet a research need unambiguously, or who asks questions of data which cannot be answered, will not long survive in a world where research contracts are based on ability to deliver the goods. Nor would the discipline as a whole benefit by such an approach. An area of knowledge can only develop when the intimate relationship is recognized between research method — in design and data analysis — and conceptual theorizing. Finney emphasized one aspect of this interdependence in his presidential address to the Royal Statistical Society, namely the role that theory has in guiding the choice of research design and analytical technique. He points out that the success of a study in addressing theoretical issues depends upon the extent to which the researcher has used existing theory to design the study and to guide statistical analysis. He says that "at the stage of planning, the inference desired should determine the structure that is acceptable; at the stage of analysis, the structure available determines the inference permissible" (Finney, 1974, p. 15).

We may illustrate this interdependence between theory and method by a trivial example which nevertheless highlights a point which we are all aware of but many seem to forget in their everyday research practice. It concerns the relationship between data and numbers. Although we all know that there is more to data than simply the numbers themselves, we often implicitly accept the reality of the myth that there is an identity between the two. But of course data and numbers are not the same thing because numbers have no history, no context, while data have both.

Consider a batch of numbers (1, 2, 2, 1, 10, 8), what can we say about them? Taking the batch as a whole we could summarize it using an index of its centre of gravity (like a mean or a median) and also an index of spread about that centre (like a variance or an index of range). We could also note that most of the numbers are small, with two large exceptions. But what else can we say? The answer to that question is that we can say very little. We noted that two numbers in the batch were large by comparison with the others and we called them "exceptions" but both of these conclusions are inferences and not facts because we have no way of knowing about the relative importance of each numerical value. Nor do we know anything about other batches which might tell us whether the higher numbers are in fact exceptional. Summary indices like mean and variance depend for their validity on knowledge of this kind. If the two higher numbers in our batch are mistakes then both summary indices are grossly misleading.

Now let us turn the batch of numbers into data by giving two examples of situations to which they might refer. Suppose that we are tossing dice and the dice you are using gave the distribution of scores in our batch — (1, 2, 2, 1, 10, 8). In other words, you achieve 8 sixes, 10 fives and so on with 24 throws of the dice. Now what can we say? The first thing is that I would want to know what is going on, because 18 out of 24 throws above four is very unusual if the dice are fair. By appealing to prior knowledge and experience I can say rather imprecisely that the first four numbers in the batch are too low and the last two are too high. Suppose I know that we each brought our own dice for the game, then I can infer from the data (not from the numbers) that you are cheating. I should either attempt to swap the dice or stop the game! None of these conclusions could have been reached from the numbers above. Only by knowing what the numbers refer to, by giving them a history and a context, do they become data.

Now consider a second application for the same batch of numbers. Suppose that we ask a group of individuals how many times they have visited their family doctor in the past year and obtain the data given in our batch (1, 2, 2, 1, 10, 8). Our interpretation of the data is very different from the previous example. First of all, it is surprising that there are no zeros in the data since it is reasonable that many people do not visit their family doctor at all in any one year. This leads us to ask how the individuals who gave us data were selected. If they were asked on entering the doctor's waiting room then any interpretation of our results must take that into account. Secondly, we might expect the data to have come from two separate populations; frequent visits from those with chronic problems, and single visits from the rest. This intuition would lead to very different forms of analysis. Clearly a mean for the whole batch of data makes little sense, since two conceptually different populations have been combined. We should instead consider ways in which to distinguish between the two groups and either analyse each group separately or incorporate the distinction between the groups in a combined analysis. We conclude, therefore, that there is a great deal more to data and to data analysis than the numbers. Without knowing what the numbers refer to, how they were arrived at, and what the question was that prompted their gathering there is little that the analyst can do that is constructive.

The same interdependence between the purposes of research and the possibilities of analysis arises in the choice of a particular form of research design. For example, when random allocation of individuals to treatment and control groups is possible then much-simplified forms of statistical model can be used, and inference is greatly eased. In other circumstances life is not so simple, and approaches such as the non-equivalent control-group design (e.g. Cook and Campbell, 1979; Kenny, 1975a) have spawned an abundance of techniques all intended to overcome the problems caused by the way individuals were assigned to groups. In the choice of variables too, forethought can make all the difference to whether a parameter can be estimated at all. This is termed the *identification* problem (Fisher, 1966; Duncan, 1975), and the use of several indicators of a construct rather than a single indicator can make life a lot easier for the researcher, for instance in the assessment of reliability and in the analysis of the relationships amongst residual terms in a model.

These examples show the productive value of the dependence of theory on method and method on theory. However, organizational psychology is characterized by a strong dependence on a limited number of research designs and analytical techniques, and this dependence has several dysfunctional aspects. First of all, it precludes the consideration of questions for which answers cannot be obtained by that limited number of techniques. Many procedures have been developed in other areas of research which are potentially legitimate for use in organizational psychology, but they are never used. Thus advancement in theory is retarded by overdependence on a few particular methods. At the same time there is less impetus for the development and application of new techniques, which to a large extent depend upon pressure from an applied problem. The second dysfunctional aspect of the dependence on a few orthodox techniques is the misuse or overgeneralization of those techniques — the application of what may be sound research practices in ways which are not appropriate, simply because the researcher is unable or unwilling to adopt new procedures or adapt existing ones.

The rest of this essay will focus on two aspects of the relationship between theory and method. First of all, issues related to research design are discussed together with illustrations of the role that theory has in guiding researchers' choices. In the second part of the essay, attention is shifted from research design to data analysis. Here, some new techniques are presented which have proved fruitful in other areas of research. The aim throughout is to demonstrate that theory guides both research design and data analysis.

1. Theory and research design

A great deal of organizational psychology is concerned with causal relationships, and the notion of cause is implicit in much of our theorizing. We talk about the *influence* of environmental deprivation on teenage delinquency, and the *dependence* of job satisfaction on characteristics of the job; we recommend changes in training curricula in order *to bring about* improvements in job transferability; we attempt to assess the *effect* of fatigue or alcohol on driving performance. In all these areas, causal relationships are central, yet often the evidence from which causal inferences are made is equivocal at best since it is based on correlational data derived from cross-sectional surveys.

The temptation to jump to causal conclusions from correlational evidence is hard to resist, despite the fact that it is impossible from such data alone to decide between A as a cause of B and B as a cause of A, or indeed neither as a cause of the other. What the researcher must do in these circumstances is to reject alternative causal hypotheses on an *a priori* basis as implausible. Thus the role of theory is pre-eminent in the analysis of cross-sectional data and clearly there are problems with taking this approach (Young, 1977). The most obvious is that many alternatives are likely to be equally plausible in an ill-defined research area. It may then be very difficult to resolve differences in the relative merits of rival theories by appeal to the data.

The problem is made all the more difficult by the fact that model-fitting procedures such as path analysis may produce a large number of models which fit the data equally well (e.g. Hilton, 1970). Many researchers consider alternative models which are nested hierarchically, and choose among them by stepwise regression. What is much less common is for researchers to consider models outside that nested sequence, which may also fit the data to an acceptable level. For example, recursive models without feedback loops are often assumed because they can be fitted quite straightforwardly by least squares. Dual causality may be more realistic and account for data equally well but is not even considered because model-fitting is much more complicated in that case.

The reliance on existing theory for substantiating the validity of causal inference with cross-sectional data has led researchers to consider ways in which alternative rival hypotheses can be ruled out on other than theoretical grounds alone. Two popular approaches are the experiment and the longitudinal panel design.

The experiment

The experimental design offers an appealing simplicity in causal inference which depends on what Campbell (1963) called "the magic of randomisation". Individuals are assigned to treatment and control groups by the researcher at random. This means that the response of the individual may be attributed to the experimental treatment itself rather than to pre-existing differences between individuals which might have led to differences in response regardless of the experimental procedure. Thus differences between treatment and control groups may be attributed to the intervention of the researcher. Needless to say, this simplicity of inference is bought at a price, and in applied psychology the price may be so high that the experiment in many cases is not likely to be useful.

This is so for practical and theoretical reasons. First of all, the experiment may be impractical in the "real world" since it involves too much disruption to normal working. Such is often the case in studies of job redesign where organizations typically will not allow the researcher to randomize work groups for the purpose of achieving experimental rigour. Moreover, the experiment may be unethical where, for instance, participants are grossly misled about what they are being asked to do or may suffer physically from an experimental treatment. Many clinical experiments cannot be performed on humans for this reason.

There are also theoretical reasons why experimental designs may not be appropriate. Even where a true experimental design can be achieved with random allocation to groups and no contamination between groups, the experiment may answer the wrong question if the performance of the experiment itself changes the phenomenon being studied. As an example, take the job-redesign situation referred to above. Few work groups comprise randomly allocated individuals; rather groups are selected to balance the experience of the individuals, their needs and wishes, and the requirements of the work process itself. A treatment effect, however significant statistically, implies nothing about the impact of the particular treatment in the work place because the conditions created by the researcher will never occur again in practice. The job-redesign experiment has bypassed constraints such as those imposed by previous work practices, the shifting constitution of work groups as members leave or pressure of work leads management to increase group sizes, and so on. A key question may be whether job redesign will increase employee performance or morale; the experiment is not likely to answer this question.

Another way in which experiments answer the wrong questions is by encouraging the researchers to think solely in a unidirectional manner. It has often been argued that individual differences are treated conceptually as independent variables simply because it is easier to allocate individuals to conditions on the basis of personality-test scores than it is to examine experimentally the determinants of these differences. In the same way, variables such as task performance or pay level tend to be seen as independent variables rather than dependent variables because they are easy to manipulate, while variables such as employee satisfaction tend to be seen as dependent variables because they are not amenable to researcher control. What this orientation neglects is the interdependence of variables and their mutual influences. Because dual causality in the experimental setting is ruled out by the intervention of the researcher, the results of an experimental study are unlikely to be broadly applicable for any variables where dual causality is in fact present. Thus the control element afforded by the experimental design makes it inapplicable for use in examining a whole range of important relationships between variables.

The panel design

Given these problems with the experiment and the many unresolved ambiguities associated with the cross-sectional survey approach to research, many applied researchers are turning to quasi-experimental designs (see e.g. Cook and Campbell, 1979). These retain elements of experimental design without random assignment while at the same time making the design workable in the real world. One of the most popular forms of quasi-experiment is the panel design. The central feature of a panel design that distinguishes it from a repeated cross-sectional survey is that data are collected from the same sample on more than one occasion, such that individuals' responses to the same questions on each occasion can be compared. The use of panel designs is discussed by, among others, Goodman (1973), Simonton (1977), Davis (1978), Goldstein (1979) and Hannan and Tuma (1979). Only a superficial acquaintance with this literature is needed in order to see that panel designs serve two main purposes in applied research: one is the study of the process of change; the other is the use of cross-lagged correlations to investigate dual causality.

(a) *Studying change.* The first use of the panel design is to study the process of change itself, where time is an integral part of the model being developed (e.g. Bock, 1976). In this context, the panel approach has two important advantages over the cross-sectional survey. First of all, a panel study nearly always measures changes with greater precision than does a series of independent samples of the same size. The standard error of a difference between means will be lower for a panel study than for completely independent samples (provided that scores to the same question on successive occasions are positively correlated, which is usually the case). The second important advantage of the panel study is that the researcher can measure not only net changes (which independent samples can also do) but in addition can identify "changers". The ability to distinguish between those who change and those who do not can often be of crucial importance, for example in Lazarfeld's (1948) classic study of voting intention, and in mover-stayer models of occupational mobility.

An example of the addition in precision afforded by the ability to distinguish changers from non-changers is given by Jackson and Stafford (1980) in a study of influences on mental health. The first phase of the panel design showed a positive correlation between mental health and work involvement for the employed but a negative correlation for the unemployed (details are given in Stafford et al., 1980). The second phase of the design replicated this result, and further support for the validity of the finding was provided by the linked longitudinal data. Those individuals whose status had not changed showed no change in the form of the relationship between work involvement and mental health. Those who did change their status, from employed to unemployed or vice versa, also showed a change in the sign of the correlation between the two variables. For both groups of status-changers, the change in correlation was consistent with the adjustment-fit model of mental health developed by the authors. Thus the panel design gave an added sensitivity to the analysis.

(b) *Cross-lagged correlation analysis.* The second use of the panel design is far more widespread. Building on the "self-evident" proposition that no effect can precede its cause, researchers have been quick to see the possibilities that the panel design brings of disentangling some of the complexities of reciprocal causation. Cross-lagged correlation analysis (Campbell, 1963; Pelz and Andrews, 1964) has generated a great deal of enthusiasm from users and at the same time almost universal disapproval from statisticians. For example, Davis (1978) is "not much impressed by the utility of panel analysis for establishing causal direction" (p. 173); Goldstein (1979) shows algebraically that a simple comparison between two cross-lagged correlations can be misleading and he argues that the technique has no place in the researcher's tool bag; Rogosa (1980) concludes that cross-lagged correlation analysis "should be set aside as a dead end" (p. 257).

Despite these arguments, however, the technique continues to be widely used (see Clegg *et al.*, 1977, for a review of users) and we must ask why this is so. One reason is that the cost to the researcher of using the technique, and to the host organization for allowing its use, is quite low by comparison with the possible pay-offs researchers see in terms of causal inference. Clegg *et al.* (1977) discuss this issue in terms of the commitment or demand a study makes on the participants. The second reason for the wide use of cross-lagged correlation analysis is that the technique *does* work *sometimes* despite blanket condemnations. Our own unpublished studies suggest that the main problem with cross-lagged correlation analysis is its low power, rather than the likelihood that the user is deceived into thinking that A leads to B when in fact B leads to A. If no lagged causal relationship is present then a difference between two cross-lagged correlations is very unlikely. On the other hand, the presence of a lagged causal relationship may lead to a cross-lagged difference; but it depends on other characteristics of the variables such as their stability and reliability.

One of the main problems with cross-lagged correlation analysis is that it encourages a single question to be asked of the data. In many research areas dual causality is much more plausible than unidirectional causal influence, yet cross-lagged correlation analysis is poorly equipped to deal with it.

Many difficulties that beset cross-lag correlation analysis can be traced to the main question: Does X cause Y or Y cause X? Though the question admits the possibility that neither effect exists, it does not anticipate that both effects may hold.

(Hannan and Tuma, 1979, p. 318)

This issue highlights a contrast between Kenny's (1975b) formulation of cross-lagged correlation analysis as a test for spuriousness, and the use that most people make of it as a means of making decisions about causal priorities. For this purpose, cross-lagged correlation analysis has low power and requires a careful examination of the variable auto-correlations and the cross-sectional relationships before any confidence can be placed in the conclusions reached. Kenny (1975b) also showed that the interpretation of results of this kind of analysis can be problematic, for many alternative rival hypotheses cannot be ruled out *a priori.* In this respect, cross-lagged correlation analysis is a poor substitute for designs which allow greater control over relevant variables and also for statistical control within a well-defined model. Kenny concludes:

> my suspicion is that its main use will be in uncovering simple causal relationships between uncontrolled variables. What would then follow is either the refinement of both the measures and the causal process in controlled settings or the estimation of causal parameters of the system by structural equation models.   (p. 901)

Most users spend far too much time on the first stage in this progression and far too little time on the second stage.

Another problem which cross-lagged correlation analysis has helped to bring out into the open is the problem of the timing of re-measurement in longitudinal studies of all kinds. The technique assumes that causal influences take time to show their effects, and so it is very important that the time-gap between measurements coincides at least approximately with the assumed causal lag. Davis (1978) gives the following example — "if weather influences one's mood, the influence probably occurs the same day; but if a college degree influences income, the effect cannot be detected the evening of commencement" (p. 173). Unpublished studies by Pelz and coworkers (e.g. Pelz and Faith, 1973) have shown that timing is important, but that it is often better to overestimate the length of causal lags since their effects tend to peak and then persist for some time. However, relatively little is known about lagged relationships in organizational research and the growth in popularity of panel studies has served to shift attention towards the latency of causal influences as well as their direction.

2.   Theory and data analysis

A.   INTRODUCTION

Data analysis serves three purposes, all interrelated but distinct. These are exploration, confirmation and communication. Techniques or methods which are adequate and useful for one purpose may be totally useless, indeed misleading, for another. Let us consider each purpose in outline first of all and then go on to a closer look at the challenges and opportunities each affords.

First of all then, the role of data analysis in *exploration*. We assume that we have gathered some data because we want to find out something about some aspect of the world that we could not find out about otherwise. Having got the data we need to explore it, just as the pioneer does on arriving at an uninhabited island. At this stage it is the major landmarks that are the focus of interest — anything that stands out in the data which may be important (or may be a response error or a freak of mispunching). We also need to know about the general shape of the data, the centre of balance of each variable and its spread about the centre. Often we use means and standard deviations for this purpose but these can be dangerously misleading, as we saw earlier. Consider, for example, the mean number of employees in a sample of organizations; what use is that? We know that most organizations are very small and few are very large, so the mean is far from democratic in what it tells us about the mass of data, and the same goes for the standard deviation — extreme data values have far greater weight than less extreme values. So we need to consider ways of viewing data and ways of summarizing data.

The second purpose of data analysis is *confirmation*; in other words, comparing the data with something we know (or hope) to be true in order to fit a model, or alternatively with something we know (or hope) not to be true in order to test a hypothesis. In this chapter we shall see what this process of confirming and disconfirming is and what it is not. What it is, is one of the fundamental cornerstones of data analysis which is essential to the effective understanding of data; what it is not is the only way of doing things or even always the best way. Confirmation and exploration go hand in hand, for data analysis is an iterative process. At each step we get further and further away from the data in modelling and theory-building; but we also keep returning to the data as a check on the validity of taking each step. The models we build can be fitted to the data in a confirmatory way but they also allow us to explore the data more effectively. This loop which brings us back to the data again cannot be missed out with impunity.

The third purpose of data analysis is *communication*. In a way we have been talking about communication all along the line. The data we have are our link with the world; they represent the communication between the world and the researcher. Exploratory and confirmatory techniques serve the same purpose of communicating what there is in the data to the researcher. Thus there are important principles of communication which we would do well to remember at all stages of analysis.

B.   METHODS OF EXPLORATION

Have you ever tried to put up a tent in a gale? You get part of it fastened
down and just as you are ready to deal with the next bit all that you have
done comes apart and you have to start again. What is needed in this
situation is several pairs of hands to keep each part of the tent under
control. Making sense of data is rather the same. Ideally, one would like
to be able to pin down each part of the data without having to worry
too much about assumptions, but none of us can afford to assume right
from the start that our data are multivariate-normally distributed or
anything-else distributed. We need to look and see first; and we need to
do the exploratory looking and seeing without first having to make the
assumptions that our exploration is designed to allow us to assess.

In recent years there have been large advances made in this area of
exploratory data analysis (see e.g. Tukey, 1977; McNeil, 1977; Mosteller and Tukey, 1977) but psychologists and social scientists in general
have been slow to take advantage of them. The new procedures are of
two general kinds. The first consists simply of procedures for looking at
the data in different ways: the development of effective forms of data
displays. Other procedures summarize the data, but rely on summary
statistics that are cheap in assumptions. Taken together, procedures for
summarizing the data can go a long way towards allowing the data to·
speak for themselves. Most important of all,

> pictures based on exploration of data should *force* their messages upon us. Pictures that
> emphasise what we already know — "security blankets" to reassure us — are frequently
> not worth the space they take. Pictures that have to be gone over with a reading glass to
> see the main point are wasteful of time and inadequate of effect. *The greatest value of a*
> *picture* is when it *forces* us to notice *what we never expected to see*.   (Tukey, 1977, p. vi)

1.   *Methods for viewing data*

Histograms are familiar devices for displaying the form of a uni-
dimensional batch of data, and scatter plots are frequently used for bivariate data. Both are easily generated by SPSS (Nie *et al.*, 1975), the
package used for the large majority of social science data analysis. Alternatives include the stem and leaf display (Tukey, 1977) and various
forms of pictogram or pie chart. Most social science data is multi-dimensional, however, and pairwise consideration of variables gives no more
than a partial insight. Of greater value are techniques which enable the
researcher to view multi-dimensional data without being forced into

accepting a battery of assumptions. None of the techniques to be described here involves high technology or sophisticated statistics, and this is taken to be a virtue rather than a failing.

Tukey and Tukey (1980) have considered displays of high-dimensional data of the following kind. First of all they choose two of the variables as the "front variables" and construct an orthodox scatter plot using these as the two defining axes. Then they take the remaining variables, the "back variables", and form a two-way grid by grouping the scores on each back variable into, say, four or five levels. Each cell in this grid then contains the scatter plot showing the relationship between the front variables for that particular combination of levels of the back variables. By judicious choice of front and back variables and of levels it is possible to view quite clearly the way in which the front variables behave together as the back variables change. An example of the application of this form of display in organizational psychology might be a plot of decision-making style and type of decision as "front" variables with size of organization and number of levels in the hierarchy as "back" variables.

Several other forms of display for multivariate data are reviewed by Gnanadesikan (1977) and Everitt (1978), and each could be adapted for use in organizational psychology to give insights into relationships among variables. The first form of display is the *glyph* (Anderson, 1960), shown in Fig. 1. Each individual case is represented by a circle and the variables are shown as rays emanating from the circle. Each variable has a fixed position and the length of the ray indicates the value of the variable for the individual. Thus a long ray represents a high score, and a short ray represents a low score. Sometimes it makes sense to differentiate among variables, as we saw in the previous example, by using two variables to define co-ordinate axes of a scatter plot, where the individual data values are shown not as points but as glyphs.

The *weathervane plot* was used by Bruntz *et al.* (1974) to display relationships among the variables of solar radiation level, ozone level, wind speed, wind direction, and temperature (see Fig. 2). Once again, each case is shown as a circle on a scatter plot defined by two of the variables. This time, however, the size of the circle is used to indicate one of the variables, daily maximum temperature. Each circle has a line emanating from it whose orientation shows wind direction and whose length shows wind speed. The success of plots of this kind depend crucially on the allocation of variables to features of the display.

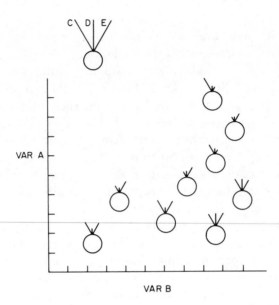

Fig. 1. A glyph display showing the levels of three variables (C, D and E) as a function of two other variables (A and B).

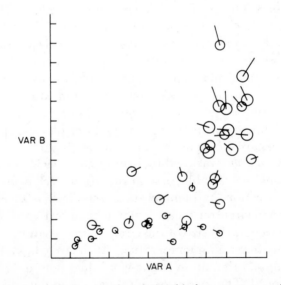

Fig. 2. A weathervane plot showing the relationship between two variables (A and B) together with three other variables.

The third kind of display (shown in Fig. 3) is the device proposed by Chernoff (1973) for representing the values of variables by different characteristics of a cartoon face. Thus, for example, the size of the eyes may code one variable and the shape of the mouth another. Some remarkable faces can be produced in this way and the technique has aroused a great deal of interest (see for example a series of papers in Wang, 1979), but there are many problems that limit its usefulness. The choice of which variables to associate with which facial characteristics needs careful thought, especially since there is a great deal of con-figurality in the perception of the human face which can easily lead to seeing more in the data than is really there. A further problem is that it is difficult to get back from a Chernoff face to the original variables since a different scale is used for each facial characteristic.

Fig. 3. Schematic representation of variables as features of a cartoon face.

Many other forms of display have been used for multivariate data, some more useful than others, but all the ones reviewed here share common characteristics. First, none is costly in assumptions—so that they may be used to see into the data without raising too many ripples. Second, they work in their particular application by capitalizing on the natural structure of the data. Thus a natural differentiation be-tween variables of primary and secondary interest suggests that dis-plays with front and back variables should be considered. The general principle is that a display is an analogue representation of the data, and the successful display is the one that captures essential structure in a natural way. The effective display enables the data to speak for them-selves, and organizational psychologists need to be more imaginative in their ways of representing data visually. The standard, low-effort forms of display that most of us are content with leave most of the work with the viewer. Not only may such displays render meaning opaque, but they may also be quite misleading. The same state of affairs is the case for the indices we use to summarize data.

2. *Methods for summarizing data*

The second stage in allowing the data to speak for themselves is concerned with methods for summarizing data. Summarizing is important
from two points of view. First of all, a summary index enables us to simplify the story the data tell and to see more easily their main features.
Secondly, the same summary index gives us a yardstick against which to
compare each data point; this is the basis for the analysis of outliers (see
e.g. Barnett and Lewis, 1978) and of residuals from a fitted model (e.g.
Mosteller and Tukey, 1977, Ch. 16).

Robust and resistant measures for location and scale. In the initial stages of
data analysis, the researcher cannot afford to take too much for granted
in his or her use of measures of location and spread. For example, it is
well known that the arithmetic mean is particularly vulnerable to the
presence of a few extremely large data values. Mosteller and Tukey
(1977) put the point this way:

> if changing a small part of the body of data, perhaps drastically, can change the value
> of the summary subsequently, the summary is not resistant. Conversely, if a change of a
> small part of the data, no matter what part or how substantially, fails to change the
> summary substantially, the summary is said to be *resistant*.   (p. 203)

The arithmetic mean is clearly non-resistant, and so too are the standard deviation and the range as measures of spread, while the median
and the inter-quartile range are resistant measures of location and
spread respectively.

A second desirable characteristic of a summary measure is robustness,
and here our concern is with the efficiency of a measure. If a measure
extracts from the data all the information that is relevant to the aspect
being summarized then that measure is efficient and is therefore said
to be robust. The virtues of the median in terms of resistance (and ease
of calculation) are counterbalanced by its inefficiency and lack of
robustness. For normally distributed data, the median has roughly two-
thirds of the efficiency of the arithmetic mean, and other more robust
measures are available which combine the resistance with a higher
degree of robustness of efficiency. Mosteller and Tukey (1977) discuss
the biweight, which is a function of the quartiles and has an efficiency
of about 90%, and other robust and resistant measures are reviewed by
Smith *et al.* (1978) and Andrews *et al.* (1972).

Most of the measures discussed by these authors are not routinely
computed by the standard packages, so what is the point of talking about

them? The answer is that robust and resistant measures are of great value, especially to the beginner and the unwary. The skilled analyst knows how much he or she can trust a set of data and measures derived from it, and can use standard procedures with due disrespect, or non-standard techniques with due sensitivity. The beginner, on the other hand, needs a set of analytic tools which will do a fair job on a wide range of problems with large safety margins built in. The routine use of linear statistics like means, standard deviations and so on just does not give the right safety margin. So robust and resistant measures are invaluable to the beginner. They are also of value to the skilled since, when used alongside non-resistant measures, they can reveal trouble spots in the data which may require attention before more detailed analysis can proceed.

C.   METHODS FOR INFORMATIVE CONFIRMATION

Confirmatory techniques have certain characteristics in common: (i) a model which is intended to capture some salient features of the data; (ii) the data itself; and (iii) a set of procedures for fitting the model to the data. These components are interdependent and, once again, all stages of the process of model-fitting are theory-driven. First of all, the model itself has its origins in theory (which might in fact just be a grand word for intuition) and its validity depends to a large extent on factors external to the data. The model derived from theory we shall call the *conceptual model*, and it defines the operationalization of the variables involved and their functional relationships. Part of the conceptual model may be the specification of relationships which are assumed to be absent, and this aspect of the definition of the model is crucial, since fixing the value of parameters at zero requires a far stronger assumption than allowing their values to vary. Block recursive path-analysis models (Land, 1969), for example, often involve the assumption of the independence of variables in the same block conditional on variables in prior blocks in the model. In other words, the correlations amongst variables in the same block are assumed to be spurious and simply the result of the causal influences of prior variables. Other conceptual models may involve constraints on variables of a different kind — for instance that the influence of one variable on another is the same for each of several sub-groups of individuals. The general applicability of a model depends on equality constraints of this kind, and they are implicit in many conceptual models (for further discussion of the notion of generalizability see Ehrenberg, 1975).

The link between the conceptual model and the data is afforded by the *statistical model*. This model is usually stated in algebraic form and its characteristics are important in several ways. First of all, the statistical model provides the means whereby the researcher may estimate the values of parameters of interest and also obtain an indication of the variability implicit in these parameter values (for example whether they are significantly different from zero or from each other). In order to achieve this end the researcher may be forced to make yet more restrictive assumptions than those involved in the formulation of the conceptual model. For example, estimating a regression coefficient by least squares involves the assumptions, among other things, that the variables are linearly related, that the cost of errors in estimation are symmetrical for over- and under-estimating, and that the residuals are independent of the predictor variables. Significance tests force the additional assumption that the residuals are independently normally distributed with constant variance. Since statements of this kind leave most of us cold, it is not surprising that there is a growth industry in assessing the robustness of model-fitting procedures (see for example, Mosteller and Tukey (1977) and Andrews *et al.* (1972)) and in defining where and when and which assumptions can be ignored with a degree of confidence.

Another important feature of the statistical model is that it is the benchmark against which the data are assessed. Whenever we calculate an index of goodness of fit (or perform a significance test for that matter) we are comparing data against a statistical model. Consequently, all tests and all model-fitting exercises are conditional on the validity of the statistical model itself. We all know that a zero product-moment correlation can mask a perfect curvilinear relationship (though how many of us have ever seen one of those, or even looked for that matter?) but the assumptions we make bite far deeper than that. Consider what we said earlier about the independence of residuals in least-squares regression. How plausible is this assumption when the predictor variables are measured at several points in time? More important still is the problem that we cannot test the assumption of independence of residuals in models fitted to panel data by recourse to the data alone. It just is not possible (except perhaps in rare, unlikely circumstances) to fit a model assuming independent residuals and then the same model with correlated residuals and compare the difference, for we come up against the identification problem again. This problem may be defined as too few independent pieces of information to estimate the unknown parameters, or more informally, getting a quart out of a pint pot. Hannan *et al.* (1974) put it this way:

we do not attempt to arrive at the appropriate error model inductively. Rather, the thrust of this chapter, and of the literature it follows, is to emphasise the practical impossibility of solving measurement problems inductively.

In these circumstances we cannot always appeal to the data for help in defining the right model; our aid comes from theory and our experience in a substantive area of research.

Now let us broaden our concept of goodness of fit a little. We have seen how confirmatory analysis involves assessing goodness of fit between statistical model and data. Another source of mismatch or badness of fit is between the conceptual model and the statistical model. This gives us two quite independent criteria for assessing the adequacy of a statistical model: we look for a statistical model that fits the data well and also for a statistical model that fits the conceptual model derived from theory. Blind pursuit of statistical significance marks one extreme position by its exclusive emphasis on fitting a statistical model to the observed data. An example of this kind of approach to data analysis is the fitting of polynomials to data for which simple linear relationships are inadequate and yet it is of little use to the researcher to know that an nth-order polynomial accounts for 99% of the variance in a dependent variable if no sense can be made of the resulting equation. In general, polynomials are a good way of opting out of the obligation for matching statistical model with conceptual model, in favour of accounting for more variance.

The adequacy of the link between statistical model and conceptual model is just as important a component of goodness of fit as the link between statistical model and data. Many false starts in research can be put down to the use of statistical models which do not capture the essence of the conceptual model. One example, taken from a very different area of research (psycholinguistics) is the use of an inappropriate analysis of variance model for testing hypotheses. Clark (1973) showed that many findings claimed in published papers disappeared when linguistic units were treated as random effects rather than fixed effects.

The literature on moderator effects provides another example of the widespread tendency to make type II errors (i.e. underestimating the size of effects) as a result of the unimaginative use of a wrong statistical model, namely that used in moderated regression analysis (Blood and Mullett, 1978; Jackson *et al.*, 1981). Moderated regression analysis was suggested by Saunders (1956) as a means of improving the prediction of variables by taking account of joint relationships amongst predictor variables. For example, recent work by many authors has considered the prediction of job satisfaction from perceptions of intrinsic job characteristics. Better predictions tend to be obtained if account is taken of the salience to the individual of these job characteristics, not just as an independent predictor but also in interaction with perceived job characteristics. Saunders' suggestion was that such interactions may be fitted by including cross-product terms in regression equations as follows:

$$Y_i = aX_i + bZ_i + cX_iZ_i$$

where Z_i is the supposed moderator variable. This procedure was supported by Zedeck (1971) in an important review of moderator-variable research and has now become almost standard practice.

How appropriate is the statistical model outlined above? What does it imply about the relationships among the variables of interest? First of all, the relationships between all three variables are linear, as one would expect. Secondly, the size of the relationship between X and Y depends on the level of Z as we want it to; and this is the sense of the interaction term in the model. The important thing, however, is the form of that interaction, for this crucially determines whether the statistical model which we propose to fit to the data is appropriate for our conceptual model.

The general form of the fitted surface given by our moderated regression model is shown in Fig. 4 (adapted from Saunders, 1956). Saunders describes it in these terms — "this model might be called the 'ruled surface regression' model — any line in the regression surface that is parallel to the XY or the YZ plane is a straight line" (p. 211). Thus at each level of Z, our moderator variable, the relationship between X and Y is linear. More important than this is the point that the change in the slope of the fitted surface is constant along any line parallel with the defining axes. Clearly we are talking here about a very restricted form of interaction, in fact the linear-by-linear component of the interaction

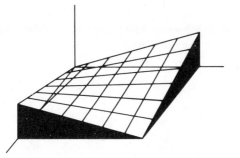

FIG. 4. The response surface fitted by moderated regression analysis.

between X and Z. This becomes clear when we see that each term in the equation above has one degree of freedom associated with it. The degrees of freedom for the X and Z terms contain the linear components of the main effects of X and Z, while the single degree of freedom for the interaction term contains *only* the interaction between these linear components. If our conceptual model also defines a linear interaction then the statistical model we have been talking about is entirely appropriate, but not otherwise.

Most predictions about moderator effects are couched in rather more general terms. By way of example we may take Hackman and Oldham's (1976) Job Characteristics Model in which those high on growth-need strength are predicted to show stronger correlations between job scope and job satisfaction than those low in growth-need strength. The strongest prediction one can make from this conceptual model is that the regression line for predicting job satisfaction from job scope should increase monotonically in slope (but not necessarily linearly) as growth-need strength increases. Threshold and ceiling effects are just as compatible with the Job Characteristics Model formulation given above as with the strictly linear interaction model of orthodox moderated regression analysis.

We conclude that the statistical model used to test hypotheses about moderator variables is not always the appropriate one, and that almost certainly its use will lead to the underestimation of effects. More generally, the goodness of fit between the conceptual model and the statistical model is a neglected but vitally important component in testing moderator effects. This problem of defining and fitting models of moderator effects is part of the much more general problem of exploring response surfaces. We need to know a lot more about how to do this in organizational research, and a good place to start is with reviews by Davies (1954) and Mead and Pike (1975).

3.   Summary

In the course of this essay we have considered many aspects of the interdependence of theory and method, and the fact that the two are interdependent is clear and inescapable. We have looked at the positive and negative implications of this relationship; but, inevitably, we have spent more time on the negative side of things — the missed opportunities and the misused orthodoxies — since here lie the greatest possibilities for progress in organizational research.

In considering issues of research design we saw how important it is in cross-sectional studies to define explicitly the plausible alternative models from existing theory before attempting to choose between them by appealing to the data. This dependence on theory makes many of us nervous, since one man's common sense is another man's prejudice; and two approaches were discussed for narrowing the range of alternative models which must be considered. One of these, the randomized experimental design, is seductively attractive in its elegance but seldom likely to be appropriate for answering questions in organizational research. Non-randomized quasi-experimental designs (of which, forms of panel design are a subset) are much more useful in many circumstances, but once again we must appeal to substantive knowledge in order to assess the vulnerability of any particular design to the various threats to internal and external validity (Cook and Campbell, 1979).

The rising popularity of the panel design illustrates at one and the same time a welcome increase in awareness of new possibilities not available with the cross-sectional design, and also a blinkered inefficiency resulting from an apparent insistence by many authors on asking the same old cross-sectional questions of longitudinal data.

The panel design offers the chance to look at change, and the chance to incorporate parameters reflecting latency, resistance and so on, but the literature on cross-lagged correlation analysis shows quite clearly that most researchers are not interested in these opportunities. It is almost as if the repeated sampling of the same individuals was no more than a replicated cross-section which coincidentally allowed matching of scores over time. Until we take time seriously in studies of this kind our use of the data obtained will be inefficient; there will always be more in the data than we are prepared to extract.

The same kinds of self-imposed limitations occur in the analysis of data itself. Of course, we cannot do without theory when we analyse our data—and we certainly should not try—but we shall seek out the technique which will answer the research question with the data we have, rather than define the research question solely in terms of the techniques that we feel at home with. In this respect, the organizational researcher can take no pride in being self-sufficient, for he needs the statistician's help in choosing the right tools and using them appropriately. When the statistician and the applied researcher meet on equal terms, each respecting the contribution the other can make, then we can look for a creative synthesis of theoretical conceptualization and research design and analysis. Meanwhile, much of our work is characterized by missed opportunities and misplaced optimism.

References

ANDERSON, E. (1960). A semi-graphical method for the analysis of complex problems. *Technometrics*, **2**, 387–392.

ANDREWS, D. F., BICKEL, P. J., HAMPEL, F. R., HUBER, P. J., ROGERS, W. H. AND TUKEY, J. W. (1972). *Robust Estimates of Location—Survey and Advances*. Princeton: Princeton University Press.

BARNETT, V. AND LEWIS, T. (1978). *Outliers in Statistical Data*. Chichester: Wiley.

BLOOD, M. R. AND MULLETT, G. M. (1978). Where have all the moderators gone? The perils of type II error. College of Industrial Management, Georgia Institute of Technology.

BOCK, R. D. (1976). Basic issues in the measurement of change. In D. N. M. Gruijter and L. J. T. van der Kamp (eds), *Advances in Psychological and Educational Measurement*. London: Wiley.

BRUNTZ, S. M., CLEVELAND, W. S., KLEINER, B. AND WARNER, J. L. (1974). The dependence of ambient ozone on solar radiation, wind, temperature and mixing height. *Proceedings of the Symposium on Atmospheric Diffusion and Air Pollution, American Meteorological Society*, 125–128.

CAMPBELL, D. T. (1963). From description to experimentation: Interpreting trends as quasi-experiments. In C. W. Harris (ed.), *Problems in Measuring Change*. Madison: University of Wisconsin Press.

CHERNOFF, H. (1973). The use of faces to represent points in k-dimensional space graphically. *Journal of the American Statistical Association*, **68**, 361–368.

CLARK, W. W. (1973). The language-as-fixed-effect fallacy: A critique of language statistics in psychological research. *Journal of Verbal Behavior*, **12**, 335–359.

CLEGG, C. W., JACKSON, P. R. AND WALL, T. D. (1977). The potential of cross-lagged correlation analysis in field research. *Journal of Occupational Psychology*, **50**, 177–196.

COOK, T. D. AND CAMPBELL, D. T. (1979). *Quasi-experimentation: Design and Analysis Issues for Field Settings*. London: Rand McNally.

DAVIES, O. L. (1954). *Design and Analysis of Industrial Experiments*. Edinburgh: Oliver and Boyd.

DAVIS, J. A. (1978). Studying categorical data over time. *Social Science Research*, **7**, 151–179.

DUNCAN, O. D. (1975). *Introduction to Structural Equation Models*. New York and London: Academic Press.

EHRENBERG, A. S. C. (1975). *Data Reduction*. London: Wiley.

EVERITT, B. S. (1978). *Graphical Techniques for Multivariate Data*. London: Heineman.

FINNEY, D. J. (1974). Problems, data and inference. *Journal of the Royal Statistical Society, Series A*, **137**, 1–22.

FISHER, F. M. (1966). *The Identification Problem in Econometrics*. New York: McGraw-Hill.

GOLDSTEIN, H. (1979). *The Design and Analysis of Longitudinal Studies*. London and New York: Academic Press.

GNANADESIKAN, R. (1977). *Methods for Statistical Data Analysis of Multivariate Observations*. New York: Wiley.

GOODMAN, L. A. (1973). Causal analysis of data from panel studies and other kinds of surveys. *American Journal of Sociology*, **78**, 1135–1191.

HACKMAN, J. R. AND OLDHAM, G. R. (1976). Motivation through the design of work: Test of a theory. *Organisational Behavior and Human Performance*, **16**, 250–279.

HANNAN, M. T. AND TUMA, N. B. (1979). Methods for temporal analysis. *Annual Review of Sociology*, **5**, 303–328.

HANNAN, M. T., RUBINSON, R. AND WARREN, J. T. (1974). The causal approach to measurement error in panel analysis: some further contingencies. In H. M. Blalock (ed.), *Measurement in the Social Sciences*. Chicago: Aldine Press.

HILTON, G. (1970). Causal inference analysis: A seductive process. *Administrative Science Quarterly*, **15**, 44–54.

JACKSON, P. R. AND STAFFORD, E. M. (1980). Work involvement and employment status as influences on mental health: A test of an interactional model. Paper presented at the BPS Social Section Conference, University of Kent at Canterbury, September 1980.

JACKSON, P. R., PAUL, L. J. AND WALL, T. D. (1981). Individual differences as moderators of reactions to job characteristics. *Journal of Occupational Psychology*, **54**, 1–8.

KENNY, D. A. (1975a). A quasi-experimental approach to assessing treatment effects in the non-equivalent control group design. *Psychological Bulletin*, **82,** 345–362.

KENNY, D. A. (1975b). Cross-lagged panel correlation: A test for spuriousness. *Psychological Bulletin*, **82,** 887–903.

LAND, K. C. (1969). Principles of path analysis. In E. F. Borgatta and E. W. Bohenstedt (eds), *Sociological Methodology 1969*. San Francisco: Jossey Bass.

LAZARFELD, P. F. (1948). The use of panels in social research. *Proceedings of the American Philosophical Society*, **92,** 405–410.

McNEIL, D. R. (1977). *Interactive Data Analysis*. New York: Wiley.

MEAD, R. AND PIKE, D. J. (1975). A review of response surface methodology from a biometric viewpoint. *Biometrics*, **31,** 803–851.

MOSTELLER, F. AND TUKEY, J. W. (1977). *Data Analysis and Regression*. Reading: Addison-Wesley.

NIE, N. H., HULL, C. H., JENKINS, J. G., STEINBRENNER, K. AND BENT, D. H. (1975). *Statistical Package for the Social Sciences*. New York: McGraw-Hill.

PELZ, D. C. AND ANDREWS, F. M. (1964). Detecting causal priorities in panel study data. *American Sociological Review*, **29,** 836–848.

PELZ, D. C. AND FAITH, R. E. (1973). Detecting causal connections in panel data: January 1971–December 1972. Interim Report No. 3, Causal Analysis Project. Surrey Research Centre, University of Michigan.

ROGOSA, D. (1980). A critique of cross-lagged correlation. *Psychological Bulletin*, **88,** 245–258.

SAUNDERS, D. R. (1956). Moderator variables in prediction. *Educational and Psychological Measurement*, **16,** 209–222.

SIMONTON, D. K. (1977). Cross-sectional time series experiments: some suggested statistical analyses. *Psychological Bulletin*, **84,** 489–502.

SMITH, G. L., MICHIE, C. AND POPE, J. A. (1978). Robust estimates of location. *Bulletin in Applied Statistics*, **5,** 8–21.

STAFFORD, E. M., JACKSON, P. R. AND BANKS, M. H. (1980). Employment, work involvement and mental health in less qualified young people. *Journal of Occupational Psychology*, **53,** 291–304.

TUKEY, J. W. (1977). *Exploratory Data Analysis*. Reading: Addison-Wesley.

TUKEY, P. A. AND TUKEY, J. W. (1980). Methods for direct and indirect graphic display for data sets in three and more dimensions. Proceedings of RSS Conference on Looking at Multivariate Data, Sheffield, 1980.

WANG, P. C. C. (Ed.) (1979). *Graphical Representation of Multivariate Data*. New York and London: Academic Press.

YOUNG, J. W. (1977). The function of theory in a dilemma of path analysis. *Journal of Applied Psychology*, **62,** 108–110.

ZEDECK, S. (1971). Problems with the use of "moderator" variables. *Psychological Bulletin*, **76,** 295–310.

8 The Research Enterprise

IAIN MANGHAM

The purpose of this essay is to provide a framework for the description of human behaviour which will be of use in understanding how the relationship between a researcher and his subject/coparticipant is initiated and sustained. The framework, which generally reflects my interest in the notion of "negotiated order" (Strauss, 1963, 1977; Bucher and Stelling, 1969; Bucher, 1970; Stelling and Bucher, 1972) is derived from a number of theoretical perspectives, the three most important being: exchange theory — particularly that branch of it reinforced by the work of Homans (1950, 1961, 1967); symbolic interactionism as reflected in the work of Mead (1934), Blumer (1969), Goffman (1959, 1961, 1967, 1969, 1972, 1974) and Strauss (1977); and, somewhat less clearly, the work of Weber (1968), notably that aspect of it which depicts society as a network of meanings. Strong if somewhat muffled echoes of phenomenological thinking may also be discernible, as may vague tinklings of other even more distant influences. After a somewhat abstract introduction to the framework, I will attempt to ground the rest of the essay in substantive issues illustrating the points I wish to make by reference to my own experience of the research enterprise. I will conclude with some comments upon the implications of these ideas for the practice of research in organizational psychology.

The relationship between the researcher and his subjects or co-participants may be seen as an example of what Allport (1962) terms "collective structure". When two people encounter one another there is some possibility that each can benefit the other; for each the contact with the other affords the opportunity to satisfy some need or achieve some end not capable of satisfaction or not achievable in isolation. Exchange theory, for such it is, rests on the assumption that people seek that which is rewarding in their lives and that they will seek to avoid that which is punishing. At root, the argument runs, behaviour is the product of conditioning and the working out of basic psycho-social needs. For Homans, and others adopting this perspective, human beings strive to satisfy their needs by entering into negotiation and bargaining with other men in a manner which resembles a marketplace barter. In subtle and not so subtle ways, men exchange aspects of their mutually exclusive advantages over one another so that each derives some measure of that which he seeks, while at the same time each is instrumental in the other achieving some measure of his interests. Social life, from this perspective, may be seen as a mutuality of satisfactions deriving from negotiation around individual needs.

Such a perspective, though unacknowledged, clearly informs Friedlander's (1968) paper on the nature of research relations. Following Berne (1964), he notes that "research may be viewed as a transactional game in which both researcher and subject co-operate, each with unexpressed (and frequently different) motivations, and each expecting and receiving some payoff" (p. 493). In a diagram (Fig. 1) similar to that used by Berne to depict parent–adult–child transactions, Friedlander outlines some of the potential transactions between researcher and subject.

The three horizontal levels of transaction range on a crude continuum from "experimental (make-believe) role behaviour" at the top to "outside-reality oriented (authentic) behaviour" at the lower part of the diagram. The hope and expectation of the researcher is that the subject will perceive him as authentic and respond in a genuine and authentic way (line RP–SP). Friedlander notes that the subject may perceive the researcher as playing a less than authentic role and may, as a consequence, respond in several ways which likewise may be termed "inauthentic". He also notes that difficulties may arise when the researcher and the subject are not playing the same game. If, however, the transaction is at the RP–SP level, "something highly constructive in terms of participation, learning and action may evolve". Whatever the level of interaction, however authentic, the framework is clearly and explicitly based upon notions of exchange. Successful transactions are characterized by "payoffs" to both parties; the payoffs to the researcher are

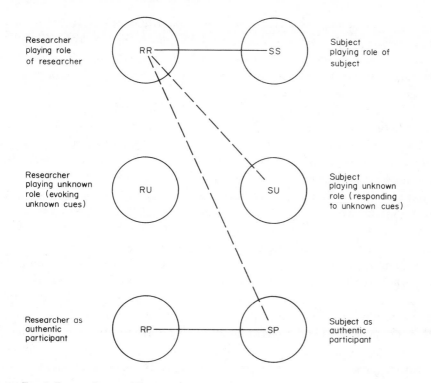

Fig. 1. Researcher–subject transaction in the conventional research paradigm.

generally those stemming from his role of social scientist — "acquisition of data in order to prove or disprove a hypothesis, recognition from his scientific colleagues, the acceptance of publications, or approval from superiors within his own institution" (p. 495). For the subject, on the other hand, since such payoffs are likely to be a matter of indifference, his payoffs may include "pleasing the experimenter and receiving his favourable evaluation . . ., satisfying his social needs . . ., and using the experimental situation for a variety of cathartic needs". These needs and purposes, notes Friedlander, though informing the whole process of interaction between the researcher and his subject, are rarely confronted by either party.

Friedlander uses the framework to explore the nature of the researcher/subject relationship, arguing throughout for a more inclusive participative approach to problem-exploration and problem-solving. "Subjects or clients who are treated as inert . . . cannot be expected to understand, accept or even care about alien descriptive analyses of a problem" (p. 502). A better payoff for all concerned, he argues, in the sense of greater mutual learning and beneficial change, will arise in circumstances where the transactions between researcher and client are "participative and confronting".

Whether he is right or wrong or, indeed, what is meant by words such as "participative" and "confronting", which on the lips of some social scientists seem to serve little more than an incantatory function, need not concern us at the moment. What does concern us is that Friedlander's paper is one of the few available that implicitly applies exchange theory, even if he does not refer to it as such, to the nature of the relations between researcher and subject. Such a framework has the strength of indicating that individuals are not simply the creatures of Fate, the playthings of the gods; rather from this perspective, man is depicted as an active agent with his own interests, needs and goals and an orientation towards achieving them. Secondly, the framework emphasizes that relations, and thus order itself, are negotiated and negotiable; man typically enters into negotiations with other men who have their own interests and goals and who are similarly motivated to achieve them. Depending on a whole range of factors—situation, resources, abilities, power and so forth—different measures of success or failure in the pursuit of self-interest will result (Mangham, 1979). Thirdly, the emphasis upon serving one's interest, the very idea of "games-playing", reinforces the idea of man as agent, man the cognitive, the calculating, the manipulating being, constantly thinking, planning and evaluating his behaviour and that of others. Transactional man, as implied in the Friedlander/Berne/Homans framework, is a variant of "economic man" who attempts to control the market-place, his competitors and his own manoeuvrings to his own advantage.

Now I happen to think that Friedlander and those writers upon whom he relies have got it about half right; the relations between researcher and subject *may* indeed be characterized as a transaction, a negotiation, a product of barter and manoeuvring. But while such a view may be a necessary element of a framework, in and of itself it is not sufficient. It rests heavily upon the notion of conscious, rational, calculating social actors. There is an underlying assumption in such a framework that a *preliminary* convergence of interest occurs because each actor in the situation anticipates that the other can benefit him and each has a similar notion of how this can be accomplished.

Exchange theory *assumes* that actors have needs and goals, *assumes* that they know what they are and *assumes* that at the onset of an encounter, the initiation of a relationship, each actor will attempt to structure his own behaviour and that of others present so as to achieve his own ends. Such a perspective pays scant attention to the problematic nature of much interaction. In many circumstances and particularly in research activities, no one is quite clear what is going on and who, if anyone, is deriving benefit from the activity. Almost by definition, research deals with uncertainty (or ought to) and my experience of relations with subjects/clients is not such that I would characterize it as a relatively unproblematic working-out of needs on the part of everyone or indeed of anyone involved in it.

So our framework needs something else which, while tempering the excessive emphasis upon rational, need-driven behaviour, does not do violence to the underlying force of the exchange analogy. Symbolic interactionism may provide a way forward in that some of its advocates hold that understanding between social actors occurs not as a consequence of factors external to the encounter — such as goals and needs — but rather as a result of "interpretive work" (Blumer, 1969; Hewitt, 1979). From this perspective order is improvised rather than negotiated. In this respect, if in no other, symbolic interactionists have a direct link with Max Weber (1968) who held that all social action depended upon interpretation: "Action is social insofar as by virtue of the subjective meaning attached to it by the acting individual (or individuals), it takes account of the behaviour of others and is thereby oriented in its course" (p.4). From such a perspective, the world is essentially without meaning and since there is no reality waiting to be discovered, any sense of reality, any understanding, that arises between myself as researcher and my subject/client is not preordained. Rather it is the product of an intricate and occasionally subtle process of improvisation in the course of which I proffer my identity, suggest courses of action and respond to his identity and his proposed courses of action. Our mutual understanding of the research relationship arises *from* our interaction, rather than *for* either of us, being entirely antecedent to it. Such a perspective renders encounters very much more problematic than that of basic exchange theory with its stress upon the rational negotiation of need satisfaction. A dash of interactionism, a hint of ethnomethodology (Garfinkel, 1967), provides the corrective and enables us to acknowledge that in a number of encounters — and research activities must surely be prominent among them — a significant part of the interaction is concerned with seeking to establish what really is going on.

One more element needs to be added before I turn to a more detailed examination of the research relationship. I have proposed that a basic exchange model tempered by a hint of symbolic interactionism will serve to analyse human interaction. I have suggested that social actors improvise relationships (not necessarily, or even often, consciously) but that improvisation and even more conscious negotiation is complicated since social actors may not only bargain about the satisfaction of needs and the achievement of personal goals, but may become involved in mutual definition of the situation such that needs and goals arise from it. Encounters have to be "made sense of" *before* we can even understand our needs, let alone satisfy them. Making sense of the world takes time and requires indulgence; interaction is not always marked by swift transactions in which each party achieves his or her ends and rapidly departs. We make sense of encounters by allowing them to unfold, interpreting and reinterpreting as we go along. In this respect interaction, particularly problematic interaction such as occurs between the researcher and his subject, may be compared to a play. Goffman (1959) has recourse to the theatrical metaphor in much of his work and it is worth turning to him for a moment:

Almost anyone can quickly learn a script well enough to give a charitable audience some sense of what is being contrived before them. And it seems this is so because ordinary social intercourse is itself put together as a scene is put together by the exchange of dramatically inflated actions, counteractions and terminating replies. Scripts even in the hands of unpracticed players can come to life because life itself is a dramatically enacted thing. . . .   (pp. 71–72)

Elsewhere (Mangham, 1979) I have commented extensively upon theatrical models of reality; for my present purpose, however, I wish to concentrate upon the phenomenon of the charitable audience. My contention is that charity does indeed begin at home; just as in the theatre it is highly unusual for a member of the audience to rise to his feet and challenge the claims to identity proffered by a particular actor, so in the drama of social life, it is equally unusual that anyone will offer an open challenge to our assumption and projection of certain roles. Indeed, as Goffman notes, when exceptions do occur and events contradict, discredit or otherwise throw doubt upon someone's claim to identity, participants "may come to feel ill at ease, nonplussed, out of countenance, embarrassed, experiencing the kind of anomy that is generated when the minute social system of face-to-face interaction breaks down" (p. 12). Goffman notes that preventative practices are constantly employed to avoid these embarrassments and that social actors go to great lengths to compensate for discrediting occurrences that have not been successfully avoided. Putting on a poor performance is to be avoided at all costs and, if unavoidable, "tact" demands that we act charitably to save the face of the other. It could be argued that the exercise of tact is conditioned by a desire to ingratiate oneself with other "performers for purposes of exploitation" or from loyalty as well as from a "desire to avoid a scene". Whichever, there appears to be in social life, in addition to interpretation and negotiation, a form of "willing suspension of disbelief", just as there is in the theatre. We each perform the function of a charitable audience to the other and are expected so to do if the very nature of social life itself is not to be threatened. As Lasky (1980) writes:

The one decisive factor which most impresses itself on any observer of these unedifying intellectual tergiversations in our time is *the will to believe* or, more accurately, *the will to be deceived*. Somewhere among all our endowed natural instincts, between (say) primordial curiosity and the so-called death-wish, there is a deep-seated desire to be gulled, hoaxed, hoodwinked, or otherwise cozened and cheated. Our species loves the specious. Dark corners of the psyche long for the fraudulent. Bamboozlement is part of the *condition humaine*.   (pp. 81–82)

Perhaps Lasky is overstating it. For my own part I want to assert nothing more, nor less, than that the processes of transaction, exchange, improvisation or negotiation between social actors occur within an overriding charitable suspension of disbelief which has, in Goffman's own words, an almost moral quality. Even if I do not perform my part as a researcher well, I can probably rely on you not to draw explicit attention to my shortcomings since we both recognize, however dimly, that social life has a fragile quality and is dependent upon both defensive and protective practices. What is more, your "tact", your co-operation in saving my face, creates an indebtedness such that, if necessary, I will exercise tact and co-operate to shore up your performance as a subject. Thus we collude and conspire to sustain encounters and to afford each other a degree of interactive security. Mutual bamboozlement sustains social life and gives an edge to each and every problematic encounter.

To summarize my argument so far: social life consists of a series of interlocked behaviours—elements of collective structure—through which an individual seeks to reduce equivocality, satisfy some personal need or achieve some specific goal, in exchange with other individuals similarly seeking satisfaction. The rational, economic nature of relations implied in such a framework is tempered by the recognition that at the onset of and during an encounter we seek to discover the "meaning" of it and by the fact that each of us, recognizing the gamble of interaction, the labour of creating understanding and the difficulty of pulling off a particular performance, indulges in mutually self-supporting conspiracies. We rarely challenge the identities proffered by others since so to do would be to invite challenge to our own identities, and, possibly, to cause the embarrassment of a total breakdown of the interaction.

In terms of the research enterprise, the proposed framework enables me to depict the researcher and the subject as each having possible interests and to the extent that they have such interests, each striving to realize them by managing those aspects of his performance which he considers will ensure their realization. For example, I may consider that in order to gain access to senior managers in a corporation, it would be worthwhile to present myself as a clever, rational, organized being (on the assumption—probably mistaken—that the denizens of higher office are of this ilk). Such a performance may, for me, be difficult to bring off, but in attempting it at all, I am relying on the fact that if my identity is in jeopardy, my subject will see enough potential benefit in the interaction for himself not to challenge my self-presentation. In essence I am claiming that all is not reason and cold calculation, rather that social actors mutually recognizing their shared precariousness conspire to suspend disbelief.

No doubt the not infrequent references to performances, audiences, actors and the like have alerted readers to the fact that my proposed framework is also heavily influenced by the dramaturgical perspective on social life. As I have stated with reference to the basic exchange model, all social action is oriented by the account the actor takes of the other; the social actor in pursuit of his own ends is aware of others and trims and shapes his own conduct in the light of this awareness. The specific contribution of the dramaturgical perspective to this discussion is my contention that Ego—the acting individual—can only become aware of Alter's definition of the situation, can only take Alter's behaviour into consideration, if Alter actually *behaves*. In other words,

Ego can trim and shape his own performance only to the extent that Alter's perceptions are dramaturgically available. The interactive world is without meaning. Meaning is created and sustained by an exchange of definitions of the situation.

> In a very fundamental sense, there is a presumption on the part of both actors that if one shows such an activity and speaks such words, they will lead to such a definition of the situation, and the interaction will be based on these definitions. Hence, each actor in a social situation must take the necessary pains to dramatize his subjective experiences, his "intentions" as he wants them to be defined or "taken account of".
>
> (Perinbanayagam, 1974, p.535)

To illustrate this last point, I invite you to consider the following exchange between myself and a senior manager. I have spent some time seeking to establish trust between us and now present the following question:

Self: What is your impression of the working of the top management team? (Presented as innocently as possible.)
Respondent: In what way? (Somewhat guarded.)
Self: Well, as a relative newcomer to it, presumably the style of operating, the flavour of discussions make some sort of impact upon you. How would you characterize them? (Seeking to present my definition that it is appropriate to talk about such issues with me.)
Respondent: Let's just say that they are "interesting" discussions, shall we? (Implying my probing will be unwelcome.)

I move on and, *for the moment*, we mutually define the situation as one in which it is not appropriate to pursue such issues. We have both taken account not only of the explicit statements we each made but also of the paralinguistic and non-verbal cues which occurred during the interchange. We each know and understand each other's actions because, in effect, we act them out, we dramatize them. My performance implies a part to be played by my respondent; he, in turn, either falls in with my casting and acts out the part assigned to him or — as is the case above — proffers another role for himself (and, implicitly, for me) and causes me to modify my performance, albeit temporarily.

The illustration, in fact, moves us forward a little bit too quickly. Let me return to the basic framework and seek to utilize it, to describe the research enterprise as it may unfold. Imagine, if you will, one novitiate researcher, Ego, and one novitiate subject, Alter. Ego is interested in, say, the distribution of influence within organizations and is to approach Alter with a view to having him comment upon patterns of influence as he sees it within his own company. It is unlikely that either party will approach the encounter without some degree of preparation; Ego will probably have undergone some training in the role of the researcher. He may have carefully thought out what he wants from Alter and may have structured a series of questions for him or, alternatively, he may have decided to conduct a relatively low-structured session. Either way he will probably realize that he must establish a good relationship with Alter if he is to get anything out of him: he will probably have decided that simply to walk in to Alter's office, flop down in a chair and demand "Now tell me who influences what around here" will not be productive. He may therefore have considered it necessary to dress appropriately and to comport himself in the manner to which he assumes Alter has become accustomed. Furthermore, he may decide to ease himself into the interview, to exchange small talk, to be sociable or whatever before moving into the sensitive areas he wishes to explore. In effect—though Ego may not be aware of it—he is seeking to present himself as straightforward and trustworthy, someone to whom confidences may be divulged, someone genuinely seeking knowledge and such a performance, if brought off, may constrain Alter to play the complementary part and to satisfy Ego's needs.

Alter, on the other hand, may have glanced in his diary, seen the appointment and wondered what it was all about. He may have had a note about it from his Managing Director or someone else and he may, as a consequence, have given the matter some thought. More likely than not, however, the subject matter of the interview will not have been previously discussed with him, and the phrase "patterns of influence"— if made available—will mean little to him. Thus, for Alter, the projected interview is problematic. He may decide to "play it by ear", or he may seek to find out from others who have been interviewed as part of the same project what it is all about. Either way he is likely to be less well-prepared for the session than is Ego. The latter has access to his researcher script either through coaching from his supervisor and colleagues or from textbooks, the former has no script readily available to him and may have to rely on experience of other types of interview, and the patterns of behaviour he has been party to in other one-to-one interactions.

From the onset of the encounter, therefore, the participants are involved in negotiating not only the substance of the questions but in exchanging definitions of the meaning of the situation. Ego may begin by outlining his area of interest and may even invite Alter to question it: "Does that seem reasonably clear to you?" Whether or not he does question it at that stage, for both Ego and Alter part of the ensuing interaction will be concerned with what really is going on. However structured his approach, Ego, as a good researcher, will want to be open to leads he discerns throughout the interaction, will want to "follow up" certain issues and will, at times, be at a loss as to where to go next with his questioning. Alter, on the other hand, may be seeking to discern what Ego is really after, may be trying to be as helpful as possible in what he takes to be Ego's purpose or, conversely, may for reasons clear or unclear to himself be intent upon frustrating these assumed purposes. He may not even be able to understand the language used by Ego and may, as a consequence, get hold of the wrong end of the stick or otherwise flounder in his role as subject. Either way, more frequently than not within a framework of mutual conspiracy not to challenge each other's performances, Ego and Alter exchange definitions and negotiate temporary working agreements as and when they respond to the overt dialogue between them.

Such a view, of course, begs the all-important question of how the would-be researcher, Ego, comes to be sitting opposite Alter at all. In my experience if Alter is a relatively low-level employee, there is little problem in securing an interview with him/her or having him/her fill out questionnaires. Providing more senior members of the organization can be persuaded that it will not take up much time and that the results will not be directly attributed to their organization, they are often willing to facilitate the study. Where the researcher wishes to study more senior people, however, and where the issues he wishes to study are of some consequence to these people, access is unlikely to be granted. It is worth noting that while there exist literally hundreds of studies of schoolchildren, students, blue-collar employees, blacks, the disadvantaged and the like from dozens of perspectives, there is no more than a handful of studies of powerful élites from any perspective. Nader (1974), an anthropologist, makes the point cogently in urging her colleagues to begin "studying up", suggesting that they:

might indeed ask themselves whether the entirety of fieldwork might not depend upon a certain power relationship in favour of the anthropologist, and whether indeed such dominant subordinate relationships may not be affecting the kinds of theories we are using. What if, in re-inventing anthropology, anthropologists were to study the colonizers rather than the colonized, the culture of power rather than the culture of the powerless, the culture of affluence rather than the culture of poverty?

(Nader, 1974, p. 289)

The central problem about "studying up", researching into the powerful and the affluent, rather than into the relatively powerless and the poor, is that of access. As Nader puts it, "the powerful are out of reach on a number of different planes: they don't want to be studied; it is dangerous to study the powerful; they are busy people; they are not all in one place, and so on". As an organizational psychologist, I can but concur; élites can and do deny access to themselves. However happy they may be for you to study their employees, their rate-payers or their constituents, they are rarely delighted that you should study their own activities. Such a position, while disheartening, is understandable and, from the perspective of the powerful, quite reasonable. What are they going to derive from the study other than possible exposure and potential embarrassment? It may be instructive for each of us to put ourselves in their shoes for a moment and ask "What's in this research for me?". I would contend that few organizational psychologists ask this question of themselves on behalf of their clients and that the failure to address this issue results quite often in the denial of access. All too often we appear to assume that we have a right to know and appear to think that reciprocal relations are for others. At its most extreme, this takes the form of "Here are a series of questions I want you to answer on a series of observations I wish to make. I am not going to tell you what this is all about because if you know that it will contaminate my findings, nor, in the interests of scientific objectivity, will I allow you to comment upon my findings until they are published. In any event you will not be able to understand them". It does not take a genius to recognize that you need to be in an extremely powerful position to negotiate or demand that sort of relationship; such a relationship, perhaps, as some have with students, shop-floor employees, prisoners and the disadvantaged?

To some extent, access is dependent upon the identity that is proffered to the potential subject/client. Offering a definition of myself as a social or organizational psychologist creates a different response to that which occurs when I volunteer my services as a professor or as a management consultant. I tend to be seen as more worthwhile in the latter identities than the former; Professor of Management is an identity which, for many senior people in organizations, is worthy of some further exploration. Status and perceived relevance of the proffered identity can be important counters in the initial stages of a research interaction. Reputation is clearly another feature which informs preliminary contacts; where I have been approached as a result of a recommendation from some third party, I have usually found it easier to negotiate some satisfaction of my needs than when I have made the initial canvass of the subject myself. Experience is another element of proffered identity which may weigh heavily with the potential host organization. My own experience as a senior manager has made it much easier for me to secure access to other senior managers; my service as a teacher has made me more welcome to teachers, and my informed interest in the theatre has facilitated my contacts with actors and directors. Perhaps beyond all of these elements of identity, however, is the one feature which may make the difference between being accepted and being rejected. And that is my own predilection to assume a specific posture towards my subjects; my desire to play my part in a certain style and, in so doing, to cast others into complementary roles.

My observation of myself and others leads me to suggest that there are four major parts or roles that are adopted by organizational psychologists, each, no doubt, stimulated by personal needs and each with consequence for at least the initial encounter with potential research participants. The first part assumed by many is that which I am tempted to term disparagingly the "boy-scientist". For present purposes I will simply term such a person as a *Scientist* with a capital *S*. Scientists tend to present themselves as controlling, objective, distant, dominant and expert. They give the impression that they have carefully designed the research project, that they know what they are doing and that questions as to purpose and method will not be tolerated or, at best, treated with condescension. Almost the polar opposite of the Scientist is the researcher who gives the impression of being ingratiating, excessively deferent and apologetic, willing to take personal abuse and to be treated with contempt. He gives little impression of being in control of his own destiny and none of having worked out what he is about; such a person I will label the *Subservient*.

Between these two extremes stand my other two types, the *Independent* and the *Participant*. The former presents himself as non-hostile, non-controlling and non-submissive; he gives the impression that he has something to offer in return for which he is willing to negotiate with his subjects. The Participant is a somewhat similar presentation with the distinction that he — unlike the Independent — makes joint commitment the central aspect of his relationship with his client. He acts so as to cast his subjects (an inappropriate word, in his view) into the role of co-researchers. The Independent does not go so far; he sees the expertise in research as his own and is less willing to share it with his subjects.

My underlying interest in spending some time in looking at the various roles assumed by would-be researchers is in understanding how it is that some encounters come to be regarded as worthwhile by all concerned and some do not. I want to understand the factors which may affect the negotiation of order within the research enterprise; to this end I have suggested four forms of self-presentation which may have significant consequences for the course of research relationships. Before turning to these consequences I wish to return to the notion of personal goals and needs which I introduced in the earlier paragraphs of this paper. While in no way wishing to become an advocate of "need psychology", it is possible to speculate that the major types of self-presentation outlined above may be related to certain conscious or unconscious interpersonal needs. Our ideal types can be distinguished according to the dimensions of interpersonal process identified by Schutz (1966): inclusion, control and affection. For Schutz — as for Homans and others in this and related traditions — needs, desires, forces, call them what you will, constitute the basis of all human interaction. They may be seen to drive the individual unconsciously towards some self-presentation or towards some aspect of behaviour. Alternatively, behaviour may be seen to be the result of conscious calculation; the individual perceives the social situation and formulates behaviours which maximize his benefits in terms of inclusion, affection and control.

Whichever way, conscious or unconscious, Schutz's dimensions of behaviour may enter into all encounters, including research ones. The Scientist may be characterized as high on control (exerted by himself) and low on inclusion and affection: he is keen to remain outside the relationship, as it were, and displays little need for warmth. The Independent is neutral on control, and shows little need for inclusion and little for affection. The Participant will probably manifest a high need for inclusion and for affection and a moderate need for control (shared with others). The Subservient will display high need for control (exerted by others) and high need for inclusion and affection (though he may not be offered it).

Whether or not such "needs" are enduring and fundamental is, of course, a matter of dispute. My purpose in bringing them into consideration is to offer some speculation as to whether or not differences in inclusion, control and affection need influence self-presentation and, in so doing, influence the entire nature of the research enterprise. A substantial part of the interpersonal literature argues that two people will work at optimum efficiency when their interpersonal needs complement each other (Schutz, 1966; McCall and Simmons, 1966). What this implies and what the basic notion of exchange implies is that a researcher and a subject will derive optimum benefit from an encounter when their self-presentations are complementary. Other things being equal, the subject who will best get along with the Scientist will be one who defers, who does not need affection and who is happy not to be included. The subject who will best get along with the Participant will be one who wishes to be included, who seeks affection and is, himself, moderate on control. The Independent should derive maximum benefit from a subject who is, in turn, neutral on control, but who can operate without warmth and inclusion. The Subservient will need someone high on inclusion, control and affection: a rare combination.

Here we begin to move into even wider speculation. "Studying up" may be difficult for the Subservient because members of élites may, almost by definition, be those who are moderate to high on need for control (for themselves) and low on affection and inclusion. The Scientist may have difficulty because of his high need for control which will conflict with his subject's needs in this area, and the Participant, although able to cope with the control dimension, will be disappointed in the affection and inclusion areas. Arguably the only person able to cope interpersonally with the study of élites is the Independent since his "needs" may complement those of all but the most controlling of his potential subjects.

Now I do not wish to overstate my case. I am arguing that interpersonal orientations as manifested in self-presentation may affect the initial research encounter, not the least because first impressions are important. Once the initial relationship has been negotiated, however, it does not necessarily persist since, as I have argued, "needs" and goals arise during interaction and affect the course of the encounter. Thus although the initial self-presentation is important, it does not necessarily *determine* the subsequent interaction. I am not, however, arguing that such factors are the only ones involved in the negotiation of research.

Clearly the nature of the research itself has an impact but is not, in and of itself, the major element in the negotiation. Research in organizations involves people and in this sense is rarely neutral; thus who is to do it and with whom becomes a critical feature of the negotiation. One final speculation before passing on to consider other factors which may influence the negotiation of the research enterprise: since all the world is a stage and since "scripts, even in the hands of unpracticed players, can come to life" (Goffman, 1959, p. 72), is it not possible to conceive of a circumstance where the would-be researcher can choose which role to adopt in a particular circumstance? In other words, none of us need be permanently cast as hero, villain or fool; Scientist, Independent, Participant or Subservient. We may indeed be disposed to play certain parts, may be experienced in only a limited range, but that need not restrict our repertoire for all time. Given the fact that in any social situation Alter will respond to that which is made dramatically available to him and that there appears to be a deep-seated willingness to suspend disbelief, most of us could make a reasonable attempt at varying our self-presentation to suit the circumstance.

In effect I am arguing that Schutz's interpersonal "needs" are not needs at all but parts to be played; if I see that my subject presents himself as one who wishes to share control (or whatever), I can choose from my repertoire an appropriate response. Neither I — nor, for that matter, he — need be constrained by our genes to respond in only one fashion. As a dramaturgical theorist, I can envisage researchers (and others, for that matter) as remaining detached from the roles they perform and "coolly alternating" presentations of self each time they enter a new situation. However, such speculation takes us a long way from the present discussion; suffice it to say that I am putting forward the notion that the researcher can control information about himself, can define situations by controlling his own self-presentation. Some situations in everyday life require more extensive interpretations, calculation and "self-work" than do others; the initial research encounter is one such situation.

A number of other commentators have attempted to characterize the roles open to researchers, though none, to the best of my knowledge, have done so in terms similar to those I have employed. Junker (1960), for example, notes that there are four roles open to the researcher using the method of participant observation. Two of these roles — complete participant and participant observer — employ an element of subjectivity, empathy and comparative involvement with the subjects. Such roles imply, in Friedlander's (1968) and Schutz's (1966) terms, a relatively inclusive process. Junker's other two roles—observer as participant and complete observer—imply a degree of distance and comparative detachment. Conceivably such roles could also be played by the subject (though Junker himself does not consider this possibility).

The adoption of a particular role can, of course, lead to problems. The literature is full of examples of researchers who have become so involved with their subjects/clients that they have found it not only difficult but undesirable to draw back from them. Such an outcome, of course, can be depicted as a consequence of a process of negotiation or as a result of the researcher not being clear as to his own needs in the circumstance. Many so-called "action-researchers" find that their role becomes more orientated towards consultancy and less towards collecting data as the project upon which they are engaged gets under way. Explicit negotiation of role, what Friedlander terms "confronting the relationship with the subject/client", can make this transaction a subject of discussion rather than an accidental and often regretted occurrence.

As I have indicated, in some circumstances the negotiation between the researcher and subject is of a very different order and may be influenced by a whole range of factors. Differences between researchers and their subjects (who in the field of organizational psychology tend to be practitioners of one kind or another) often give rise to conflicts and to negotiations which make it difficult for the particular relationship always—or even often—to be fruitful. McNaul (1972), writing about relations between physical scientists and practitioners, makes a number of points which are equally valid in the social sciences. He notes six areas of potential conflict—evaluation of knowledge, methods of communication, time frame, uniqueness versus patterns, the degree of finality of knowledge and the use of environmental controls. In particular he notes that the researcher is often motivated by the chance to increase knowledge, whereas practitioners have an equally strong motivation to apply knowledge. Thus I as a researcher may be interested in the behaviour of a particular group of powerful individuals for what it tells me about the nature of power with no end other than the advancement of knowledge. The manager, on the other hand, is much more likely to be interested in learning about the dynamics of "his" team in order that he may operate more effectively within it. Likewise, I may be happy to devote months, even years, to the study of power (or some aspect of it), whereas a manager measures the use of his time in days, if not hours. I may be interested in the managers' team behaviour as examples contributing to a pattern. Some researchers, by no means all, are interested only in the particular insofar as it can be seen to fit and enlarge the pattern. Practitioners, on the other hand, may be more concerned with the specific and the particular events or circumstances with which they find themselves and may thus be much less tolerant of those who seek to discern principles and laws. Equally, for many researchers, scientific knowledge is never final; it is always open to further refining and modification. Practitioners are generally less interested in such a stance of professional if passionate scepticism and seek to apply what is known with a conviction and finality it may not warrant.

Glatt (1968) gives a clear account of the problems inherent in this kind of interaction when he notes the mutual misunderstanding which occurs when the researcher, unable to imagine in what way the practitioner could contribute to his research design, interacts with the practitioner, unable to perceive what the "scientist" is getting at. Thus, from a number of perspectives, the relationship between a Scientist and a "traditional" practitioner may be difficult to initiate, let alone sustain.

The negotiated order between researcher and researched may be further complicated by the specialized techniques, skills and frameworks that the researcher brings to the situation. Tests, questionnaires, attitude scales, etc. often, not always, tend to exclude the client or subject from any meaningful involvement in the problem-exploration and problem-solving process. As Friedlander (1968) notes: "In this sense the more esoteric and sophisticated the specialization, the more vulnerable it is to impotence due to the non-involvement of those for whom its benefit is introduced."

I believe it to be incontestable that subjects or clients who are treated as so much computer fodder cannot be expected to understand, care about or accept the resultant analyses of problems, let alone to implement the suggested remedies, if any. In effect, such activities imply a "negotiation" whereby the researcher is allowed to play his role as Scientist and the subject is expected to play his part as a docile and relatively inert being around whom various manipulations are made and from whose reactions a number of inferences are drawn. Not surprisingly, few with the power to resist such "games" actively engage in them; quite aside from the ease of access is it not to be expected that most of what passes for research in organizational psychology is "negotiated" with students and low-level employees? Those who may challenge the game are studiously avoided by those who seek to perpetrate it.

Thus the research enterprise is the product of the needs of each party and in particular of the posture adopted by the researcher. By and large, he who would have access to relatively private data needs to negotiate a very different relationship with his subject than does he who requires no more than public data. He who would treat subjects as relatively inert needs to acquire a pool of inert, docile souls upon which to experiment. If, on the other hand, he wishes to penetrate the public front of, say, an organization, the researcher must recognize that which many in the organization subconsciously if not consciously recognize: that

a study that purports to deal with social structure . . . inevitably will reveal that the organization or community is not all it claims to be, not all it would like to be able to feel itself to be. A good study, therefore, will make somebody angry.   (Becker, 1964)

He must be prepared to negotiate a very different kind of relationship if he wants to succeed in making someone very angry indeed.

Either way, whether in exclusive "game"-playing research or inclusive approaches, the process of research may fruitfully be depicted as a negotiating of reality, a complex system of bargains to be struck between individuals and groups. It may be characterized by an asymmetry of power (most organizational psychologists are one-down in the power stakes and feel they must accept whatever crumbs are thrown their way by sponsors), and it may be marked by a desire to remain detached from the subjects or by a desire to become almost one with them. Whichever, the relationship is a shifting one wherein to a greater or lesser extent those party to it express their needs and purposes and manoeuvre so as to have them satisfied at the least cost to themselves.

Finally, the depiction of the research enterprise as characterized by the negotiation and improvisation of reality has implications for the intending researcher. The practice of organizational psychology is unlikely to be advanced by either sociologists or psychologists armed with batteries of theories and cases of questionnaires. What is needed is more intimate familiarity with the processes which occur within organizations which, in itself, can only come by gaining access to the "backstage" regions (Goffman, 1959). Such access is not granted easily and is often dependent upon an explicit exchange between those party to it.

Unfortunately, few of those who purport to be organizational psychologists have anything to offer in return for access and few of those who have something to offer have interests in the development of organizational psychology. This circumstance can, however, be rendered less unfortunate if the intending researcher is prepared to abandon his "scientific" stance and enter into a collaborative relationship with his potential client; if, for example, he is prepared to reveal what he is seeking to discover and enter into a discussion as to how such discoveries would be of help to the subject or client. Lacking the experience and the ability to help directly with the manager's problems, the would-be researcher can none the less offer a collaboration which may create opportunities for mutual benefit.

Such an orientation, of course, with its heavy emphasis upon working with people, argues that skill in handling social relationships is a necessity for researchers. Interestingly enough, few social or organizational psychologists have any direct training in social skills — some interviewing sessions, perhaps, but often little else. If it is accepted that much of what comes out of a research enterprise is dependent upon the nature of the interaction between the researcher and his subjects or clients, it follows that the training of researchers will need to encompass much more of the dynamics of such interactions and correspondingly much less of questionnaire design, statistical manipulation and the like. Training in counselling and consultancy would appear to be as worthwhile as training in computer programming and research method.

The research enterprise in social science is a social process. It is not a process in which a detached observer studies activities unaffected by his or her presence; even in physical science this is not the case, one cannot dip one's foot in the same river twice. The organizational psychologist must recognize the dynamics of the circumstance in which he finds himself as he seeks to initiate and prosecute his research and, if he is to be successful, he must seek to capitalize upon this recognition.

Approaching senior members of organizations as a supplicant with a begging bowl will ensure that you are treated as a beggar and, perhaps, that you be given some crumbs for your comfort. Approaching them with the confidence that you have a trained ability to describe and analyse and, more importantly, a conviction that the utilization of those abilities in helping to resolve organizational problems is not intellectual prostitution, may result in very different outcomes.

References

ALLPORT, F. H. (1962). A structuronomic conception of behaviour: individual and collective. *Journal of Abnormal and Social Psychology*, **64**, 3–30.

BECKER, H. S. (1964). Problems in the publication of field studies. In A. Vidich, J. Bensman and M. R. Stein (eds), *Problems in the Publication of Field Studies*. New York: Wiley.

BERNE, E. (1964). *Games People Play*. New York: Grove Press.

BLUMER, H. (1969). *Symbolic Interactionism*. Englewood Cliffs: Prentice Hall.

BUCHER, R. (1970). Social process and power in a medical school. In M. Zald (ed.), *Power in Organizations*. Nashville: Vanderbilt University Press.

BUCHER, R. AND STELLING, J. (1969). Characteristics of professional organizations. *Journal of Health and Social Behaviour*, **10**, 3–15.

FRIEDLANDER, F. (1968). Researcher-subject alienation in behavior research. In E. Glatt and M. W. Shelly (eds), *The Research Society*. New York: Gordon and Breach.

GARFINKEL, H. (1967). *Studies in Ethnomethodology*. Englewood Cliffs: Prentice Hall.

GLATT, E. (1968). In E. Glatt and M. W. Shelly (eds), *The Research Society*. New York: Gordon and Breach.

GOFFMAN, E. (1959). *The Presentation of Self in Everyday Life*. Garden City: Doubleday.

GOFFMAN, E. (1961). *Encounters*. Indianapolis: Bobbs-Merrill.

GOFFMAN, E. (1967). *Interaction Ritual*. New York: Aldine.

GOFFMAN, E. (1969). *Strategic Interaction*. New York: Ballantine Books.

GOFFMAN, E. (1972). *Relations in Public*. New York: Harper and Row.

GOFFMAN, E. (1974). *Frame Analysis*. Cambridge: Harvard University Press.

HEWITT, J. P. (1979). *Self and Society*. Boston: Allyn and Bacon.

HOMANS, G. (1950). *The Human Group*. New York: Harcourt Brace.

HOMANS, G. (1961). *Social Behavior: Its Elementary Forms*. New York: Harcourt Brace.

HOMANS, G. (1967). Fundamental social processes. In N. J. Smelser (ed.), *Sociology*. New York: Wiley.

JUNKER, B. H. (1960). *Field Work: An Introduction to the Social Sciences*. Chicago: University of Chicago Press.

LASKY, M. J. (1980). 1917 and all that. *Encounter*, **54**, 79–82.

McCALL, G. J. AND SIMMONS, J. L. (1966). *Identities and Interactions*. New York: Free Press.

McNAUL, J. P. (1972). Relations between researchers and practitioners. In S. Z. Nagii and R. G. Corwin (eds), *The Social Contexts of Research*. New York: Wiley Interscience.

MANGHAM, I. L. (1978). *Interactions and Interventions in Organizations*. Chichester: Wiley.

MANGHAM, I. L. (1979). *The Politics of Organizational Change*. London: Associated Business Press.

MEAD, G. H. (1934). *Mind, Self and Society*. Chicago: University of Chicago Press.

NADER, L. (1974). Up the anthropologist — perspectives gained from studying up. In D. Hymes (ed.), *Rethinking Anthropology*. New York: Random House.

PERINBANAYAGAM, R. S. (1974). The definition of the situation. *Sociological Quarterly*, **15,** 521–541.

SCHUTZ, W. (1966). *The Interpersonal Underworld*. Palo Alto: Science and Behavior Books.

STELLING, J. AND BUCHER, R. (1972). Autonomy and monitoring on hospital wards. *Sociological Quarterly*, **13,** 421–446.

STRAUSS, A. AND SCHATZMAN, L. (1963). The hospital and its negotiated order. In E. Freidson (ed.), *The Hospital in Modern Society*. New York: Free Press.

STRAUSS, A. L. (1977). *Mirrors and Masks: The Search for Identity*. London: Martin Robertson.

WEBER, M. (1968). *Economy and Society*. New York: Bedminster Press.

9 Research as Action: Usable Knowledge for Understanding and Changing the *Status Quo*

CHRIS ARGYRIS

Social scientists believe that the purpose of their research is to describe reality so that the order that they assume it contains can be understood and explained. Successful prediction is the test and the fruit of valid description and explanation. Social scientists also believe that their research should ultimately be useful to human beings throughout the world. They are the first to admit, however, that it takes a long time for rigorous descriptive-explanatory research to add up to, and become especially relevant for, producing knowledge about new and liberating alternatives.

I should like to advocate that the barriers to progress in applicability of social science knowledge are at least as much related to certain taken-for-granted views about "normal science" methodology as they are related to the inherent complexity of the subject matter. More specifically, the axiom that social scientists should conduct research that is descriptive-explanatory and the technology to assure internal and external validity appear to contain inner contradictions that make it highly unlikely that social scientists will produce usable knowledge about genuine liberating alternatives.

In making the argument, I am not allying myself with those who appear to condemn the necessity for empirical research that adheres to the requirements of: (1) public disconfirmability or falsifiability; (2) causality; and (3) elegance (valid explanatory theories that combine simplicity with comprehensibility). I believe empirical research should strive to approximate these features for two reasons. First, as social scientists we must be vigilant about testing the validity of the knowledge that we produce. Second, if human beings are to increase the effectiveness of their actions they also require skills in testing their views, in understanding their own and others' causal responsibility, and they, too, require parsimonious models that can be used to understand complexity in everyday life as it is occurring. In other words, some of the most basic requirements for the conduct of social science research may also be basic to human beings' effectiveness in designing and implementing their actions in everyday life (Argyris, 1980).

This leads, I hope to show, to a paradox. The paradox is that the research methods presently used to conduct rigorous research appear to lead to conditions that inhibit the production and the falsifiability of useful knowledge, especially if that knowledge challenges the *status quo*. Yet one reason for rigorous research methods is to facilitate falsifiability and a reason for scientific research is to encourage an ever-expanding inquiry into the universe.

This paradox may have remained unwittingly covered up by the present conceptions of rigorous research that polarize basic from applied research. To be sure, many basic researchers will support the position that both types of research are needed. But this olive branch misses the boat and reinforces the *status quo*. It misses the boat because most applied researchers also aspire to be rigorous and hence they strive to follow the established technology of rigorous research. It reinforces the *status quo* because too often applied researchers define their problems in terms of the existing universe and hence remain within the confines of the *status quo*. If the purpose of knowledge is to inform the everyday citizen, then there can only be basic research and that research may have to have additional and different features from those presently used.

There are two intellectual fields from which the argument draws heavily. One is the literature on rigorous research methodologies; the other is a theory of action about individuals and systems. I will assume that the readers are familiar with the first and will introduce some concepts from the latter below.[1]

1. A theory of action perspective

The theory of action perspective assumes that human beings hold designs in their heads about how to manage their actions in order to achieve their intentions. Actions are behaviours imbued with meanings. The designs are largely culturally taught and maintained. Individuals therefore are able to design actions within the constraints to which their societies socialize them.

Understanding or explanation and prediction are key processes in everyday life but they are penultimate; they are necessary but not sufficient for taking action. Taking action is the ultimate and most basic activity of human beings. When people take action, they typically do it under severe time and resource constraints. The world does not slow down to give them all the time they need. Moreover, other human beings are interacting with them who have their own intentions which may include modifying their actions. All these features add up to the proposition that is so basic it is probably an axiom: the environment is always significantly more complex than the individual's information capabilities. Hence, individuals must decompose the complexity into manageable sub-parts and use external aids such as external memories to assist them in their information-processing (Simon, 1969).

One way to deal with these complexities is for human beings to come to a situation with a master design about how to manage their actions. Schön and I have found that people may hold two types of master designs. One is the theory they espouse and the other the theory that they use (theory-in-use). Both of these theories are maps about effectiveness. Effectiveness is defined as accomplishing one's intentions in such a way as to continue to do so in the future. Embedded in this requirement is the capacity to learn to detect and correct error. We define learning as those activities that lead to a match between intentions and outcomes or those that lead to the detection and the correction of a mismatch. Note that learning is not simply inquiry. Learning occurs when inquiry leads to action that produces a match, or if a mismatch, to action that detects and corrects the error.

We have found much variance in individuals' espoused theories, much variance in their behavioural or action strategies, and almost no variance in their interpersonal theories-in-use. That is, individuals who are young or old, male or female, white or black, rich or poor, powerful or powerless, may hold different espoused theories; they may act differently but their interpersonal theories-in-use do not seem to vary. We find similar results with individuals from Africa, South America and India. But these results may be due to the fact that most of our clients from these locations have been educated in universities dominated by American–West European traditions and thought.

We have developed a model of this theory-in-use and have called it Model I. Model I theory-in-use has several major components. The first is the governing values which actors strive to satisfy. They are: (1) control the purpose of the situation; (2) minimize losing and maximize winning; (3) suppress negative feelings; and (4) emphasize rationality. These values are never fully actualized. They do act as the foundation for the design of actions. The second component is the action strategies. Two of the most frequent action strategies observed are: (1) advocate one's position while unilaterally controlling others (in order to win and not lose); and (2) save one's own and others' face, usually through unilateral and covert action (in order not to produce negative feelings). The third component is the consequences of the governing values and the action strategies on the behavioural environment. For example, action strategies combined with the governing values create a defensive environment (e.g. conformity, low trust) which in turn leads to miscommunication, ineffective problem-solving and decision-making.

People appear to realize that a map for action must be necessarily incomplete because they rarely, if ever, have all the time that they require to get all the information that they need. Also, the very act of collecting information may induce others to alter their intentions and their actions. Individuals appear less aware that one of their key skills is designing for valid ignorance and valid attention. Their theories-in-use tell them what to pay attention to and what to ignore. Hence, Model I informs the actors to advocate their position and strive to control others so that they will not lose. Model I also alerts the actors to expect that from others and informs the actors not to make these strivings and expectations discussable. Model I does not encourage advocacy combined with inquiry, nor does it encourage the creation of valid information of informed choice.

If the above is valid, then Model I would encourage people to detect and correct those errors that are routine and that do not require changing the underlying values of the theory-in-use. Such learning is called *single-loop learning*. It is like a thermostat that knows how to detect when the room is too cold or too warm. If the thermostat ever asked why it was set at 65 degrees or why it was measuring heat, that would be *double-loop learning*. Double-loop learning occurs when, in order to correct error, the underlying assumptions and values are questioned and altered.

So far, the maps people use to take action appear to be low on precision and high on accuracy. Low precision means that the maps may contain highly subjective views, metaphors, guideposts or heuristics that may be organized in a loosely coupled manner. Accuracy is defined as the degree to which the individual is behaving effectively. Effectiveness, the reader may recall, is achieving one's objective or solving problems in such a way that they can continue to be handled.

Human beings may strive to make up for low precision and to achieve high accuracy by on-line iterative learning. That they do not succeed as well as they intend is evident by all the problems that can be observed in everyday life. But the failure, I suggest, is only partly due to the feature of using maps with low precision or trying to perform on-line iterative learning. The failures are more related to the theories-in-use they hold to accomplish their activities. People hold theories-in-use that make matching more likely for the routine, programmable, non-threatening issues. The more the issues involved are threatening, complex, and require changing basic values and underlying designs, the greater the likelihood of escalating error, self-fulfilling prophecies, and self-sealing processes. (A self-fulfilling prophecy is making something come about and a self-sealing process is being unaware of having made a self-fulfilling prophecy.)

2.   The type of knowledge that social scientists strive to produce

Let us now examine the features of the knowledge social scientists produce and package. We aspire to produce knowledge that is high on precision and high on accuracy. Precision is more important at any given moment than accuracy because the latter can be increased through the additive feature of the knowledge that we produce.

Precision usually means quantitative specification of the invariant relationships between or among the relevant variables. In order to produce quantitative data, it is necessary to extract from reality in a way that leads to precise definition of abstract concepts. In order to produce propositions about invariant relationships, one must select a few of those concepts and plot their relationship quantitatively. This usually results in statements such as "X is some quantitatively specified function of Y".

It can be shown that to accomplish the above, social scientists frequently uncouple variables that are coupled and couple variables that are uncoupled in the action context (Argyris, 1976b; Brunswick, 1955). The concepts that are quantified often no longer contain the meanings that are understood and used in everyday life.

Moreover, propositions that X is some quantitative function of Y are information-rich. In order for human beings to use such propositions to design and implement their actions in a given situation, they would have to identify X and Y from all other variables and then identify the specific points on the graph on which they are located. By the time they accomplish these tasks, the events may have passed them by or others may have become upset or bewildered by their trying to slow down the pace of everyday life in order to use an abstract model. Such reactions may lead the others to react differently and hence to change the meaning of the situation.

Take, for example, the research on leadership. Stogdill (1974) has codified systematically most of the empirical research. Note two important features about that knowledge. First, as Stogdill points out, it is not additive. After fifty years of research, it is very difficult to find propositions which, when combined, account for more than 20–30% of the non-random variance. Moreover, as he and others note, the additivity is highly unlikely because researchers are using different theories, concepts, and operational definitions. The assumption that precision should dominate accuracy in any given research project because the latter will increase as knowledge becomes additive is questionable.

Secondly, let us assume the opposite. Let us say that the leadership research accounts for all the variance. What does a leader do with it? The way it is packaged, it is doubtful that it could be stored and retrieved under on-line conditions. The leader would have to use an external memory (i.e. a book). But the very act of referring to a book in front of those being led could alter the situation significantly. For example, if human beings used the rigorous knowledge as presently packaged in the handbook on leadership, they would require a high degree of unilateral control over others. Not surprisingly, this is the condition under which most of social science knowledge is produced—i.e.

under conditions where the researcher maintains unilateι
over the subjects (see Campbell and Stanley (1963) on ma.
internal validity).

For example, leaders using Fiedler's (1967) contingency apprι
would have difficulties if they told their subordinates that they wι
using a particular leadership style because, let us say, the task uncertainty was high and the quality of the interpersonal relationships was
low. Or, if someone were trying to change the minds of an audience,
they would be advised to present both sides of the issue if the audience
was composed of primarily bright people. If the audience contained
people who were not so bright, then only one side of the issue should be
presented. If human beings who used these propositions told the audiences why they were behaving towards them as they were, they might
anger the "dumb" group or put off the "smart" group which may be
smart enough to interpret such comments as buttering them up
(Argyris, 1980).

3. The type of knowledge that human beings require in designing and implementing their actions

Human beings, in order to design and to take action, require social
science knowledge that is understandable, retrievable under on-line
conditions, high on accuracy and low on precision, yet which is highly
generalizable, publicly disconfirmable, and whose validity is not dependent upon unilateral control by the actor over others.

These are not easy requirements to fulfil, especially with our commitment to public disconfirmability, causality and elegance. Knowledge
that is "understandable" will require a knowledge of the sociocultural
conditions. Cognitive psychology may help us to understand what
information, and in what form, the human mind can organize, store
and retrieve while cognitive sociology and anthropology may tell us the
probable meanings that will be stored and the way the environment
reinforces them.

Lewin (1940) represents one of the few models of how to develop
knowledge that may be low on precision and high on accuracy. Elsewhere (Argyris, 1980) I have tried to show how the original autocratic-
democratic climate studies contained some of the key features of knowledge that is low on precision yet can be used to produce accurate

results. I also attempted to show that the follow-up studies by Lewin's colleagues (Lewin *et al.*, 1939), which were done in order to make the original studies more rigorous, may have produced knowledge that was so distant from the action context that it would be unlikely to contribute to accuracy as much as it contributed to precision.

The gatekeeper concept is an example of a concept that is low on precision and high on accuracy. Briefly, Lewin constructed a genotype situation where there are superiors and subordinates, where the latter cannot achieve their goals without going through the gate controlled by the superiors, where no one can go through at any time that he or she wishes, and where the goals are important to all the actors involved. Lewin depicted the situation as follows:

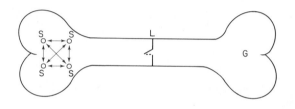

FIG. 1. Gatekeeper. S = Subordinate; L = leader; G = subordinate's goals.

Lewin stated that under these conditions one could predict that the subordinates would become leader-centred and dependent, that they would compete against each other to get through the gate, that within- and between-group rivalries would occur. These predictions should hold for any such situation: the superior could be a boss, a parent, a teacher, a minister, while the subordinates could be workers, children, students, or parishioners. Furthermore, there should be no exceptions to these predictions. If exceptions were found, they should become tests of the theory (because, for example, a set of conditions obtained which, once realized, make it possible to show that the exception is a test of the theory).

Lewin's topological drawings could have the features that make it possible for the human mind to organize, store, and retrieve complex sets of knowledge. For example, I think of the picture as a dog bone and that, in turn, makes it easier to retrieve the remainder of the findings. Moreover, it is easier to communicate to others by using these graphics.

Many felt that Lewin's models were not mathematically rigorous but were useful graphics. But what the critics may have overlooked is that the graphics may be more than pictures; they may hold some of the keys to packaging generalizable knowledge in ways that it is understandable, easily retrievable, and easily usable in everyday life.

4. Co-operative subjects may not be able to reveal key features of selves and their environment

Researchers have always known that subjects may be unable or unwilling to provide valid responses to their questions. One reason may be that the research settings may be threatening, uncomfortable, or that the results may be threatening, or that the subjects may see no particular payoff for them. Researchers have developed many ways of handling these problems, ranging from sampling, to more effective designs, to greater attention for the needs of the subjects (such as debriefing). A second reason is related to the subjects' apparent inability to describe their actions because they are taken for granted. Yet what is taken for granted may be the most important features of the universe. Researchers have developed more sophisticated ways to observe subjects in everyday non-contrived settings and then to interrogate them on what they may have been taking for granted.

There is a third domain that has surfaced recently with the development of intervention research where the purpose is to understand the *status quo* with a view to altering it. We have found, in addition to the two causes of invalidity just described, that individuals and social systems may have characteristic ways of dealing with basic changes in their world that they are unaware of. They become aware of these ways of dealing with change when the attempts at change are real. Unless the requirements of effecting this change threaten individuals' sense of competence as well as the equilibrium of their social systems, they may never become aware of how they would react under these conditions. (Yet such knowledge is necessary if social science is to have a complete picture of the *status quo*.)

I am not referring simply to the observation that people know more than they can tell, which may be overcome by observing individuals in "difficult" situations (including changes in their world) and then interrogating them to explain their actions. I am referring to conditions where people are required to design and implement actions that have not, up until now, been achievable and hence they do not have the individual skills nor do they have the necessary societal support. For example, many organizations have "living systems" at the middle and upper levels where people experience conformity, mistrust, and minimal risk-taking which in turn makes it difficult to have effective problem-solving on issues that are basic and threatening (Argyris and Schön, 1978). Many of these people evaluate these living systems as counterproductive. Yet there are few cases where genuine change attempts have been tried, and even fewer where there has been evidence of success. Two of the most important reasons for the failure are the inability of individuals to learn the skills to produce conditions of trust, candidness and risk-taking under on-line conditions, and the lack of organizational support for such changes (Argyris, 1976a, b).

Why it is that people have difficulty in learning these skills, even if they understand them, if they want to learn them, and if they are given the proper opportunity to practise them, especially intrigues us. An example is the case of Y that has been used a dozen times with groups from 20 to 120. In all cases, the members have learned (at the espoused level) a new model (called Model II) which, if implemented, could lead to double-loop learning. The members are given a short verbatim transcript of Y's conversation with X. To date, all the participants have evaluated Y's action strategies in such terms as "dogmatic", "coming on too strong", "unilateral", "authoritarian", and "unilaterally judgemental". We have then asked the participants to write a scenario of how they would help Y to behave more effectively with X. In all cases, the written scenarios may be described as judgemental, authoritarian, dogmatic, and "coming on too strong". These evaluations are made by the participants as they read each other's scenarios. So we have "consultants" trying to help Y by using actions that they tell Y are counterproductive to helping X. The consultants are saying in effect, "Such and such behaviour should not be used to help others; I will use it to help you".

After there is consensus on the counterproductivity of the helping behaviour, the participants are asked to redesign their helping actions to reduce or eliminate the counterproductivity by using Model II which they have learned and which they are committed to use. Yet they continue to produce counterproductive actions even if they have several overnight opportunities to think about and redesign their actions (alone or in small groups). The staff then produces possible Model II action strategies which the class members identify as genuinely different and lacking the counterproductive features. Hence, what they have been asked to do is producible.

These results are predictible from Model I. The participants should not be able, if left to their own devices, to produce the new actions which are congruent with Model II. The reason is that it is not possible for people to produce meanings consonant with theories-in-use that they do not hold. The conscious design and production by a Model I participant of one Model II intervention would disconfirm this prediction.

What is it that the participants should not be able to produce? They should not be able, for example, to combine advocacy with inquiry in such a way as to enhance the Model II governing values of valid information, informed choice, and internal commitment to that choice. They should not be able to act in ways that their meanings are publicly disconfirmable. They should not be able to detect *and* correct double-loop errors. *And* they should be unaware of these features.

The feature of unawareness is important. If all actions are designed, if it is true that no one can knowingly design for error, then the unawareness must be the result of a design and it cannot be an error. Moreover, if unawareness is the result of skilful behaviour, then the actors must have automatic reactions that keep them unaware about which they are unaware! The feature of being unaware that one is unaware leads us to the domain of defences of human beings. Being unaware that one is unaware of the features that inhibit double-loop learning helps keep people relatively safe and simultaneously helps them to maintain a Model I world.

If I have a theory-in-use that leads me to produce error, if I am unaware of the error, then I hold an error-producing design, part of whose feature is to keep me unaware of my inability to produce actions that I desire to produce. Moreover, the defences that keep me unaware are societally sanctioned. Otherwise, the Model I world would be shattered.

Understanding the depth and scope of our theories-in-use and experiencing the degree to which they appear unalterable is, to date, an experience that most of our clients see as bewildering to frightening. Overcoming these features and learning new theories-in-use becomes a very bewildering learning experience because it begins with the dilemma that one must experience a genuine sense of failure in order to begin to succeed. These and many other features become important challenges which we are now able to help people achieve.

The point, however, is that none of these features (and others that have been published) could have been told to us by the respondents, neither through interviews nor through observation, nor could we have observed them if we were trying to understand the world as it is. They would not have been able to tell us because they would be unaware, and unaware that they were unaware. We would not have observed them because they would have no reason to produce them since they are programmed not to challenge their theories-in-use, nor society's theories-in-use, and because they are embedded in social systems that reinforce the unawareness.[2]

5. Conclusions

To the extent that the analysis made above is valid, there are several requirements that should be added to the social scientists' rules for, and skills in, conducting research. The first is that in order to describe the universe accurately and fully, we must also describe its innermost mechanisms against double-loop change. As we have seen in the example of Y, people are unaware of their mechanisms against double-loop change. Moreover, the environment in which they are embedded reinforces the unawareness and makes it unlikely that actions will occur that will surface these mechanisms. Hence, the only way to surface these individual and social mechanisms for change is to place people in situations where double-loop changes are required.

This requires that people be asked to learn about and to produce genuinely new alternatives. But researchers cannot design these possibilities unless they produce models of worlds that do not presently exist; hence, the need for normative theories. Also, they cannot help people to strive to move from here to there without becoming interventionists.

Secondly, the diagnosis and the movement cannot remain only at the espoused level. Evidence must be given that the individual and societal theories-in-use have been altered. The only way theories-in-use can be inferred is from actual behaviour. Hence, a critical basis for research is conversations and other actions whose meanings can be inferred and related to theories-in-use.

Intervention research, which combines description of the world as it is in order to alter it, means that the researchers and the subjects are interacting for serious stakes. It is not a simple matter to consider learning new theories-in-use and to design new social systems. People will have to move from the role of subjects to clients. They will have to see that the research is of important value to them. Discovery for the sake of discovery will not be adequate motivation for them to participate. They will require some assurances that the result will at least not reduce their present effectiveness and that there is a reasonable probability for enhancing this effectiveness. These assurances need not be given at the outset; indeed, to try to do so would be foolish if not dishonest. Ways could be developed by which researcher and clients jointly monitor the progress and by which either group can stop the experiment.

Interventions to change theories-in-use are experiments. Admittedly, the researcher is not in unilateral control over the subjects. Nor is the researcher in control over the variables that may impact upon the situation. But this does not mean that *a priori* hypotheses cannot be stated in such ways that they can be falsified. Indeed, as has been shown above, it has been possible for us to tell people who are programmed with Model I theory-in-use that they will be unable to produce Model II interventions even when they understand the theory, they wish to do so, they have the opportunity to practise, and they can watch others do the same. People then attempt to produce Model II interventions and they are unable to do so.

Under these conditions, the criteria for disconfirmability are actually tougher than those typically used. In our case, predictions about how people will or will not act have been repeatedly disconfirmed even though the researchers have had little unilateral control over the situation, even though all the clients were aware of the predictions, and even though in many cases they disagreed with the predictions.

The clients will also seek the tough criteria because they want continuing evidence that they are not kidding or harming themselves or their social systems. Thus they will make demands of the interventionists that are much tougher than subjects make of researchers in the more descriptive studies.

Finally, the use of qualitative data to design and produce rigorous falsification suggests that a re-examination of the meaning of rigour may be important. Once application of knowledge is seen as the ultimate criterion, then it may be that rigour should mean high accuracy even though there is low precision. One is reminded of Von

Neumann's (1950) observation that the human brain differs significantly from the computer because it can operate accurately under conditions of lots of noise and with an apparently sloppy calculus.

Much of this depends upon developing powerful theories. These theories must be subject to as tough tests about their connectivity to the action context as they are about their inner consistency. Moreover, the nature and structure of the theories that we design should be consonant with the nature and structure of the kinds of theories people actually use. Such components as governing values, action strategies, and consequences are assumed to exist in the heads of individuals. If we try to teach them new theories-in-use, we must define new governing values, action strategies, and specify the consequences.

Finally, we also need theories of how to get from here to there. There is a dilemma that these theories of intervention and instruction must resolve. In order for people to produce new actions, they must have a new theory-in-use, such as Model II. But they do not have a new theory-in-use, and Model I theory-in-use acts to inhibit the learning of Model II.

Somehow we must find features in the old that can be used to help bridge to the new. One example of such a bridge is the concepts of valid information, disconfirmability, and implementation. People who hold Model I and II theories-in-use are able to understand this importance for effective action. Another set of important concepts are those of competence or effectiveness. People who hold Model I and Model II theories-in-use agree that creating actions that are counterproductive to their intentions is not a sign of competence or effectiveness. Finally, all the clients that we have dealt with also hold some common criteria for justice. For example, if I am a superior to Y and if I tell Y not to use certain behaviour to help others, and if I then proceed to use it, and if I ignore protestations of inconsistency (as was the case with Y above), then all of our clients to date would assert that I am creating a world of injustice. There appear to be embedded in the logics of producing valid information (which have been specified by logicians) the conditions for competence and justice. If this continues to be the case, then we have some very strong bridges to the new alternatives as well as reasons for conducting "action science" whose penultimate goals are explanation and prediction in the service of the ultimate goal, namely, implemental or usable knowledge.

Notes

1. In order to minimize repetitive references to my work, I will mention that my most recent view of normal science methodology is to be found in my book *Inner Contradictions of Rigorous Research* (1980). The views and research on theory of action may be found in Argyris and Schön (1974, 1978) and Argyris (1976a and 1976b).
2. This analysis provides some clues as to why most of the alternative schools that espoused Model II environments failed even when they had adequate funds, students and teachers who volunteered to join them, and the freedom to establish their curriculum and their organization (Argyris, 1974).

References

ARGYRIS, C. (1974). Alternative schools: a behavioural analysis. *Teachers College Record*, **75,** 429–252.

ARGYRIS, C. (1976a). *Increasing Leadership Effectiveness*. New York. Wiley Interscience.

ARGYRIS, C. (1976b). Theories of action that inhibit learning. *American Psychologist*, **31,** 638–654.

ARGYRIS, C. (1980). *Inner Contradictions of Rigorous Research*. New York and London: Academic Press.

ARGYRIS, C. AND SCHÖN, D. (1974). *Theory in Practice*. San Francisco: Jossey Bass.

ARGYRIS, C. AND SCHÖN, D. (1978). *Organizational Learning: A Theory of Action Perspective*. Reading: Addison-Wesley.

BRUNSWICK, E. (1955). Representative designs and probalistic theory in a functional psychology. *Psychological Review*, **62,** 193–217.

CAMPBELL, D. T. AND STANLEY, J. C. (1963). Experimental and quasi-experimental designs for research. In N. L. Gage (ed.), *Handbook of Research on Teaching*. Chicago: Rand McNally.

FIEDLER, F. E. (1967). *A Theory of Leadership Effectiveness*. New York: McGraw-Hill.

LEWIN, K. (1940). Formalization and progress in psychology. In K. Lewin, R. Lippitt and S. K. Escalona (eds), *Studies in Topological and Vector Psychology 1*. University of Iowa Studies in Child Welfare, University of Iowa Press, XVI, No. 3, No. 380, 9–42.

LEWIN, K., LIPPITT, R. AND WHITE, R. K. (1939). Patterns of aggressive behavior in experimentally created social climates. *Journal of Social Psychology*, **10,** 271–301.

SIMON, H. A. (1969). *The Science of the Artificial*. Cambridge: Massachusetts Institute of Technology Press.

STOGDILL, R. M. (1974). *Handbook of Leadership: A Survey of Theory and Research*. New York: The Free Press.

VON NEUMAN, J. (1958). *The Computer and the Brain*. New Haven: Yale University Press.

10 Emancipation and Organization

DENIS PYM

1. Values and orientations

Some time ago I began an article with the assertion, "Emancipation
provides the one continuing thread of idealism in psychology" (Pym,
1974). This claim was made more in hope than in realization and I cling
to it in the face of considerable odds. Little of consequence has occurred
in the name of either psychology or organizational psychology over the
past decade to dispute Illich's (1977) view of the featherbedding and
disabling preoccupations of professions.

My second theme provides the means for achieving the first, but it
also represents a shift in the focus of research and thinking, from the
study of organizations to a concern with organization. It is this theme
which needs elaboration and explanation and I shall leave the subject
of emancipation to later.

The quest for an alternative view of organization must, I believe,
hold closer to human nature, to man's whole being, than we have succeeded in achieving with bureaucracy in advanced industrial societies.
This position implies that the quest for "alternatives", as soft-energy
exponents are finding, is misleading. In our minds, primary sources
have more to do with fundamentals than alternatives. Too often the
search for "alternative organizations" leads us to those very distortions
which make for the current crisis. Different descriptions and labels do
not necessarily lead to different experiences. "Alternative" cannot
mean something with which we are unfamiliar, nor can it be some more

elaborate form of bureaucracy, nor can it be the same machinery favouring different class-ends. The search must start from fundamentals, from nature itself, from human nature.

My objections to orthodoxy are all of a piece.[1] They begin with the question of authority. Why is it that those who study organization prefer to locate authority in some abstract object out there — the Government, BP, the TUC, the BBC — rather than in man's head? Of course the question is politically naive. Nevertheless, from this choice the reification of organizations is practically inevitable. Better surely to deify man who built these edifices and must personally acknowledge them if they are to exist in any sense at all? Sociologists might be excused their anti-personal stance but not psychologists who claim the person as their concern and then go and direct their attentions to his artefacts or at best locate their attentions between man and his appendages in a concept-like role. In short, I am disputing the easy cop-out of those who live most comfortably with the label "organizational psychology".

The answer to the question, "Why locate authority outside man?" can be usefully pursued through an examination of the problematic relationship between nature and culture. This is not an orientation shared by the nature/nurture protagonists but is more familiar to some social anthropologists — I am thinking particularly of the French social anthropologist Levi-Strauss.

For industrial man there *is* no problem in the relationship between nature and culture. The belief in environmental mastery, the subjection of nature by culture is central to the culture of industrial literate man.

We have this value deeply ingrained in our academic tradition, in the conquest of reality by increasingly precise, abstract (written), concepts. But there is a catch in this view of the world. Man is also a part of nature, of this reality. The price we pay for the belief in environmental mastery is the conquest of our own natures. In Freudian terms, so unequal is the fight between Super-Ego and Id within the person of advanced industrial man that the old arbiter, the Ego, is of little consequence. It's a knock-out for Super-Ego depending on the intervention of neither referee nor judge. If man cannot believe in his own nature he can hardly believe in the nature of others. Our anti-personal stances derive directly from a lack of love for self. Pirsig (1976) thinks a lot of our troubles are a consequence of putting truth before good and I agree. It may be true that my behaviour can be explained by my level of intelligence, sexual potency, status, class, roles, the culture and structure of the organizations I work for and what you will, but such explanations do not elevate Pym they just reduce him.

So it is that the crises we acknowledge are those of our authorities and institutions, organizations out there, not the crises of our souls. Yet it is important to remember when New York and Gothenberg are facing "financial ruin", Italy and Britain are gripped by "the chaos of industrial unrest", governments in Latin America are tottering or inflation in the Argentine is running at x hundred per cent per annum, that the threat is nearly always worse than the reality. Because, whatever the mess we foist on ourselves through our public roles, the bulk of men and women are struggling through their everyday exchanges to make sense of their existence and order their own lives. The only crisis of organization "out there" is that industrial man suffers too much of it.

I fear the reader is still able to escape the implications of what I write. I shall labour the point a little. The public view of reality he and I share, for all the good things associated with it, leads to many of the insanities of our time and space. The very tradition which governs "legitimate" communication in academia, as it does in this book, requires self-denial and the elevation of other authorities — "evidence", "documentation", "founding fathers". The quantity of reference and deference will be inversely related to self-respect. In this race to hell, format Marxists and Positivists run neck and neck.

2.   The problematic relationship between nature and culture

Organization is natural to man but, because of his hostile view of nature, industrial man discounts this. He becomes insensitive to the natural origins of his cultural artefacts. Those insanities of organizations, which we widely acknowledge, grow, in the main, from the loss of contact between our cultural elaborations and nature. This break triggers organizational excess.

The stress on difference in social intercourse has cultural origins. It is also in part a response to the uniformity imposed by mechanical technologies which are burdened by some of our hostilities to nature because, in nature, we are all of the same species. Whatever our differences we have the same brain, same body, same sensory apparatus. True there are quantitative and qualitative differences between us in terms, for

example, of visual, auditory, olfactory, tactile, gustatory and extra-
sensory acuity but what are we to emphasize where and when—our
sameness or our differences?

Industrial man has no doubt: psychology is the study of differences in
behaviour. The task is to discriminate. To think about ourselves and the
world around us we need to distinguish between events. This fits in
nicely with our belief in the authority of the written word. Through
literacy the capacity to discriminate is practically limitless. I am not
stupid enough to question the value of thinking, but there must be a
limit to conceptualizing, bureaucratizing or whatever you like to call
it if nuances are not to become nonsenses. But without this hold on our
own nature, our capacities and inclinations, we don't know when to
stop. We lose our sensitivity for those limits. Abstractions are piled on
abstractions and then some academic gangsters invent "integration" or
"systems thinking" to plug the gap. But these panaceas turn out to be
more of the same. This kind of problem-solving, "the irrationality of
the rational" Marcuse (1964) called it, has all the characteristics of unauthentic ritual (Pym, 1978).

Literacy, the medium of middle-class industrial man, is, as McLuhan
(1964) tells us, an extension of a natural phenomenon, the eye. Our first
words have visual representations but more sophisticated words like
those in the terminology of organization theorists—"role", "motivation", "boundaries"—have no visual forms. These are abstract words
but they may still have natural, observable expressions. Humanistic
psychologists are particularly concerned about the way in which values
of the eye, like measurement, come to be imposed on our other senses. I
call this "sensory colonialism" because the effect of this imposition is to
reduce the values or quality of our other senses. If Laing (1960) is right
in proclaiming insanity as a sane response to an insane world then the
role of the all-powerful eye in much psychiatric art tells us a lot about
industrial society. Industrial society is a visual and literary culture
McLuhan says, and literacy, the life-blood of the edifices we call modern
organizations, is germane to our assertions of the authority of culture
over nature.

In the past decade we have seen visual representations, words for
naturally occurring phenomena, give way to abstractions in place
names, phone numbers, postal codes, regions and the rest. The same
developments can be seen in cultural pursuits—David Hockney links
the dominance of abstract art in recent gallery acquisitions to the

bureaucratization of art. Abstract art, he argues, is the art of bureaucrats.

The new EEC colour code for electrical cables aptly demonstrates the advance of disorder. To remind the reader, they are brown, blue and green/yellow. They have a scientific base. They make recognition possible for those who are colour blind. They also represent, I understand, a concession to the Germans who adopted the EEC code some time ago. No doubt the reader is impressed with the logic behind this new convention. The colour code it replaces is red (for danger), green (earth) and black (neutral). In most societies, equivalent to the percentage of people who aren't colour-blind, these colours carry the same meaning—they happen to derive their associations from nature. We have just replaced a meaningful convention which protects the interests of man with a dangerous nonsense which some fools somewhere will describe as progress.

I have been studying business rituals over the past 10 years (see Pym, 1973, 1978). Business doesn't make much of its rituals. We deny the emotional basis of activities we claim as rational. But business has many rites, the best of which are based on task, product, process or event. Again these are observable phenomena. Rites so based articulate meaning, reduce anxieties and enhance social cohesion. These are good rituals. But one effect of professionalizing the work-force has been the conversion of rites based on natural events and entities to those based on abstractions like budgets, accounts, cost reductions, job descriptions, plans and productivity. Examination of these newer rituals shows their lack of meaning and significance to the participants. They are unauthentic. The worst aspects of the "participation movement" include the attempts to get people more involved in such nonsenses.

I am using a range of examples to draw the reader's attention to the price we pay for ignoring the natural origins of cultural activities. Illich (1973) makes much of the convivial basis of those social orders he finds more satisfying than our own. But without "conviviality" the industrial order would not function. In a recent piece of research, Gorley (1978) found that concern with equity and reciprocity dominates even apparently instrumental activities like selling on commission. Tapes of transactions between buyer and seller revealed markedly little selling behaviour on the part of salesmen but, once the buyer had allowed the salesman to enter his network of association, they do show a great deal of effort put in by both parties to establish a relationship around the theme of two people trying to make some sort of sense of their situation.

Bureaucratic organizations depend on convivial relations to operate but they exploit these relations without nurturing them. Personal dignity and integrity are enhanced by social exchanges which allow some kind of balance between giving and receiving behaviours. Everyday relations between people allow opportunity for this balance to emerge, and if it fails to materialize we can always withdraw from the association. Within the prison of our occupational roles this opportunity is thwarted by the formalizing of giving and receiving activities. This is particularly true of bureaucratized welfare where the roles of giver (expert, professional, teacher, bureaucrat) and receiver (delinquent, sick, old, destitute, learner) are more or less fixed. The scope for reciprocity in exchange is denied by divisions of labour and controls. That is, imposed organization rides rough-shod over behaviour fundamental to human dignity. Every time the receiver of advice, clothes, attention or money goes through this experience he is reduced by it. Those in giving roles soon sense this dependence and cease to rate the receiver as somebody worthy of checking the efficacy of their services. Expert arrogance and ultimately disservice is inevitable (see Pym, 1980a). In a social setting where community relations are stronger, the survival of the self-employed doctor, social worker or lawyer depends much more on their capacity to provide a service and recognize the importance of equity in social exchange. By ignoring a fundamental feature of human transaction, bureaucratized welfare achieves conditions which are the reverse of those ideals sought by social welfare reformers who depend on the mechanisms of the state to achieve their aims.

The discussion so far on natural limits to organization has focused on issues of space but, in the context of Einsteinian relativities, space and time are as one. Mechanized time probably represents the single most powerful instrument of social control in industrial society. The success of centralized authority in getting man to synchronize his life to the mechanisms of the clock must number among its most remarkable achievements in coercion. So brainwashed are we that any other concept of time belongs to the realm of fantasy. Yet our complaints about the pace and pressure of modern life—the rat race—are not receding, quite the reverse. The extent to which we allow our lives to be divided between unrelated activities depends considerably on how we use time. In my studies of subterranean excellence the personal use of time and space, as against conventional use, is a distinguishing characteristic of those for whom we have high private regard (see Pym, 1974). Natural time involves discrimination between the seasons and night and day, for example. These have clock and calendar equivalents. Industrialization has fragmented time as well as space. Over the past six centuries significant time has passed from the day to the fraction of a second. Long before we get to the nanosecond but somewhere between the minute and the day, the organization of time becomes excessive for man.

These limits might be explored within the enterprise in a study of executive stress, for example. How does the notion of critical time vary between executives. Do they make appointments and undertake tasks by the day, half-day, hour or even quarter hour? A more human use of time would probably see the day as the critical unit and, with the technology available, this should be well within our reach now.

I have reviewed a mere handful of examples which show how man's condition can be elevated by formulating concepts of organization closer to nature and the nature of man. In essence this implies shifting authority away from the objective and abstract out there towards the subjective in here, from organization*s* to organization.

3. Technology and human nature

Much has been written by social scientists on the link between technology and organization*s*, rather too much of it on the techniques of production. Since most people now "work" in offices and the more recent electronic developments have a lot of relevance for home-based activities, our focus ought to be on communication technologies in and between employment and home.

The confusion surrounding technology comes in part from our visual and literary content-bound perspective. By and large, systems approaches and contingency models have added to that confusion (Pym, 1980a). Our interest in technology is in terms both of organization and emancipation. All technologies are cultural artefacts but the dominant technologies of industrial society have required a subservience of man to machine that electronics does not. Mechanical technologies have played a major part in the reduction of man. Electronics offers us the opportunity to evolve notions of organization closer to the nature of man.

The diagrams below (Fig. 1) hopefully make this point clearer. The mechanical system underlying industrialization lacks the self-regulating characteristic. When machines became too large, costly and complex for their use around the home, men and women had to go out to operate them. Factories were built for machines not people. In matters of control, where two systems (the technical and social) interact, control must derive from the lowest common denominator. The linear sequential, rational view of the world inherent in the mechanical sequence is reinforced in our minds by literary-based education. Organization out there, as bureaucracy, is extended and modified by the principles of subdivision and external regulation—a response to crisis which now carries all the hallmarks of an unauthentic ritual.

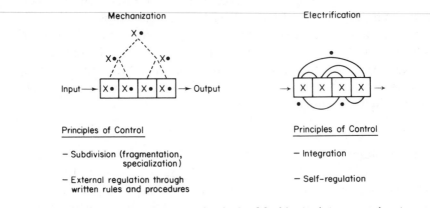

FIG. 1. Machines and people in two technologies. Machine/task (**X**); people (•).

Electrification provides the missing link in the mechanic sequence. Feedback loops integrate the various operations in such a way that self-regulating technical systems are now possible on a substantial scale. These organizing principles reverse those of mechanization and bureaucratization and make it possible for the social system to operate, in large measure, independently from many technical systems. The constraints to the advance of electronics are social and political. One of these, universal employment, we will be considering shortly. Electronics offers us choices that mechanization does not and with the application of electronics to production and communication, the dominant social system can now be geared more closely to man's personal and collective needs.

However, as McLuhan (1964) tells us, electronics does not dictate what we should do. Thus far we have deployed it to extend the industrial order and bureaucracy. We can also use electronics to erode dichotomies like those between subject and object, and reality and fantasy. No longer do the source of energy and its use have to be in close proximity. With the saturation of institutional organization by computers and duplicated materials, the scope for microprocessors in production and communication lies in freeing man from the dictates of employment, i.e. in eroding the powerful division between economic activity and the rest of life. Whether we can live with the political and social consequences will determine the speed with which the microprocessor revolution takes place.

4. Scope for emancipation through the failures of the institutional economy

Let us now turn to the question of man's emancipation from the dominant institutions of industrial society. During the past few decades the myth of all-powerful organizations has been exposed, not the least because self-denigration inevitably leads to the deterioration of the extensions of ourselves. The problem as always is our continuing dependence, even on institutions which fail us — we have to learn to be free and no authority out there can be our educator in this most serious of ventures. However, I shall attempt to sketch an outline of circumstances and forces outside the person which make our emancipation from employment possible.

Reduced man is man as consumer, welfarist and participant on terms offered by authorities out there. His subordinate state is compounded by a view of economic activity which equates work with employment. The question of integrating individual and organization, which many organizational psychologists take as their central concern, begins with accepting the industrial establishment as a legitimate authority. Thus far we have proved more willing slaves to employment and its institutions — governments, employers, trade unions, education and the mass media — than medieval man was to church, king, baron and manor. But the crisis of industrial society, of our own being, is the consequence of a dependence on institutions whose own deficiencies grow by the day.

The failure of the institutional economy — falling production, inflation, unemployment, overmanning and a general loss of spirit — is the failure of employment to provide an adequate basis for social life in general and the creation of wealth and provision of service in particular. While the work to be done is limitless, our capacity to undertake work through employment is not. There are social as well as technical reasons for this. We are unable to sustain the central value(s) of industrial society through employment. Yet, so great is our dependence on its organizational vehicle, bureaucracy, that its effectiveness declines by the day because we use it to excess. We are witnessing too the rapid decline of a welfare system based on employment. Along with these processes we have seen the erosion of notions of ownership, however we choose to define it. Increasingly employment fails to meet our life expectations, to enable the production of quality goods and services, to facilitate the reconstruction of town and village communities and the protection and enhancement of the natural environment. Yet we cling to its illusory magic and the desperate search for more employment-based work.

Let us look at some of the claims I have made in more detail. The belief which once aroused human energy in industrial society and still legitimizes our institutional actions is loosely described as "the work ethic". There are some industries, like aspects of the construction industry, where it still matters. The mythology of early industrial expansion is littered with stories of the Wittingtons, Arkwrights, Bridgewaters, Wedgwoods, Wilkinsons and Macadams upholding the belief that effort and ingenuity have their rewards. Modern industrial heroes like the property-developers and asset-strippers do little to sustain the work ethic. Nor do advertisers who promote sales on the basis of getting something for nothing. Though the present government pays lip service to the worth of hard work, like governments before it, it does so against a background of failing manufacture. Success, 1980s-style, in terms of profits, comes mostly to the money-shufflers like banks and insurance companies and to the extractive industry which lives less off its industry than its property rights over the world's non-renewable resources.

Within employment itself, the problem of sustaining the work ethic is no less serious. The transfer of people from agriculture and manufacture to service is accompanied by the mystification and/or loss of task. Many people must be of the opinion that the less tangible the task performed the greater the rewards. Large enterprise using advanced production and communication techniques cannot easily sustain the importance of collective efforts, still less those of the individual. A loss of direction and considerable confusion is inevitable. In response to this predicament, we find much energy in large enterprise diverted to a literary shoring-up of the work ethic in the belief, one assumes, that written words and numbers are not just abstractions but have a reality all of their own. Objective setting exercises, formalized planning, budgets, job descriptions, appraisals and computer print-outs, have emerged to clarify the unclarifiable. For man as employee they represent still more fragmented time and space, more paper work, and a cancerous pile of unauthentic ritual undermining organizations. The wreckers of the industrial order are not its critics but those who do things in its name. Quite simply, modern employment cannot sustain its central belief.

The work ethic has not been helped by our fudging of the ownership issue. Nineteenth-century critics of industrialization, like Marx, drew attention to the alienating aspects of a social order which advanced on man's loss of ownership of his time, space, skills and products. At least the early owners of the employee's labour were, for the most part, known to their employees. Today we are more concerned about property, while ownership is typically in the hold of abstractions like the State or the stockholders. State office-holders are familiar to us through the media but their temporariness and the gulf between their public postures and private games leave us confused. The average employee knows little about shareholders save through a ceremonial deference shown them by senior executives once or twice a year. As for managers, why is it that organizational theorists show an acute concern with the manager's leadership role while ignoring his role as employee? Of course, leadership is a necessary myth. It helps to legitimize the unequal distribution of power in hierarchies within an order which purports to hold all men equal. But there is more to it which our collusive dealings and the perks and trappings of office hardly conceal — there is also the manager's role as servant of the organization. At least the largely futile efforts to extend industrial democracy, co-ownership and co-operatives within employment serve to remind us that, as employees, we all suffer from the loss of ownership of our own time and space.

Bureaucratic organizations now dominate employment. The case against the alienating features of bureaucracy is well-documented. But our relationships with this abstract parent to which we owe much of our material well-being is not simple. Success not failure has led to its excess and individually we demonstrate a remarkable ability to dissociate our own actions from those excesses.

Over-organization comes from underestimating the extent to which our upbringing and education train us to think bureaucratically. We are all bureaucrats now, living in our own fragmented time and space. The primacy of visual and literary detail as fact in industrial man's frame of reference, and the linear, sequential, rational mode of thought reinforced by literacy lend themselves to the advance of bureaucracy and the authority of organizations.

Bureaucracy is an easy form of organization for industrial man to set up and operate. New divisions of labour and additional rules and procedures only impinge on current practice in a marginal way. But what begins as a natural response to the need to organize the world for ourselves gets lost in overlays of abstraction as the process of fragmentation and formalization decreases the meaning and understanding of the whole. There are fewer steps than we recognize between the void and organized confusion — and describing the process as conceptualizing should not legitimize it. What we seem to have here is a logic trap — more of a good thing is not always better.

I have always been suspicious of the manner in which social psychologists associated with studies of the authoritarian personality (Adorno *et al.* (1950) and Rokeach (1960)) were able to persuade us so easily that the worst villanies of our time against man could be heaped conveniently on prejudice and the closed mind (i.e. bad beliefs). These doubts were kindled some 12 years ago by a visit to Strutoff, a preserved Nazi concentration camp in the Vosges. For me the remarkable feature of this story of horror was its organization. The many activities in the killing process were carefully refined and fitted together to minimize personal responsibility. Most tasks involved no more violence than one might expect in a modern welfare agency. Rationality not madness was the foundation of this horror.

The same organization existed in the Milgram experiments (1965). I am not referring to the authority of science or education or even to the manner in which the experiments were conducted, but to the immediate situation facing the real subject. Picture him confronted by a row of keys to be pressed in ascending order of shock severity carefully denoted by occasional words and symbols. The large number of keys suggests to the operator that the differences between adjacent keys is slight (i.e. may not matter). So, beginning with the first key, he starts on a familiar treadmill and goes on to the end. What would have happened if the subject had been faced with only two choices — harmless

and dangerous? At least the choice would have been real. But the proliferation of keys is familiar, reassuring and comforting. He knows this
game. He can trust it. But this comfortably logical task is a deception,
just as the process of conceptualization takes the academic from concepts to decepts. Not "blind, emotional prejudice" but belief in organization out there, the location of authority beyond ourselves, provides
the essential ingredient for the worst villanies man can bestow on his
fellows.

5. The retreat from employment

While men in their institutional roles seem powerless to reverse what
they see as a deteriorating industrial situation, privately we appear to
be evolving strategies which may be convergent enough to form the
basis of an alternative model. More and more people are shifting their
life concerns away from employment-based work. In short they are
transferring their energies out of the institutional economy.

Our failure to sustain the work ethic in employment, the consequent
loss of a meaningful link between effort and reward, and organizational
excess are undoubtedly major factors in this phenomenon. But new
technologies, changing values and resource problems in general also
suggest that our private strategies are, in the main, correct.

Identifying the nature, forms and extent of this withdrawal is not
easy because of its invisibility. We can hardly be expected to keep
records which reflect on the declining potency of our institutions. For
example, the information on absences from employment is interesting
but completely inadequate — we only know about certified absences of
more than three days for *part* of the working population. Manning
figures which compare UK performances with specific industries in
other countries and show us up badly can be explained away. Even
attitudes to work tell us little. The percentage of the population satisfied with their work is remarkably stable. The writers of a report on
extensive surveys of workforce attitudes in the United States (see Sheppard and Herrick, 1972) were hard put to make much of the more
questioning attitudes they sought to find. We are it seems "satisfied
with our work", in much the same way that we can usually find a
religious denomination for questionnaire surveyors. The question, "Are
you satisfied with your job?" is probably unaskable in industrial society.

To complicate matters, withdrawal is not just a physical phenomenon. Employment is increasingly about people going through the motions of work. We even have a word for it, *satisficing*. Working to rule, pushing paper, shortened working days, extended lunches, excessive travel, busying ourselves in a sea of bad ritual, the loss of concern for quality on all fronts are signs of withdrawal on a psychological level. Our friends across the Channel, who are certainly busier in a visible sense than we are, complain that the British do not work. The evidence is everywhere save in official documents it seems.

Where comparisons of a kind are possible on manning levels, for example, in steel-making, car production and coal-mining, much of British industry appears to be overmanned, moderately so compared with the Germans and grossly so compared with the Japanese. But the capital investments in these industries are also vastly different and could account for some of the differences.

Over the past three decades the time lost through certified absence has increased steadily with a trend towards more frequent but shorter spells of absence (according to the Department of Health and Social Security statistics). This development has been most marked among men. Furthermore, figures cited in an Office of Health Economic Report (1970) shows big increases in less serious illnesses (sprains, strains, headaches, nervousness) and some decline in more serious illnesses as causes of absence. This evidence supports the theory of a declining commitment to employment.

When uncertified absence figures are collected they are mostly limited to hourly paid staff. In respect of all absences the evidence from secondary schools is more useful. Reports from the Inner London Education Authority (1979) show an absence level of 15%. Over the past 10 years daily attendances in comprehensive classrooms have dropped from 90 to 85%. Again, for obvious reasons, evidence collected from *within* schools is likely to be on the conservative side.

Another survey in the north-west of England (Barnes, 1979) among 450,000 children showed absence levels ranging from 18 to 31% depending on the school—somewhat below the average four-day week that some observers believe many British employees to be approaching. In this enquiry mention was made of the widespread connivance of parents in pupil truancy—signs of a "ganging up" against our institutions!

Nearly all statistics, from the abuse of employment and "scrounging-off-the-state" to forms of work-avoidance are least adequate for managerial and professional classes of employee. These groups enjoy the privilege of greater personal control over time and space than other office workers and their factory counterparts. In my view one major reason for our reluctance to take on manufacturing jobs, particularly in production, is due to the extent to which both technical and social systems greatly reduce the freedom of movement, and therefore association and activity, for those engaged in production.

Many of the perks managers enjoy, like cars and travel, provide a line to sanctioned forms of work-avoidance. Three-quarters of new cars on British roads are company-owned. Indeed many executives now spend so much of their time away from their place of work that the unavailability of bosses along with their indecisiveness has become a major complaint among subordinates in non-production jobs in surveys I have conducted in airline, electronics and tobacco industries. The growth of professional services, larger enterprises and the importance of marketing in a more competitive economic system inevitably lead to greater emphasis on lateral communications and boundary relations. Whereas executives once claimed man management as their major task, now in my own enquiries I find them talking more and more about managing situations. Delegation, Theory Y management and participation have enjoyed some popularity in management circles of late, not least because they appear to sanction abdication. I *frequently* have considerable difficulty linking executive and professional travel to task and this, no doubt, is one good reason for playing down the importance of task. What I am arguing here is that there is much collusion in professional and management circles to protect and maintain work-avoidance opportunities (see Pym, 1980a).

Recent figures in the *Department of Employment Gazette* also support the "retreat theory". Over the past three years to the end of 1979, in spite of a net gain of nearly one quarter of a million men in the labour market, the numbers of men either employed or claiming unemployment relief in Britain has *dropped* by 160,000. The "disappearance" of 400,000 men can only be partly explained by early retirement. More helpful is the equivalent *increase* in women in or seeking employment. The economic independence being won by the men from employment may not infrequently be aided by women taking over as key earners of income in the institutional economy.

On the basis of the "conservation of energy", where, it ought to be asked, are we taking our energies? There are at least two factors characteristic of living in Britain which nurture alternative uses. One is the emphasis on private individualism in the British culture. This reality lies behind much public acquiescence and subservience to authority. The outsider soon observes, however, that whatever the Englishman makes of his public life, he regards his private world as sacrosanct. It is a domain seldom penetrated except by the closest of friends and relatives.

Supporting this private individualism is the role of house and home. The depression of the 1930s seems to have convinced the average Englishman that his home is his castle. With little government aid, 3 million houses were built in Britain during the hard times of the 1930s in contrast with the 1920s when with considerable government support only half that number of houses were completed. Today the British are among the greatest home-owners in the industrialized world and, thanks to the policies of successive governments, our working people enjoy the advantages of greater living space both inside and outside the home than any other people in Europe with the exception of the Norwegians. Nobody in Europe spends as much money on do-it-yourself materials as the British. We have uses for our energies outside employment and all the signs suggest that we are transferring our energies back into the home and community as our disaffections with employment grow.

6. The domestic or free economy

From the point of view of advanced industrial man there is little sense in continuing with our policies of patching up the institutional economy based on employment. This is not in the interests of man nor is it an effective way of creating wealth and providing service. I shall begin this section with an analogy.

Consider a man who catches a bus every day to his place of employment. Over the years the reliability and comfort of this service deteriorates. For a time our man complains to his fellow passengers and to the bus conductor. In exasperation he even writes to the owners of the bus. Although companies do not like customer complaints they ought to recognize them, in part, as expressions of concern. The customer cares. Silence which follows concern is much more serious. In the case of our man silence may signify resignation or even that he has found alternative transport. But in neither case does it matter any longer what the bus company does to improve its services. IT IS TOO LATE. Our passenger has given up. Physically and/or mentally he has gone. This situation now applies to much of British industry. Tinkering with the internal mechanics will not improve it. Only radical solutions will do now. The seeds of these solutions are to be found in the ways in which people are privately coping with the increasing insanities of life built around employment.

So let us get to essentials. We cannot do without the institutional economy. However, we do not need compulsory employment nor is it good for us. The technical means are available to create the wealth and service currently met by the formal economy with a fraction of the workforce. There are many economic and social tasks which the institutional economy seems incapable of meeting, including the provision of meaningful work for all.

Western societies, and Britain in particular, have now reached a stage in their evolution when the revival of an old form of economic organization to operate alongside the institutional economy offers the advantages of each without all the disadvantages that either alone brings. We need a revived domestic or home-based, people-intensive economy to operate alongside the institutional, technically intensive economy. We need a dual economy.

Governments and men in their institutional roles do not recognize the domestic economy, yet we are all part of it. By way of acknowledging the material achievements of the institutional economy and the obligatory nature of employment let us call this other economy in "advanced" societies, *the free economy*. While the formal economy flounders throughout much of the industrial world, the free economy is emerging and prospering. But the failings of the former are not unrelated to the illegitimacy of the latter which exists beyond the black economy with its pilfering, fiddling, second jobs and tax evasion.

The comments and statements which follow are based on personal observations in city and country. They should accord in many respects with the observations of others. Social commentators like Stretton (1976), Gershuny (1978) and Kumar (1979) hold broadly similar views.

The domestic economy is as old as civilization. In traditional societies it is *the* economy. Stretton has made the following points to establish the significance of economic activity in home and community even within industrial societies. He tells us that more than half our waking lives are spent in and around the home. More than a third of all work is done there. More than a third of all capital is invested there. More than three-quarters of all subsistence, leisure and recreational activity is centred there. Yet, we discount it completely in economic terms.

Many activities unsuited to employment are best undertaken within the free economy, including the production of arts and crafts, many quality goods, people-intensive community services, city, town and village reconstruction, professional services, and environmental protection. The free economy embraces the work of the self-employed, voluntary services, house- and home-keepers, do-it-yourselfers, home and allotment gardeners — the list is endless.

Unlike the institutional economy, the free economy is rooted in community life. Community life in industrial society suffers because so many people residing within the community have no socioeconomic relations with it save through taxes.

We are *all* party to the free economy. Its conventions are therefore familiar to us. It is born out of an informal network of people living in relatively close proximity to each other and is dominated by convivial relations. The focus of authority rests in people's heads rather than in some abstract edifice out there. Its codes, signs, norms and values remain relatively close to human nature.

In its current form the free economy revolves around home, pub and club. Transactions are seldom written, indeed the eschewing of written agreements and procedures is one of its distinguishing features. It depends for communication on an amalgam of oral tradition and electronics-based media, like the telephone, where two-way exchanges are possible. Transactions are based on trust. Therefore, the relations sustaining them require constant and careful attention. Its values and norms are exacting. Notions of community evolve out of lasting contacts and associations. The contravention of that trust is not a matter to be taken lightly by people who live, more or less permanently, near each other.

Man owns his own skills and products and exercises considerable control over his own use of time and space in the free economy. It is labour-intensive and depends more on barter and the exchange of goods and services and less on money than the institutional economy. Relatively fixed bases of exchange and the low hourly rates of payment suggest that this is not an inflationary economic system. Being a people-intensive economy, the choice of technologies is much more governed by man's own capacities and limitations, it is ready-made for the use of intermediate technologies.

As the free economy emerges in strength and influence we will come to recognize the advantages it affords women, those with manual skills and permanent residents. It does not favour geographically mobile, middle-class males.

The free economy offers scope for the economic traditionalists, those who believe in work and the link between effort and reward. It is not surprising to find that the modern achiever also feels at home in the free economy.

7. Towards the dual economy

The free economy can only grow and prosper if we collectively use the formal economy in the most socially effective manner. Neither system can operate in isolation and conflicts of interests between people whose lives are centred in different economies are inevitable. I have considered at some length some measures for achieving the dual economy (see Pym, 1980b), the major points are summarized below.

The first task is to find ways and means of enabling and encouraging people to relinquish their places in the institutional economy. Those who do least good and are most wasteful of resources may also be the easiest to persuade to go. Governments and large enterprise could aid this process just by dropping their hostile attitudes to legitimate social and economic activities outside employment. Exchanging the dole for a minimum wage for all adults would help even more but it would be expecting far too much of government to have it support a process which returns power and authority to the people. Even many of those who advocate less government cling to the centralized control of energy in their support of expensive nuclear power.

Employers, particularly large employers of people, will see the economic advantages of moving people out of employment provided their purchasing powers are retained. Changes in employment contracts — more part-time work, more employed people working from home — would help employers to cut their costs and enable the better use of technology. It would also give employees a secure base from which to find a niche in the free economy.

But the way into the dual economy lies with people rather than old institutions and in the attractiveness of the free economy to the adventurer and idealist: to those who can live with their freedom. For a country with many people and limited resources the ethic to stir our imaginations must derive from *resourcefulness*.[2] Whether expressed in physical or mental terms, it forges dignity and self-respect. Resourcefulness is the ethic of elevated man and the enemy of gross organization, professionalization, old corporatism and welfarism. Its message is their containment and even their irrelevance. It is through the perspectives this ethic provides that the strategies most appropriate to the post-industrial world will emerge.

8.   Methods

The view of man and organization I am advancing here is as old as Adam. It just hasn't had much going for it lately. In our politico-philosophical tradition it has its origins in existentialism and anarchism. My sympathies derive from early experiences which find their expression in a romantic's reluctance to pay lip-service to ideals and a naive predisposition to accept, for a time, whatever others are asserting. I find rhetoric far less imposing on my person than dialogue as it is shaped by our academic conventions. There is something intensely hostile about demolishing the arguments of others, or proving their logical inconsistencies or damning a view for lack of evidence. There are an awful lot of people wedded to that game who wonder why they are short on love. Other aspects of our academic tradition also disturb me — the authority of the literary medium in communication, the authority of knowledge over wisdom, of truth over good and the maintenance of the subject–object dualism.

The prejudices I hold are reinforced daily. For example, each year I get my small group of Ph.D. students to select some ten well-known texts in the organizational field and we read, review and criticize them (orthodoxy is not beyond my pale). Those texts which stand the passage of time like Whyte's *Street Corner Society* (1967) or Gouldner's *Patterns of Industrial Bureaucracy* (1955) or Burns and Stalker's *Management of Innovation* (1961) are not beyond criticism but they stimulate. The "good" books never include studies heavily based on statistics and questionnaires (a characteristic of much of my own earlier work), and seldom those on comparative techniques and experiments or those which ignore or abstract context (i.e. nearly all psychological studies). In fact the students prefer the best of the case studies, books positivists malign so much.

The message here is obvious. Studies based on observation and the close proximity of observer to the subject of his enquiries cannot easily ignore the complexity and variability of human nature. What many of our observational studies lack is a legitimate part for the observer's imagination, but that will come. When we observe we use all of our senses not just one, provided the exchanges are not reduced to written transcripts, which seems to me to be a retrogressive practice.

Research is always directed, the scientific method recommends hypotheses to be tested. Any enquirer who lives comfortably with his prejudices needs no hypothesis. In terms of the other paradigm therefore, our attentions might be directed towards the odd, discrepant, nonsensical and contradictory. These are misfits with respect to our beliefs and they lead to different perceptions of our problems and to different problems. My own interests in the collusive relationships between professionals and managers (see Pym, 1980a) has such origins — namely the public demand for technologists in the 1960s and 70s and the experiences of those technologists in employment. I depend on this strategy in all my research now. Perhaps I depend on it too much, but it leads to interesting perspectives and stimulates a dull mind.

This strategy *uses* prejudice, which personally I cannot distinguish from theory, instead of *denying* it. A few years ago, following a study in the petrochemical industry where there is generally an excess of management, I became involved in a study of air transport. The usual introductions and interviews with a cross-section of employees in the relevant departments were completed. From these, just two discrepancies emerged. Neither had anything to do with what I found in the interviews directly but helped to make sense of them. The first was the numbers of people bearing the title "manager" — everybody in an airline is a manager or so it seems. The second was the large number of people who failed to keep appointments for the interview. Airline employees are the best consumers of their own advertising. Travel is prestigious — so much so that the failure to keep an appointment can be justified with a "he or she is in Beirut, Brussels or Barcelona". But why the profusion of managers? The airline culture is not a managerial culture, unlike ICI, people in airlines don't know what management means. Its history is short and entrepreneurial. As airlines grew so the need for rules and regulations compounded by the close association between airlines and government grew also. Airlines are not managed but are run on a curious amalgam of *implicit* entrepreneurship and procedures. The much-criticized failings of employees in the managerial role came down to their inadequate perception of what "manager" means and the proliferation of a role which few attempt to fulfil. The key to my reaching these conclusions depended on discrepant information.

Notes

1. This orthodoxy is well represented in the contributions to this book and *does not* exclude most sociological writers on organization, least of all contemporary, middle-class, "format Marxists". By contrast, those with whose work I have much sympathy include: Cobbett (1979), Mailer (1962), Orwell (in Orwell and Angus, 1968), McLuhan (1964), Illich (1973), Roszak (1969), Pirsig (1976) and Gouldner (1976). None are psychologists but all are organization theorists if they but knew it.
2. Blake (see Wilson, 1978) and Cobbett (1822, 1979) personify this ethic for me. The modern heroes have yet to emerge.

References

ADORNO, T. W., FRENKEL-BRUNSWICK, E. LEVINSON, D. J. AND SANFORD, R. N. (1950). *The Authoritarian Personality*. New York: Harper.

BARNES, J. A. (1979). *Observations and the Report of Irregular School Attendance Survey 1979*. North Western Regional Society of Education Officers (UK). (Mimeo.)

BURNS, T. AND STALKER, G. M. (1961). *The Management of Innovation*. London: Tavistock Publications.

COBBETT, W. (1979—originally published 1822). *Cottage Economy*. Oxford: Oxford University Press.

GERSHUNY, J. (1978). *After Industrial Society*. London: Macmillan.

GORLEY, P. (1978). *In the Sales Call: A Study of the Industrial Sales Interview*. Unpublished Ph.D. Thesis, University of London.

GOULDNER, A. W. (1955). *Patterns of Industrial Bureaucracy*. New York: Free Press.

GOULDNER, A. W. (1976). *The Dialectic of Ideology and Technology*. London: Macmillan.

ILLICH, I. (1973). *Tools for Conviviality*. London: Fontana.

ILLICH, I., *et al.* (1977). *Disabling Professions*. London: Marion Boyars.

INNER LONDON EDUCATION AUTHORITY REPORT (1979). *School Attendance*. (Mimeo.)

KUMAR, K. (1979). *Prophecy and Progress*. Harmondsworth: Penguin.

LAING, R. D. (1960). *The Divided Self: An Existentialist Study of Insanity and Madness*. London: Tavistock Publications.

MAILER, N. (1968). *Advertisements for Myself*. London: Panther.

MARCUSE, H. (1964). *One Dimensional Man*. Boston: Beacon Press.

McLUHAN, M. (1964). *Understanding Media*. New York: McGraw-Hill.

MILGRAM, S. (1965). Some conditions of obedience and disobedience to authority. *Human Relations*, **18,** 57–76.

OFFICE OF HEALTH ECONOMICS (1970). *Off Sick*. London: HMSO.

ORWELL, S. AND ANGUS, K. (eds) (1968). *The Collected Essays, Journalism and Letters of George Orwell*. London: Secker and Warburg.

PIRSIG, R. (1976). *Zen and the Art of Motor Cycle Maintenance*. London: Corgi.

PYM, D. (1973). The politics and ritual of appraisals. *Occupational Psychology*, **47,** 231–235.

PYM, D. (1974). In quest of post-industrial man. In N. Armisted (ed.), *Reconstructuring Social Psychology*. Harmondsworth: Penguin.

PYM, D. (1978). Employment as bad ritual. *London Business School Journal*, **3,** 25–35.

PYM, D. (1980a). Professional mismanagement. *Futures*, April, 142–150.

PYM, D. (1980b). Towards the dual economy and emancipation from employment. *Futures*, June, 223–237.

ROKEACH, M. (1960). *The Open and Closed Mind*. New York: Basic Books.

SHEPPARD, H. AND HERRICK, N. (1972). *Where Have All The Robots Gone?* New York: The Free Press.

STRETTON, H. (1976). *Capitalism, Socialism and the Environment*. London: Cambridge University Press.

WHYTE, W. F. (1967). *Street Corner Society: The Social Structure of an Italian Slum*. Chicago: University of Chicago Press.

WILSON, M. (1978). *The Life of William Blake*. London: Paladin.

11 The Future of Organizational Psychology

SYLVIA SHIMMIN

In his review article of the first introductory texts bearing the title "Organizational Psychology", Gardner (1966) referred to "this hungry child seeking admission to the family of Social Sciences" and asked "is it really a new child, or one which is attempting to attract attention by adopting a new name?" His conclusion was that it was more than a new name, that an emergent multi-disciplinary area of study could be discerned which required multi-disciplinary training in the social sciences. As such, he observed that it could be disputed whether it lay within the realm of psychology, noting that Mayntz (1964), for example, designated the same area as "organizational sociology", and he suggested that a multi-disciplinary field requires a neutral name, perhaps "organizational science".

These terms and other variants, for example "organizational behaviour", persist today and it is widely acknowledged that several disciplines contribute to the study of organizations. However, it is still an open question whether this is a field of study in its own right or an area of application to be approached via a basic training in a more established discipline. Among the plethora of books and articles pertaining to organizations, some are slanted towards a particular discipline, others are eclectic in their approach and yet others focus on the work of practitioners, who come from a variety of backgrounds, and their efforts to improve organizational effectiveness or bring about organizational change.

How one views the future of organizational psychology, therefore, depends on the relative emphasis given to each of the two words. If "organizational" is stressed, indicating that the focus of endeavour is developing knowledge of organizations, the perspective differs from that which sees "psychology" as the key word and considers developments in terms of the discipline as a whole. Although these orientations are not mutually exclusive, the ways in which organizational psychologists define themselves and the peer and reference groups with whom they identify usually show a bias in one or other direction. For example, those in the "organizational" category may associate more with researchers and practitioners from other fields than they do with psychologists, whereas the "psychology" group may tend to work mainly with others from their own discipline. The difference in emphasis is reflected also in the kinds of research undertaken, journals read, publication outlets sought and often in the ideological and philosophical positions espoused.

An important question, therefore, is the degree of coherence and consensus within organizational psychology. The duality of outlook mentioned above is often ignored or tacitly accepted, but it is an issue which has to be confronted in looking to the future, not least because of the implications for education and training. To produce psychologists specializing in organizational applications of their subject requires a different programme from one designed for organizational specialists operating in a multi-disciplinary or interdisciplinary mode (following Peston (1977) in defining "interdisciplinarity" as the approach to a problem emphasizing its many *aspects* and "multi-disciplinarity" as the approach using many different *methods*). At least we are accustomed to think so — to see the former as based in academic psychology departments and the latter as located in business schools, centres of management education and institutes of applied social research. Graduates from both types of programme may join the relevant branch of the psychological professional association (for example, Division 14 of the American Psychological Association), provided that the latter considers that the business school or other training includes sufficient psychology to admit to membership, and they may take up similar employment. But the chances are, in Britain at any rate, that they are likely to proceed in different directions, reflecting the differing orientations of their respective institutions.

There is also another group, who may be described as "organizational practitioners", who may or may not have had a formal training in psychology, but who have acquired a fair knowledge of the subject through their own reading, short courses, working associations with organizational social scientists, and so on. Many of those concerned with organizational development would come within this category. If organizational psychology were to be embraced within a new profession of organizational science, comprising the several disciplines concerned with the study of organizations and responsible for validating generalist training programmes, these organizational practitioners would doubtless be included. At present, however, they are a marginal group, worrying to those for whom the scientific "purity" of their discipline is of paramount importance and yet, perhaps, better equipped than the latter for general practice.

The boundaries of the field are therefore far from clear. Indeed, the scene is rather like a picture with a reversible perspective in which "psychology" is to the fore at one moment and "organizations" the next. Although the contributions of several disciplines are recognized and a good deal of borrowing of ideas and methods occurs across disciplinary boundaries, there have been few sustained attempts to deal with problems of aggregation and integration. As Roberts *et al.* (1978) observe, there is no cumulative development in organizational research and theory because "integrating data bases, languages, models and theories from different perspectives is well nigh impossible, given the present scattered state of our knowledge and lack of integrating framework". Their book is an attempt to provide such a framework, in which they stress not only the need to identify and make explicit the paradigms underlying organizational studies but also suggest that the way forward lies in moving away from the paradigms of psychology, human factors and sociology and establishing new paradigms designed specifically for organizational science.

Questioning conventional assumptions and methods is a first step in this direction and, by this token, what appears as fragmentation or disarray within the field may be a sign of progress. For there is little doubt that the study of organizations is characterized by controversy and questions about research and theory. These range from the challenges presented to the functionalist tradition of psychology by the changing views of science held by historians and philosophers, to problems of ethics in professional practice and the social responsibilities of researchers and consultants. In contrast with the prevailing mood of the

1960s, when organizational psychology was seen as an essentially "applied" subject with the potential to contribute to the solution of many problems, there is now a far greater critical awareness of its limitations and anxious debate about the legitimacy of various research strategies (for example, interventionist approaches underpinned by particular social values or beliefs). Further tension is created by the paradox that, while many of those working in the field have become increasingly self-critical of their activities, popularization of the subject through the media and books and journals aimed at the non-specialist reader has gathered momentum. Thus, concepts and findings may be used by others in ways which those responsible for these ideas never intended. A good example is how "job satisfaction" has become an embarrassment to psychologists, so that, as Cherns notes (in Chapter 2), having fashioned the term they cannot get rid of it and "the more elusive and unsatisfactory the concept turns out to be, the more firmly it enters the non-technical literature".

Does this matter? There are those who would say that it does not, that the confused scene outlined above is inevitable and that, faced with such complex and conflicting influences, a policy of "live and let live" is the only expedient. The contrary view is that it behoves those disturbed or frustrated by the present situation to take a fresh look at themselves and their activities, and to seek a new perspective. What this might involve is discussed by a number of contributors to this volume. Hage, for example (Chapter 6), considers that the time is ripe for merging qualitative and quantitative approaches in organizational research, and Landy (Chapter 5) suggests that inductive and deductive strategies are not mutually exclusive, as is frequently assumed, but have a co-ordinate or sequential relationship. Gowler and Legge (Chapter 4) examine the problems and possibilities of integrating individual, group and organizational levels of analysis and different disciplinary perspectives, but feel constrained to point out in their conclusions that the different levels and perspectives are more easily juxtaposed than integrated.

The same can be said about the essays in this book. If one strives to find them, one can identify some common elements in different contributions, the significance of which lies in the contrasts between them. Two examples are the references made to the value of case studies in empirical work by Payne (Chapter 3) and Pym (Chapter 10) and the discussions of the researcher–client relationship by Argyris (Chapter 9) and Mangham (Chapter 8). They indicate different personal experiences and biographies, cultural and intellectual traditions, reflection on which might provide cues to the influences shaping the direction of the field. The study of history through autobiography has much to offer and, in this respect, the publication in the *Journal of Occupational Psychology* of invited personal accounts by those who have made their mark on the development of the subject is to be welcomed.

Unlike clinical and educational psychology, organizational psychology offers no well-structured career pattern to psychologists, not least because their discipline has no monopoly of the field. As indicated earlier, the study of organizations is part of the domain of practitioners from many disciplines and, in terms of employment opportunities, it is often the "organizational" rather than the "psychology" part of the label which counts. In other words, psychologists are not distinguished from other social scientists concerned with organizations, with whom they are expected to work and with whom they are in competition for jobs.

Until recently, universities and research institutions were the major employers of organizational psychologists and it is noteworthy that most contemporary writers on organizational theory hold tenured academic appointments. In the 1960s, it was realistic for organizational psychologists to aspire to an academic career and, in some cases, demand exceeded the supply of adequately trained specialists. Expansion then slowed down and finally ceased during the 1970s. Now, in the 1980s, we are faced with projected cutbacks in expenditure on universities and other institutes of higher education. As a result, those who aspire to academic posts are now faced with very limited opportunities in this sphere.

How this will affect the development of organizational psychology is a matter of speculation, but it is likely that, in order to secure their bread and butter, new graduates will take up a variety of jobs which will lead them to define the field differently from those employed in academic settings. If the latter continue to regard themselves as the dominant faction in the domain and do not recognize the claims and contributions of the others, there is a risk of splintering and isolationism. If, on the other hand, this is seen as a unique opportunity for dialogue and establishing intersubjectively shared understandings, as advocated by Shotter (1975), then the outcome could be very different. One of the limitations of organization theory at present, however radical the form presented, is that it has not been produced by those in precarious, arduous or monotonous jobs, located outside the academic establishment, but by people in positions of privilege and security compared with most of the working population. There are now likely to be increasing numbers of (would-be) organizational psychologists compelled to live dangerously, with first-hand experience of organizational processes and practices not shared by their mentors, inclusion of whom in the dialogue and debate about what the subject is all about and what direction it should take would be invaluable.

Another feature of the present situation is the way in which the domain is subject increasingly to the direct and indirect influence of governments. Thus, in Europe, most educational institutions are financed mainly by the State, and a great deal of research-funding comes from government sources. There has been a marked growth in applied research commissioned by government agencies, whereby researchers become agents or contractors dealing with a problem which is presented to them. As such they are not the prime movers in initiating or determining their research activity. In Britain, the principle that applied research and development should be done on a customer–contractor basis is associated particularly with Lord Rothschild (1971) who recommended it as the basis for Government Research and Development. As he puts it: "The customer says what he wants; the contractor does it (if he can); and the customer pays".

This principle applied to much traditional industrial psychology and, indeed, to other applications of social science in industry. It led Baritz (1960) to make the charge that the social scientists concerned were "the servants of power", that is, of the managers who hired them. But, as Eldridge and Crombie (1974) point out, social scientists *may* choose to serve powerful interests in other kinds of organization, for instance the trade unions, and "to this extent, just as the technologist may exercise some choice over the sphere in which he allows his skills to be utilised, so may the social scientist". Today, this degree of choice looks much more restricted, both to those seeking employment and to those responsible for research staff on short-term contracts who wish to keep the latter in their jobs for a further period, and who find themselves drawn to projects for which finance is available. One is reminded of the man who is said to have advised his son: "Don't 'ee marry for money, but go where money is", especially in a situation in which success is judged by the amount of research income generated, seemingly without too much concern about the sense or futility of the exercise, the source of funding, and so on. Announce that a sum of money has been earmarked for research on a certain topic, or indicate that a government department would like to commission work in a certain area, and the enquiries will come flocking in, and not just from those already familiar with the problem. This may not be altogether a bad thing — it certainly counteracts any tendency towards ossification of the field — but it also raises a number of ethical issues.

The first of these is the question of the extent to which the provision of jobs, albeit on a short-term basis, and the survival of one's institution, department or research group, justify a chameleon-like attitude and approach to organizational research. While it is seldom that any commissioned research project is undertaken without negotiation between sponsors and researchers, with a view to reaching an agreed definition of the problem and terms of reference, desire to get the grant or contract may lead to an unwillingness by the researcher to consider, say, the political dimensions involved. For example, policy-makers may commission research in order to delay making a decision, or they may be seeking data to support a policy already determined. Butler (1979), giving his personal view as Principal Psychologist in the Department of Employment, notes the tendency for administrators to formulate research needs in terms of "instant research" and "packaged solutions". He also thinks there are real difficulties in reconciling appropriate timescales for research with administrative thinking influenced by a parliamentary lifetime of no more than five years.

Once the contract is agreed, there is the question of how much freedom is given to the investigators to carry out the research without close monitoring or intervention by the sponsoring body. There is also the related issue of making known the results, especially when these are not of the kind hoped for by the sponsor. Although practice varies (for example, some sponsoring bodies try to exercise fairly tight control over their projects, others over the form and publication of the final report, while others appear to show little interest), research staff are often uncertain as to how far they should accommodate their work to the perceived requirements of the funding agency. This applies particularly to young research assistants who, as Platt (1976) observes, frequently enter research with unrealistic expectations. It is often difficult enough for them to carry out the day-to-day operational tasks on a project which they did not initiate or design, but their frustration and bewilderment are all the greater when they discover that, in addition to their supervisor or director, there is, say, a committee of the funding body whom it is judged important to please. Under these circumstances, it is hardly surprising that the current plea for new directions in research seems to go largely unanswered.

One way forward for organizational psychology would be to cease to assume that research is necessarily a paid activity. Of course, research workers have to live and it is unlikely that our present system of support, whether from research councils, charitable trusts, or commissions from the public or private sector, will alter greatly in the immediate future. But if, as the sociologists of knowledge suggest (Mulkay, 1979), there is no clear separation in science between the negotiation of social meaning and the acceptance of knowledge-claims, it means that we have a potential army of researchers who can help to elucidate this complex area and the influence of the wider society on organizational psychology. These are the members of organizations of all kinds who are prepared to observe, document, discuss and reflect upon their experiences through mutual interest and a desire to understand, for whom such activity is a hobby rather than a means of livelihood and who, therefore, are not preoccupied with research careerism. To judge from informal conversations in many quarters, there are numerous individuals who are trying to make sense of their organizational worlds who would welcome the opportunity to engage in such an enterprise. Furthermore, they are not necessarily the people who would represent client organizations in action research (although some may come into this category), but men and women from positions in all walks of life with a curiosity and enquiring outlook.

If this suggestion is seen as implying the erosion of expertise by including amateurs with professionals in our endeavours, then it is a measure of the élitism to which we have become accustomed in our view of the way in which knowledge is produced. Similarly, although university teachers are expected to engage in research alongside their teaching and administrative duties, the prevailing idea that this requires funding to employ research staff, with the commensurate institutional rewards of enlarging one's territory and sphere of influence, obscures the possibility of one-person research efforts, undertaken solely within the limits of an individual's timetable and salary. Here again, the mere suggestion may seem absurd to those taught to think in terms of large samples, a steady stream of publications and the prestige associated with big research awards. However, it should be noted that a few organizational psychologists do pursue their research in the individual manner described, but, unless they are already established figures in the domain, their efforts are apt to be overlooked or discounted by their contemporaries.

Another reason for involving a wider group of people in questions and discussions about organizational psychology is that many of the problems in which we are interested, and for which our help is sought, come into the category identified by Hardin (1968) as those for which there is no technical solution. This class of problems depends for their resolution on changes in human values or ideas of morality leading to mutually agreed social arrangements. They cannot be dealt with solely through a scientific, technical approach, to which the education of psychologists is still largely directed. Hardin is a biologist, writing about the population problem, but Behrend (1977) considers the problem of inflation to be of the same order. Structural unemployment, likewise, is another contemporary example which has no technical solution. Psychological research can assist in identifying the dimensions of the problem, but how the available jobs are to be distributed and what provision should be made for those without work is a social, moral and political issue.

The likelihood of encountering problems for which there is no technical solution, the increasing centralized control of resources, the diversity of the field, and the lack of a clear occupational identity for organizational psychologists are not encouraging signs. However, they do not necessarily lead to a pessimistic conclusion. The present uncertainty, doubt and sometimes agonizing debate, provided that it does not turn into self-destructive cynicism or despair, is an advance on facile and misleading optimism. To name but a few positive indicators: we are beginning to appreciate the importance of identifying the assumptions which underlie social theory and their implications for organizational analysis, to understand more of the dynamics of knowledge-production in their cultural context, to recognize that how and to whom we gain access in organizational research has considerable influence on its outcome and interpretation, and to learn that we must consider and make explicit our own scientific and social values. These suggest movement towards a break with past traditions and the development of new approaches.

Nevertheless, the difficulties should not be underestimated. Thus, the term "organizational psychology" itself is problematic and psychologists themselves differ as to whether the way forward lies in cross-disciplinary studies under the rubric of "organizational behaviour" or "organizational science" or in concentrating on distinctive psychological research. Much that passes for interdisciplinary or multi-disciplinary activity involves specialists working in parallel, rather than interactively, and there is a lot of dialogue and development work needed to achieve the latter. The scientist/practitioner split is likely to continue, with educational programmes geared towards producing research scientists, as long as the present appointment and promotion system in universities persists, with its emphasis on scientific research and number of publications. In the interests of quality control and social responsibility, there is also still much to be done to educate potential clients and the wider public as to what we can and cannot do, as well as being prepared ourselves to be held publicly accountable for our mistakes.

Finally, and most important of all, we need to recognize that the organizations we study and the tenor of much of our writing derive from outmoded assumptions about the availability of material resources, about the life-style and expectations of different groups and about the political configuration of the world. The future of organizational psychology, therefore, depends on its ability to help members of advanced industrial societies come to terms with this situation and deal with the dilemmas arising from what Katz and Kahn (1978) describe graphically as "the human race engaged in a kind of Faustian exchange with its own organizational creations". It is by no means clear whether, on present showing, it is equal to this task, but, as a matter of sheer survival, the challenge is one which cannot be ignored.

References

BARITZ, L. (1960). *The Servants of Power*. Middletown: Wesleyan University Press.

BEHREND, H. (1977). Research into inflation and conceptions of earnings. *Journal of Occupational Psychology*, **50,** 169–176.

BUTLER, F. (1979). Government policy in Great Britain and the social psychology of industrial relations. In G. M. Stephenson and C. J. Brotherton (eds), *Industrial Relations: A Social Psychological Approach*. Chichester: Wiley.

ELDRIDGE, J. E. T. AND CROMBIE, A. D. (1974). *A Sociology of Organisations*. London: Allen and Unwin.

GARDNER, G. (1966). Organisational psychology. *Occupational Psychology*, **40,** 101–106.

HARDIN, G. (1968). The tragedy of the commons. *Science*, **162,** 1243–1248.

KATZ, D. AND KAHN, R. L. (1978). *The Social Psychology of Organizations* (2nd edition). New York: Wiley.

MAYNTZ, R. (1964). The study of organizations—a trend report and bibliography. *Current Sociology*, **13,** 95–176.

MULKAY, M. (1979). *Science and the Sociology of Knowledge*. London: Allen and Unwin.

PESTON, M. (1977). Some thoughts on the evaluation of interdisciplinary research. Paper presented at Imperial College, London. (Mimeo.)

PLATT, J. (1976). *Realities of Social Research*. Sussex University Press.

ROBERTS, K. H., HULIN, C. L. AND ROUSSEAU, D. M. (1978). *Developing an Interdisciplinary Science of Organizations*. San Francisco: Jossey Bass.

ROTHSCHILD, LORD (1971). The organisation and management of Government R. and D. In *A Framework for Government Research and Development*. Cmd. 4814. London: HMSO.

SHOTTER, J. (1975). *Images of Man in Psychological Research*. London: Methuen.

Author Index

Subject Index